STAR WARS®

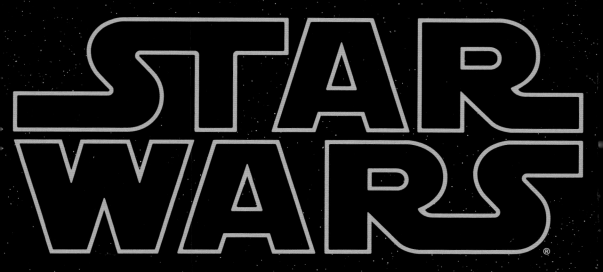

SKYWALKER STRIKES

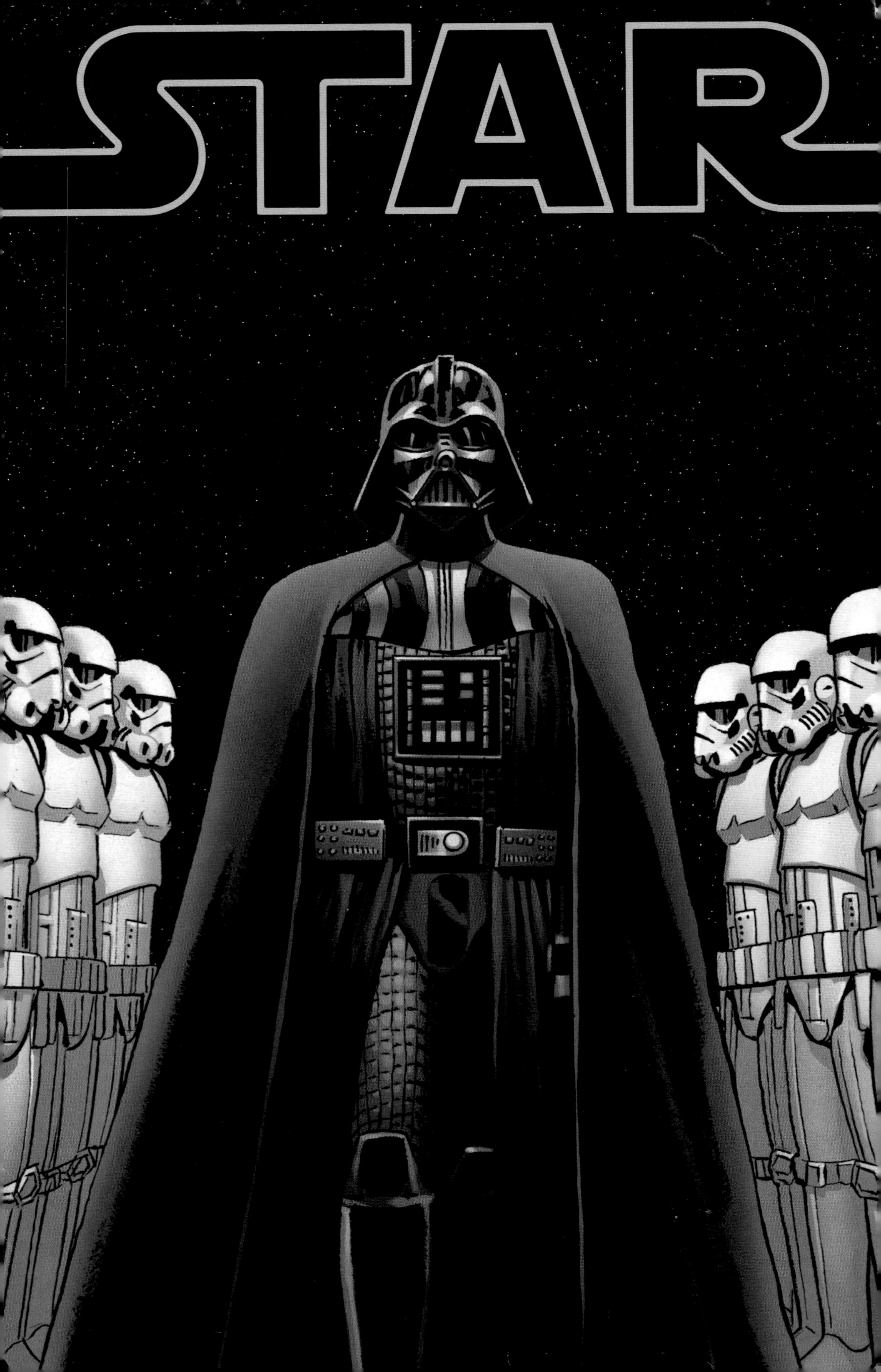
STAR

SKYWALKER STRIKES

Writer	**JASON AARON**
Artist	**JOHN CASSADAY**
Colorist	**LAURA MARTIN**
Letterer	**CHRIS ELIOPOULOS**
Cover Art	**JOHN CASSADAY**
	WITH **LAURA MARTIN** (#1-3 & #5-6)
	& PAUL MOUNTS (#4)
Assistant Editors	**CHARLES BEACHAM &**
	HEATHER ANTOS
Editor	**JORDAN D. WHITE**
Executive Editors	**C.B. CEBULSKI & MIKE MARTS**

Editor in Chief	**AXEL ALONSO**
Chief Creative Officer	**JOE QUESADA**
Publisher	**DAN BUCKLEY**

For Lucasfilm:

Creative Director	**MICHAEL SIGLAIN**
Senior Editors	**JENNIFER HEDDLE, FRANK PARISI**
Lucasfilm Story Group	**RAYNE ROBERTS, PABLO HIDALGO,**
	LELAND CHEE

Collection Editor	**JENNIFER GRÜNWALD**
Assistant Editor	**SARAH BRUNSTAD**
Associate Managing Editor	**ALEX STARBUCK**
Editor, Special Projects	**MARK D. BEAZLEY**
Senior Editor, Special Projects	**JEFF YOUNGQUIST**
SVP Print, Sales & Marketing	**DAVID GABRIEL**
Book Designer	**ADAM DEL RE**

STAR WARS VOL. 1: SKYWALKER STRIKES (SCHOLASTIC EDITION). Contains material originally published in magazine form as STAR WARS #1-6. First printing 2016. ISBN# 978-1-302-90078-6. Published by MARVEL WORLDWIDE, INC., a subsidiary of MARVEL ENTERTAINMENT, LLC. OFFICE OF PUBLICATION: 135 West 50th Street, New York, NY 10020. STAR WARS and related text and illustrations are trademarks and/or copyrights, in the United States and other countries, of Lucasfilm Ltd. and/or its affiliates. © & TM Lucasfilm Ltd. No similarity between any of the names, characters, persons, end/or institutions in this magazine with those of any living or dead person or institution is intended, and any such similarity which may exist is purely coincidental. Marvel and its logos are TM Marvel Characters, Inc. **Printed in the U.S.A.** ALAN FINE, President, Marvel Entertainment; DAN BUCKLEY, President, TV, Publishing and Brand Management; JOE QUESADA, Chief Creative Officer; TOM BREVOORT, SVP of Publishing; DAVID BOGART, SVP of Operations & Procurement, Publishing; C.B. CEBULSKI, VP of International Development & Brand Management; DAVID GABRIEL, SVP Print, Sales & Marketing; JIM O'KEEFE, VP of Operations & Logistics; DAN CARR, Executive Director of Publishing Technology; SUSAN CRESPI, Editorial Operations Manager; ALEX MORALES, Publishing Operations Manager; STAN LEE, Chairman Emeritus. For information regarding advertising in Marvel Comics or on Marvel.com, please contact Jonathan Rheingold, VP of Custom Solutions & Ad Sales, at jrheingold@marvel.com. For Marvel subscription inquiries, please call 800-217-9158. **Manufactured between 10/13/2015 and 11/21/2015 by HESS PRINT SOLUTIONS, A DIVISION OF BANG PRINTING, BRIMFIELD, OH, USA.**

10 9 8 7 6 5 4 3 2 1

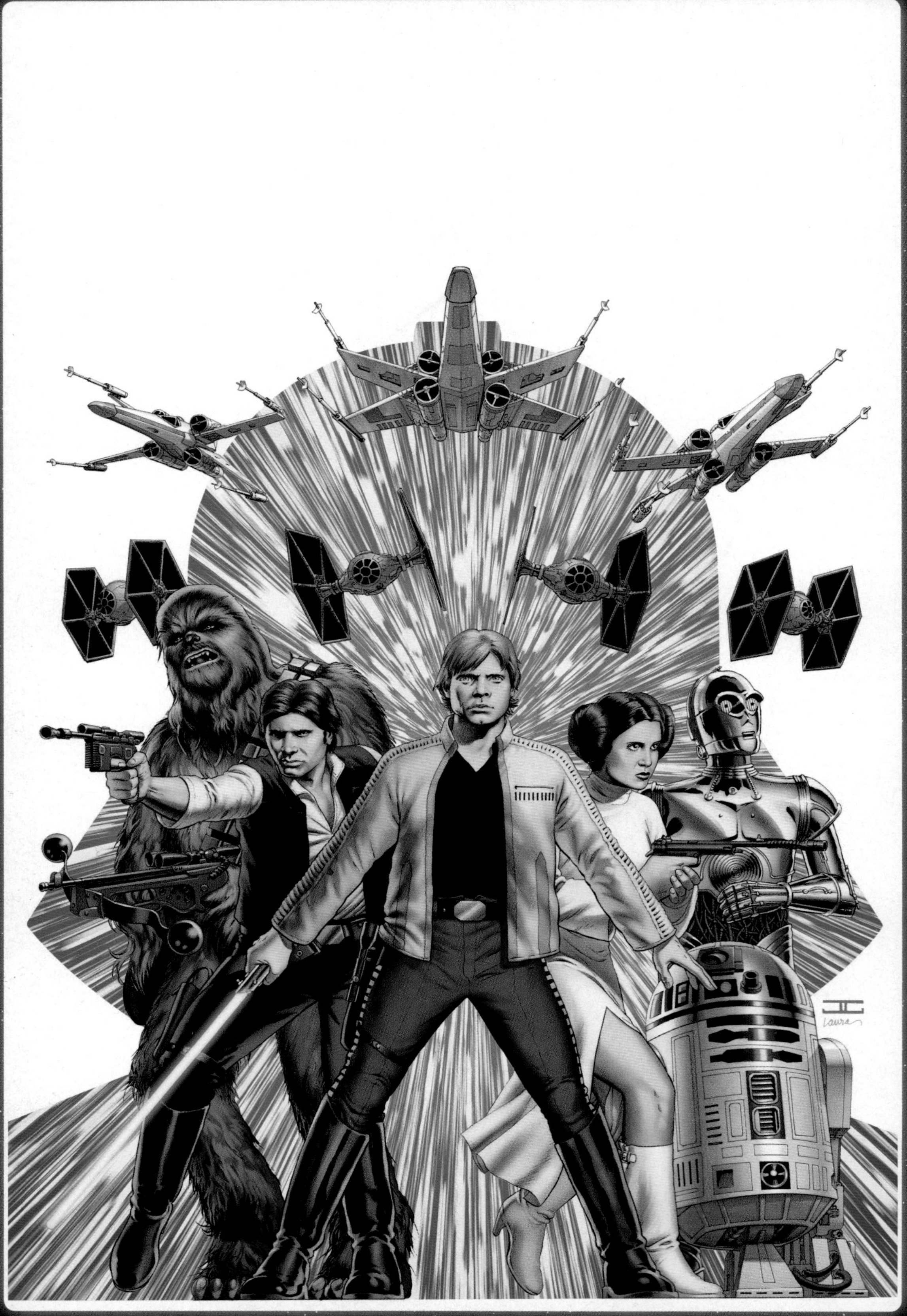

1

A long time ago in a galaxy far, far away....

ST
WA

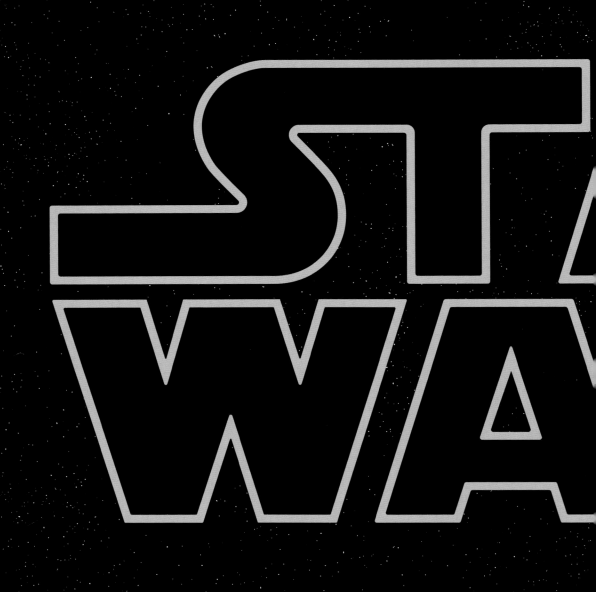

AR
RS

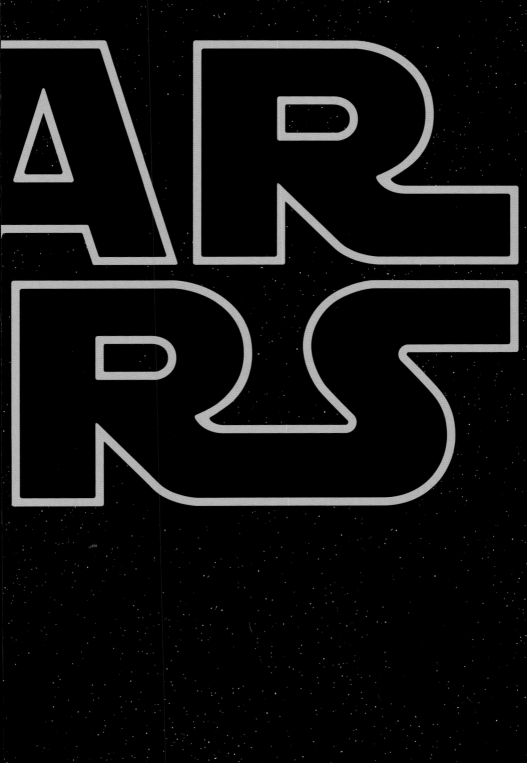

Book I

SKYWALKER STRIKES

It is a period of renewed hope for the Rebellion.

The evil Galactic Empire's greatest weapon, the Death Star, has been destroyed by the young Rebel pilot, Luke Skywalker.

With the Imperial Forces in disarray, the Rebels look to press their advantage by unleashing a daring offensive throughout the far reaches of space, hoping to defeat the Empire once and for all and at last restore freedom to the galaxy....

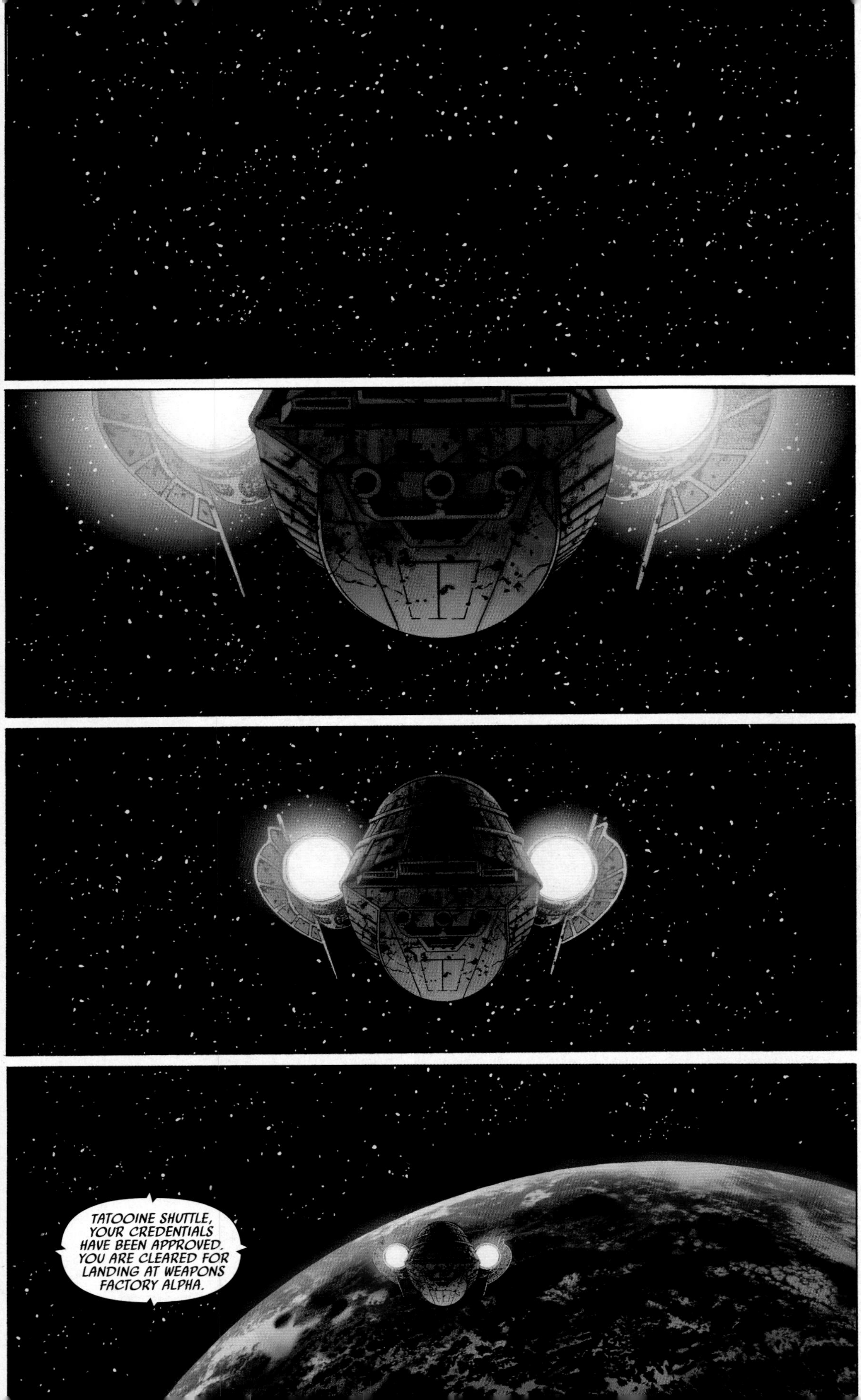
TATOOINE SHUTTLE, YOUR CREDENTIALS HAVE BEEN APPROVED. YOU ARE CLEARED FOR LANDING AT WEAPONS FACTORY ALPHA.

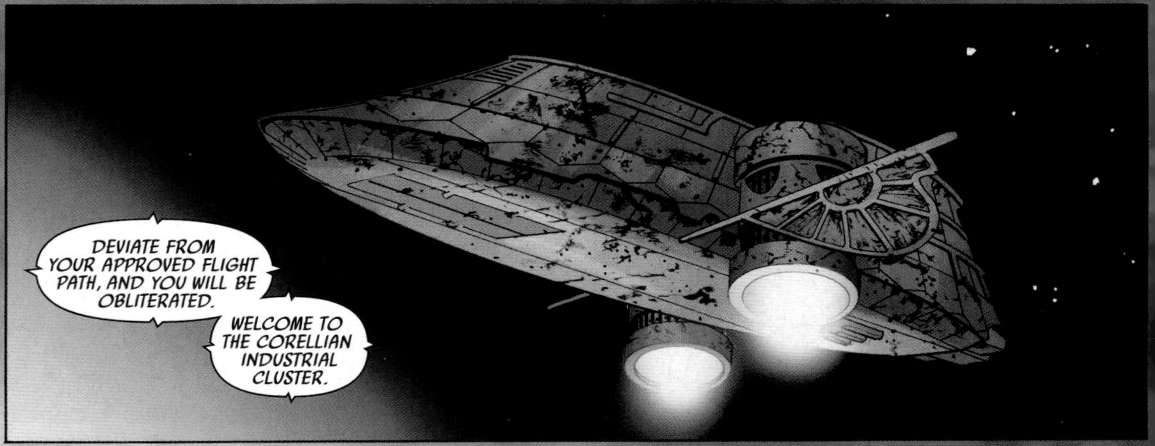
DEVIATE FROM YOUR APPROVED FLIGHT PATH, AND YOU WILL BE OBLITERATED.
WELCOME TO THE CORELLIAN INDUSTRIAL CLUSTER.
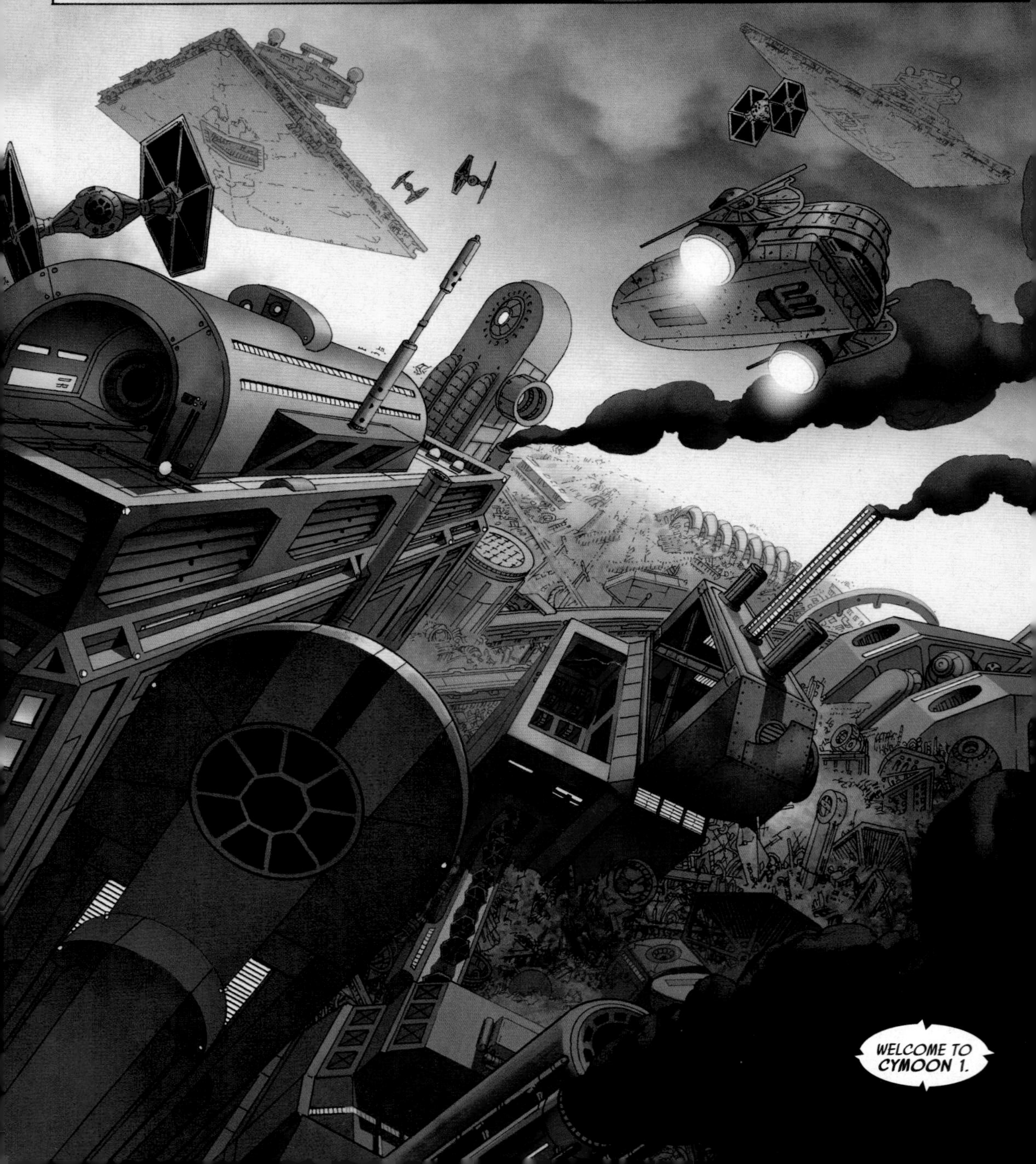
WELCOME TO CYMOON 1.

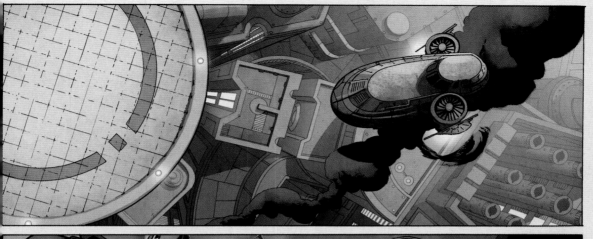

OUTER RIM SCUM, I CAN *SMELL* THEM ALREADY.

BE ON THE ALERT. IF ANYTHING SEEMS EVEN *REMOTELY* SUSPICIOUS...

...*KILL THEM ALL.*

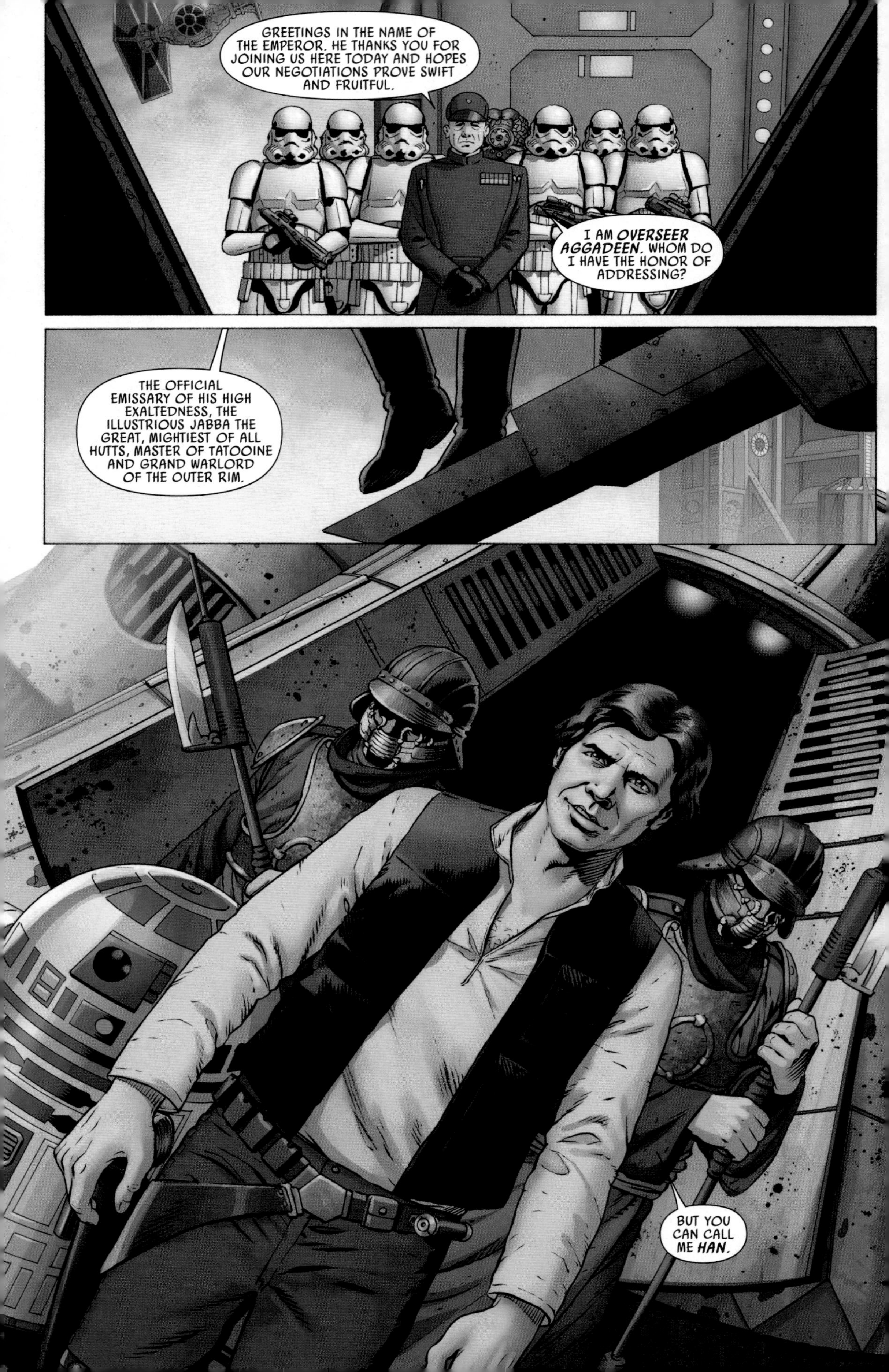
GREETINGS IN THE NAME OF THE EMPEROR. HE THANKS YOU FOR JOINING US HERE TODAY AND HOPES OUR NEGOTIATIONS PROVE SWIFT AND FRUITFUL.
I AM OVERSEER AGGADEEN. WHOM DO I HAVE THE HONOR OF ADDRESSING?
THE OFFICIAL EMISSARY OF HIS HIGH EXALTEDNESS, THE ILLUSTRIOUS JABBA THE GREAT, MIGHTIEST OF ALL HUTTS, MASTER OF TATOOINE AND GRAND WARLORD OF THE OUTER RIM.
BUT YOU CAN CALL ME HAN.

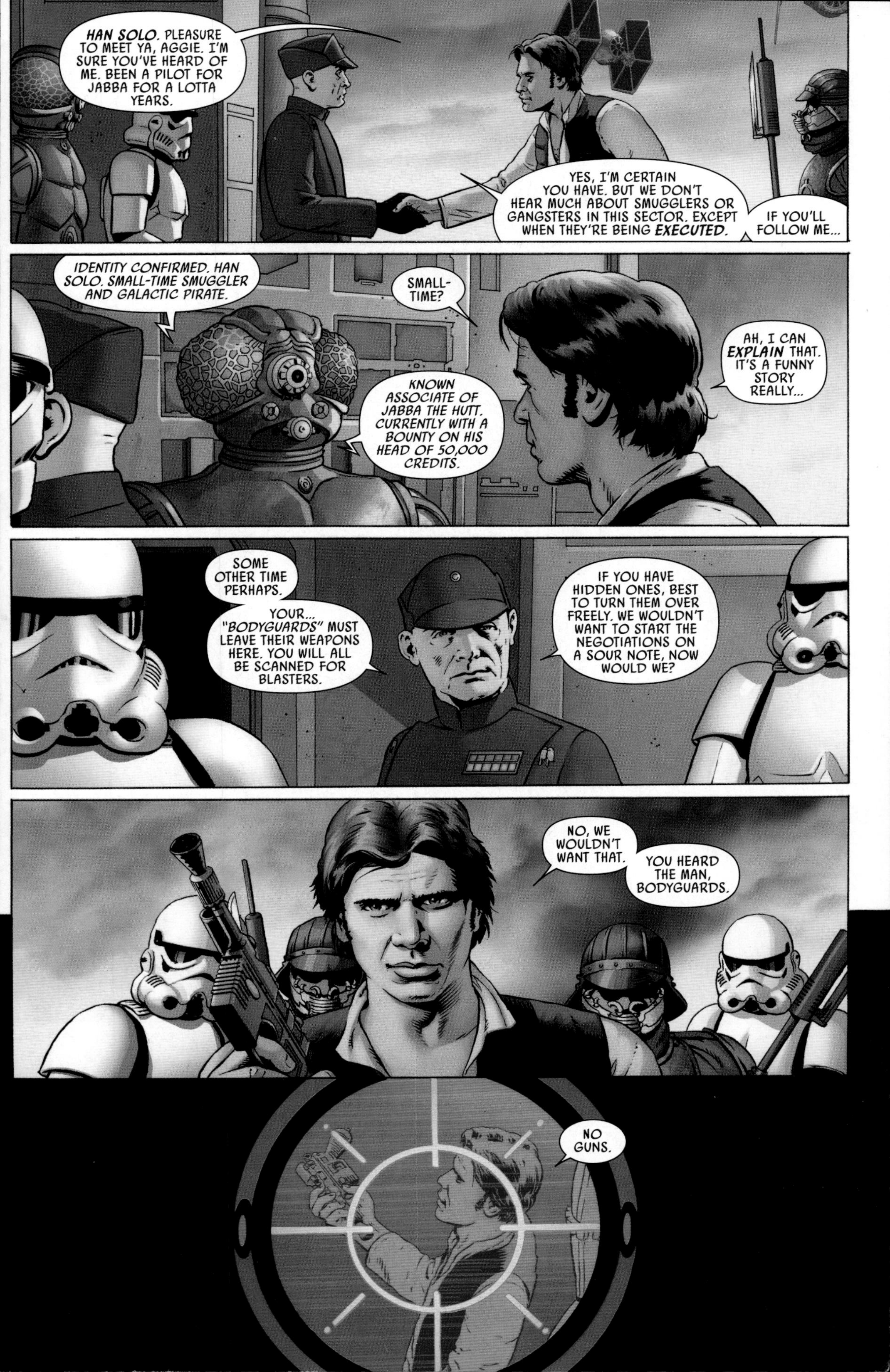

HAN SOLO. PLEASURE TO MEET YA, AGGIE. I'M SURE YOU'VE HEARD OF ME. BEEN A PILOT FOR JABBA FOR A LOTTA YEARS.
YES, I'M CERTAIN YOU HAVE. BUT WE DON'T HEAR MUCH ABOUT SMUGGLERS OR GANGSTERS IN THIS SECTOR. EXCEPT WHEN THEY'RE BEING EXECUTED.
IF YOU'LL FOLLOW ME...
IDENTITY CONFIRMED. HAN SOLO. SMALL-TIME SMUGGLER AND GALACTIC PIRATE.
SMALL-TIME?
KNOWN ASSOCIATE OF JABBA THE HUTT. CURRENTLY WITH A BOUNTY ON HIS HEAD OF 50,000 CREDITS.
AH, I CAN EXPLAIN THAT. IT'S A FUNNY STORY REALLY...
SOME OTHER TIME PERHAPS.
YOUR... "BODYGUARDS" MUST LEAVE THEIR WEAPONS HERE. YOU WILL ALL BE SCANNED FOR BLASTERS.
IF YOU HAVE HIDDEN ONES, BEST TO TURN THEM OVER FREELY. WE WOULDN'T WANT TO START THE NEGOTIATIONS ON A SOUR NOTE, NOW WOULD WE?
NO, WE WOULDN'T WANT THAT.
YOU HEARD THE MAN, BODYGUARDS.
NO GUNS.

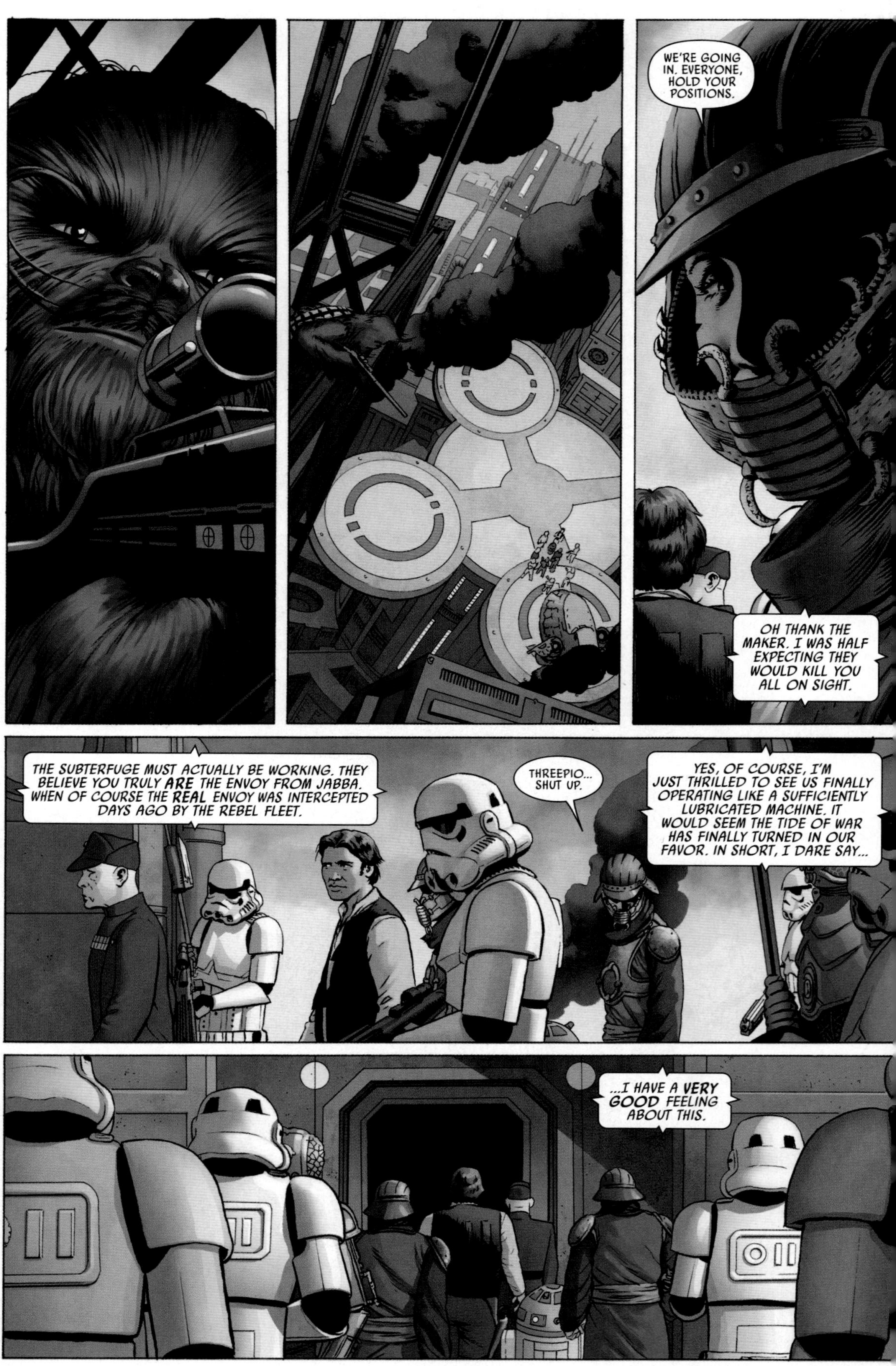

WE'RE GOING IN. EVERYONE, HOLD YOUR POSITIONS.
OH THANK THE MAKER. I WAS HALF EXPECTING THEY WOULD KILL YOU ALL ON SIGHT.
THE SUBTERFUGE MUST ACTUALLY BE WORKING. THEY BELIEVE YOU TRULY ARE THE ENVOY FROM JABBA. WHEN OF COURSE THE REAL ENVOY WAS INTERCEPTED DAYS AGO BY THE REBEL FLEET.
THREEPIO... SHUT UP.
YES, OF COURSE, I'M JUST THRILLED TO SEE US FINALLY OPERATING LIKE A SUFFICIENTLY LUBRICATED MACHINE. IT WOULD SEEM THE TIDE OF WAR HAS FINALLY TURNED IN OUR FAVOR. IN SHORT, I DARE SAY...
...I HAVE A VERY GOOD FEELING ABOUT THIS.

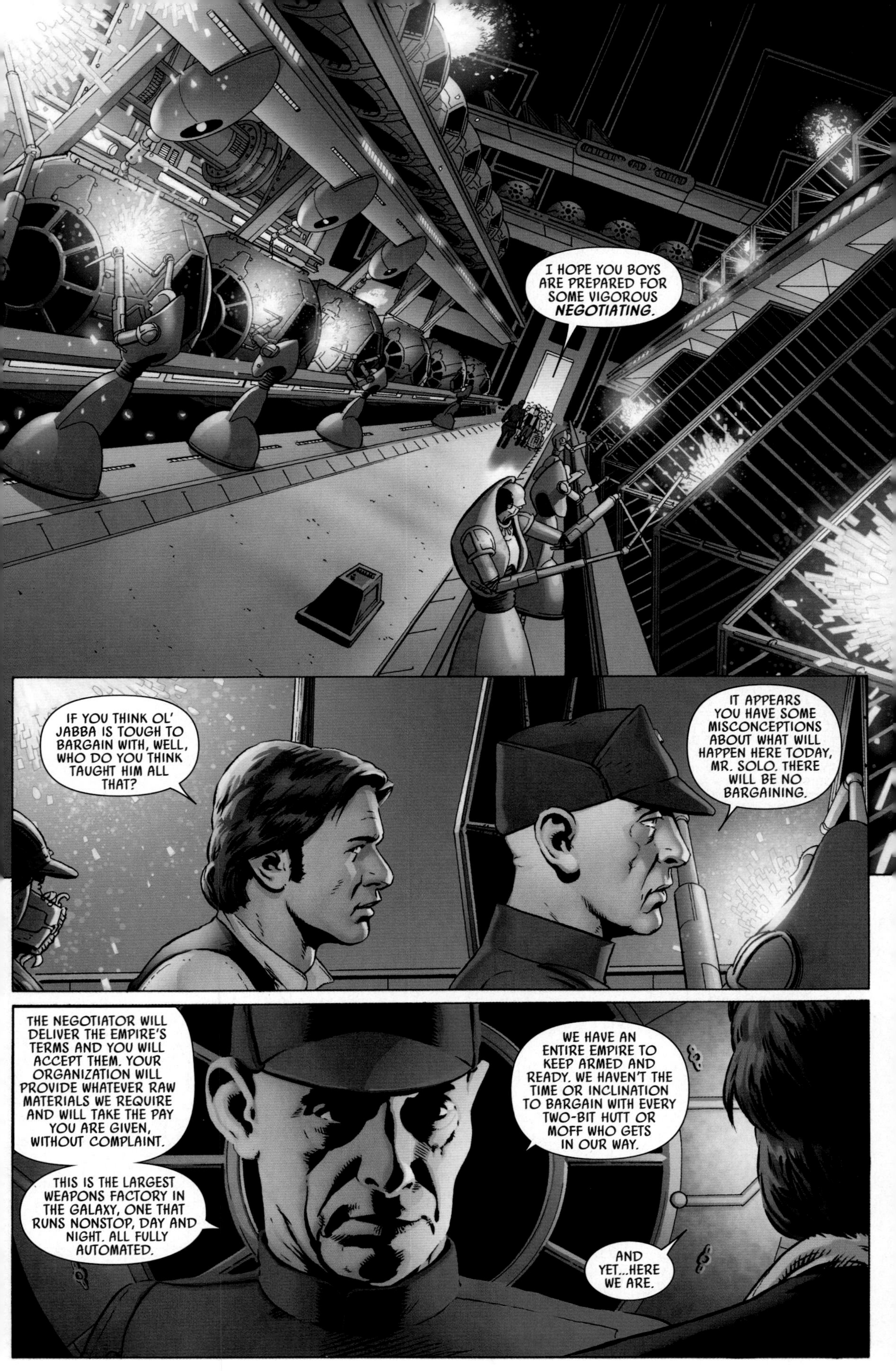
I HOPE YOU BOYS ARE PREPARED FOR SOME VIGOROUS ***NEGOTIATING.***
IF YOU THINK OL' JABBA IS TOUGH TO BARGAIN WITH, WELL, WHO DO YOU THINK TAUGHT HIM ALL THAT?
IT APPEARS YOU HAVE SOME MISCONCEPTIONS ABOUT WHAT WILL HAPPEN HERE TODAY, MR. SOLO. THERE WILL BE NO BARGAINING.
THE NEGOTIATOR WILL DELIVER THE EMPIRE'S TERMS AND YOU WILL ACCEPT THEM. YOUR ORGANIZATION WILL PROVIDE WHATEVER RAW MATERIALS WE REQUIRE AND WILL TAKE THE PAY YOU ARE GIVEN, WITHOUT COMPLAINT.
THIS IS THE LARGEST WEAPONS FACTORY IN THE GALAXY, ONE THAT RUNS NONSTOP, DAY AND NIGHT. ALL FULLY AUTOMATED.
WE HAVE AN ENTIRE EMPIRE TO KEEP ARMED AND READY. WE HAVEN'T THE TIME OR INCLINATION TO BARGAIN WITH EVERY TWO-BIT HUTT OR MOFF WHO GETS IN OUR WAY.
AND YET...HERE WE ARE.

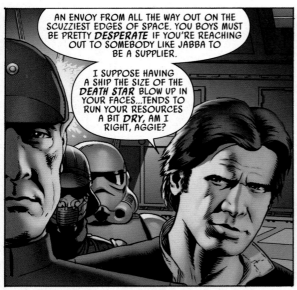

AN ENVOY FROM ALL THE WAY OUT ON THE SCUZZIEST EDGES OF SPACE. YOU BOYS MUST BE PRETTY *DESPERATE* IF YOU'RE REACHING OUT TO SOMEBODY LIKE JABBA TO BE A SUPPLIER.

I SUPPOSE HAVING A SHIP THE SIZE OF THE *DEATH STAR* BLOW UP IN YOUR FACES...TENDS TO RUN YOUR RESOURCES A BIT *DRY*, AM I RIGHT, AGGIE?

THE NEGOTIATOR WILL ARRIVE SHORTLY.

YOU WILL AWAIT HIM WITHIN.

I BET IT'S NICE AND QUIET IN THERE.

IT IS SHIELDED, YES.

YOU KNOW, I KINDA PREFER IT OUT HERE WHERE IT'S ALL LOUD AND NOISY.

DON'T BE IDIOTIC. WHY IN THE WORLD WOULD WE HOLD NEGOTIATIONS ON THE FACTORY FLOOR?

DON'T YOU REMEMBER? YOU SAID IT YOURSELF...

WE AREN'T HERE TO NEGOTIATE.

ARTOO...

YOUR DROID APPEARS TO BE LEAKING FLUIDS.

UM... ARTOO?

KZZZT

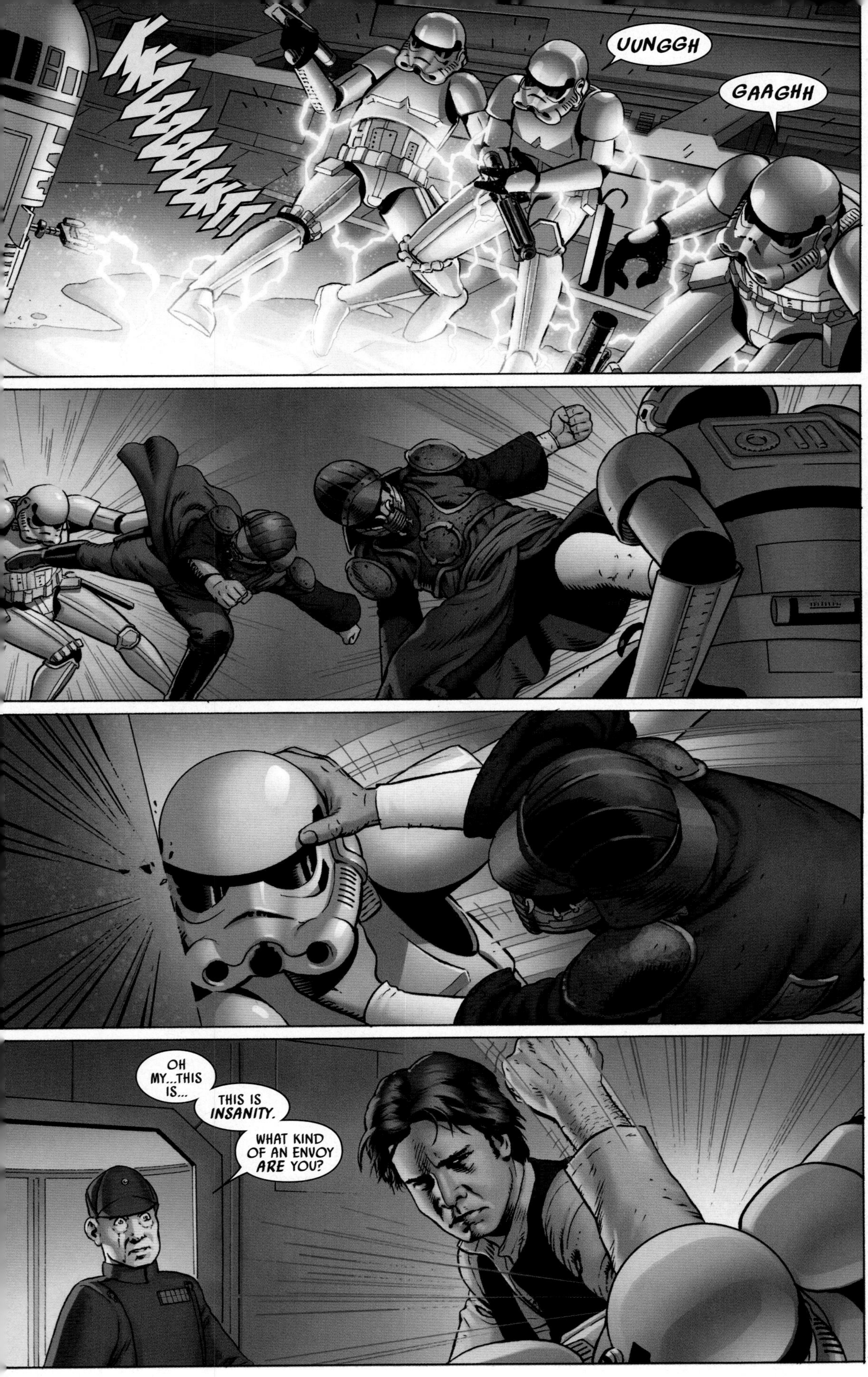
KKZZZZZZKTT
UUNGGH
GAAGHH
OH MY...THIS IS...
THIS IS INSANITY.
WHAT KIND OF AN ENVOY ARE YOU?

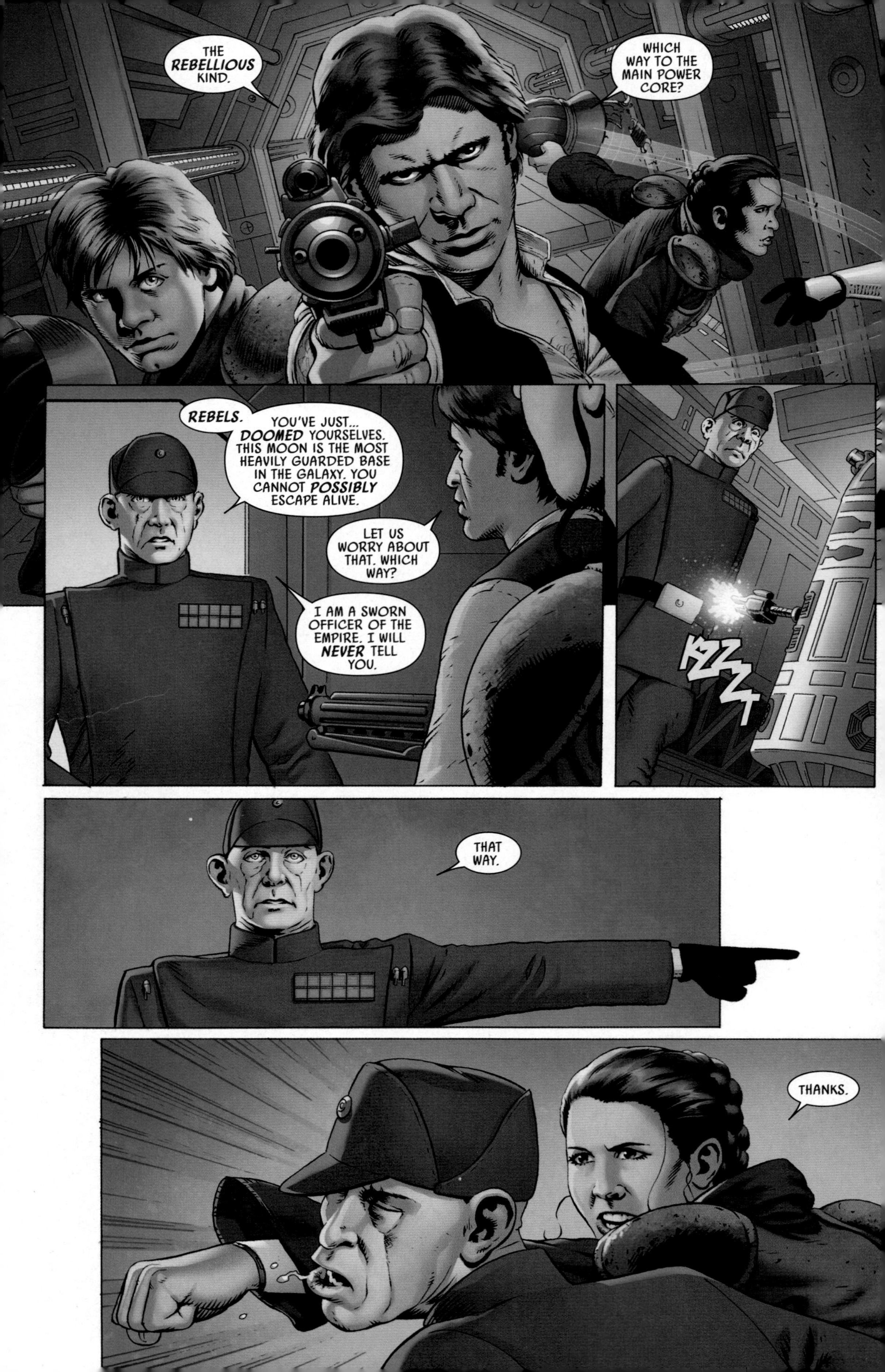
THE REBELLIOUS KIND.
WHICH WAY TO THE MAIN POWER CORE?
REBELS.
YOU'VE JUST... DOOMED YOURSELVES. THIS MOON IS THE MOST HEAVILY GUARDED BASE IN THE GALAXY. YOU CANNOT POSSIBLY ESCAPE ALIVE.
LET US WORRY ABOUT THAT. WHICH WAY?
I AM A SWORN OFFICER OF THE EMPIRE. I WILL NEVER TELL YOU.
KZZZT
THAT WAY.
THANKS.

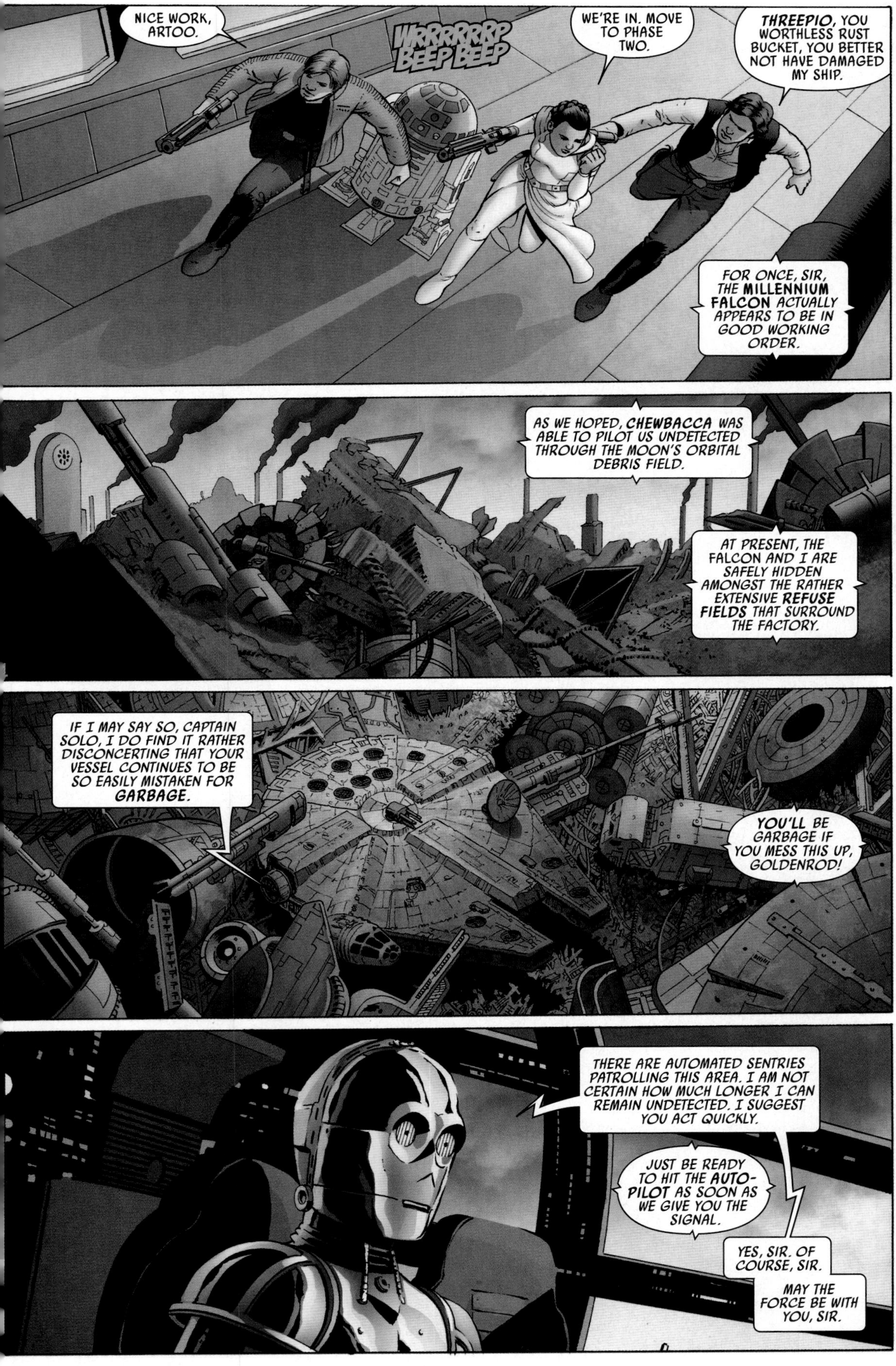
NICE WORK, ARTOO.
WRRRRRRP BEEP BEEP
WE'RE IN. MOVE TO PHASE TWO.
THREEPIO, YOU WORTHLESS RUST BUCKET, YOU BETTER NOT HAVE DAMAGED MY SHIP.
FOR ONCE, SIR, THE MILLENNIUM FALCON ACTUALLY APPEARS TO BE IN GOOD WORKING ORDER.
AS WE HOPED, CHEWBACCA WAS ABLE TO PILOT US UNDETECTED THROUGH THE MOON'S ORBITAL DEBRIS FIELD.
AT PRESENT, THE FALCON AND I ARE SAFELY HIDDEN AMONGST THE RATHER EXTENSIVE REFUSE FIELDS THAT SURROUND THE FACTORY.
IF I MAY SAY SO, CAPTAIN SOLO, I DO FIND IT RATHER DISCONCERTING THAT YOUR VESSEL CONTINUES TO BE SO EASILY MISTAKEN FOR GARBAGE.
YOU'LL BE GARBAGE IF YOU MESS THIS UP, GOLDENROD!
THERE ARE AUTOMATED SENTRIES PATROLLING THIS AREA. I AM NOT CERTAIN HOW MUCH LONGER I CAN REMAIN UNDETECTED. I SUGGEST YOU ACT QUICKLY.
JUST BE READY TO HIT THE AUTO-PILOT AS SOON AS WE GIVE YOU THE SIGNAL.
YES, SIR. OF COURSE, SIR.
MAY THE FORCE BE WITH YOU, SIR.

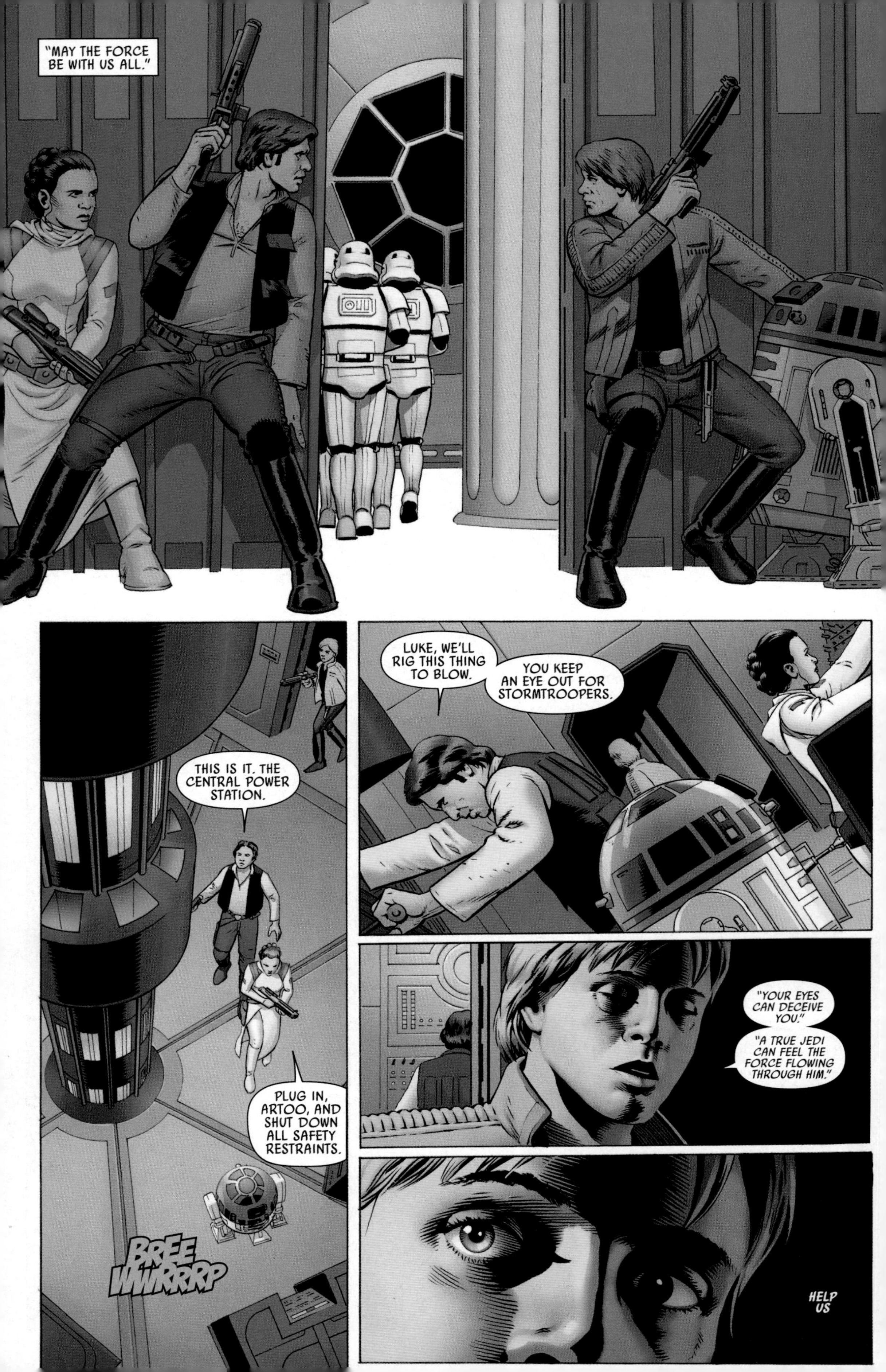
"MAY THE FORCE BE WITH US ALL."
THIS IS IT. THE CENTRAL POWER STATION.
PLUG IN, ARTOO, AND SHUT DOWN ALL SAFETY RESTRAINTS.
BREEWWRRRP
LUKE, WE'LL RIG THIS THING TO BLOW.
YOU KEEP AN EYE OUT FOR STORMTROOPERS.
"YOUR EYES CAN DECEIVE YOU."
"A TRUE JEDI CAN FEEL THE FORCE FLOWING THROUGH HIM."
HELP US

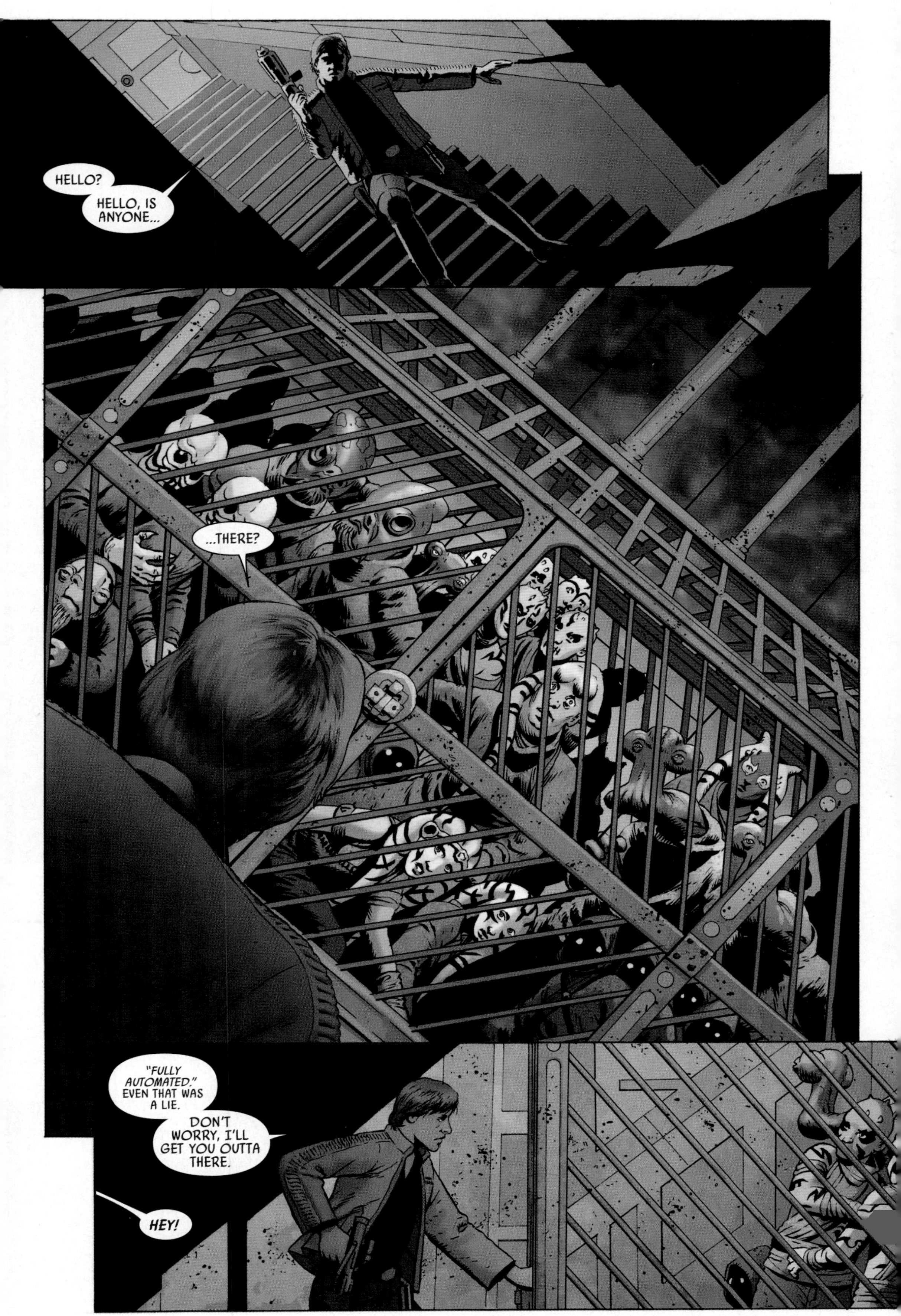
HELLO?
HELLO, IS ANYONE...
...THERE?
"FULLY AUTOMATED." EVEN THAT WAS A LIE.
DON'T WORRY, I'LL GET YOU OUTTA THERE.
HEY!

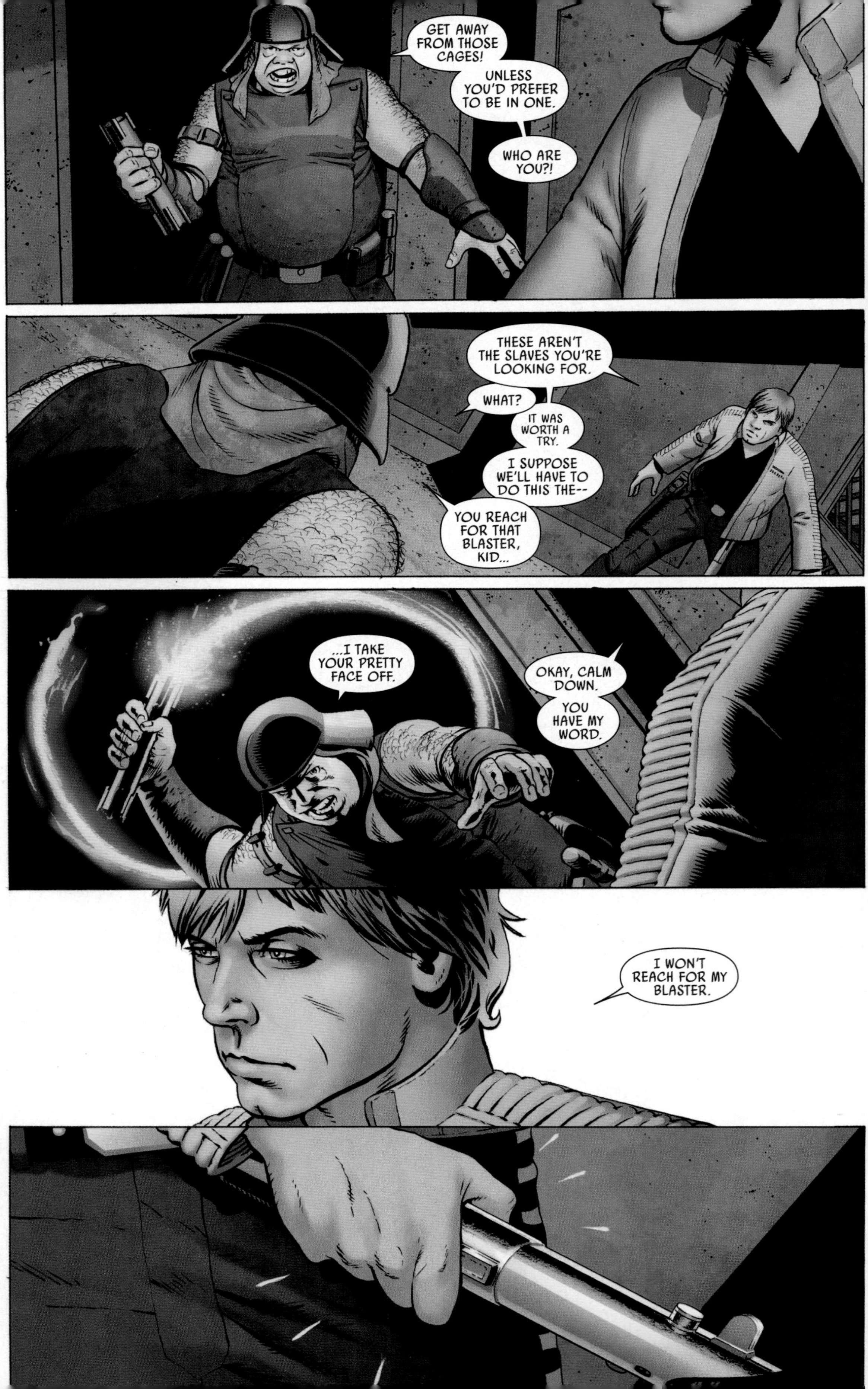
GET AWAY FROM THOSE CAGES!
UNLESS YOU'D PREFER TO BE IN ONE.
WHO ARE YOU?!
THESE AREN'T THE SLAVES YOU'RE LOOKING FOR.
WHAT?
IT WAS WORTH A TRY.
I SUPPOSE WE'LL HAVE TO DO THIS THE--
YOU REACH FOR THAT BLASTER, KID...
...I TAKE YOUR PRETTY FACE OFF.
OKAY, CALM DOWN.
YOU HAVE MY WORD.
I WON'T REACH FOR MY BLASTER.

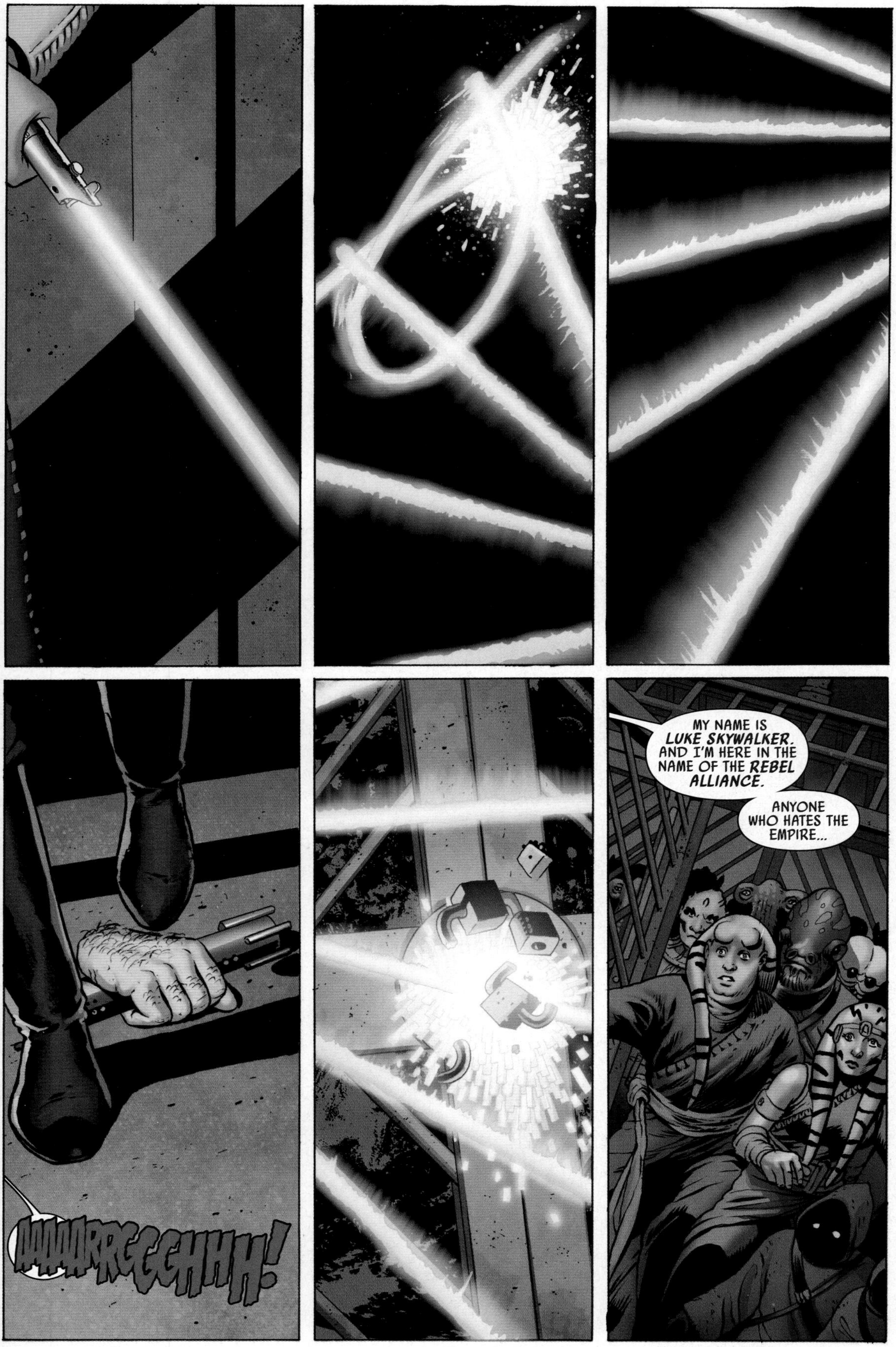
AAAAARRGGGHHHH!
MY NAME IS LUKE SKYWALKER. AND I'M HERE IN THE NAME OF THE REBEL ALLIANCE.
ANYONE WHO HATES THE EMPIRE...

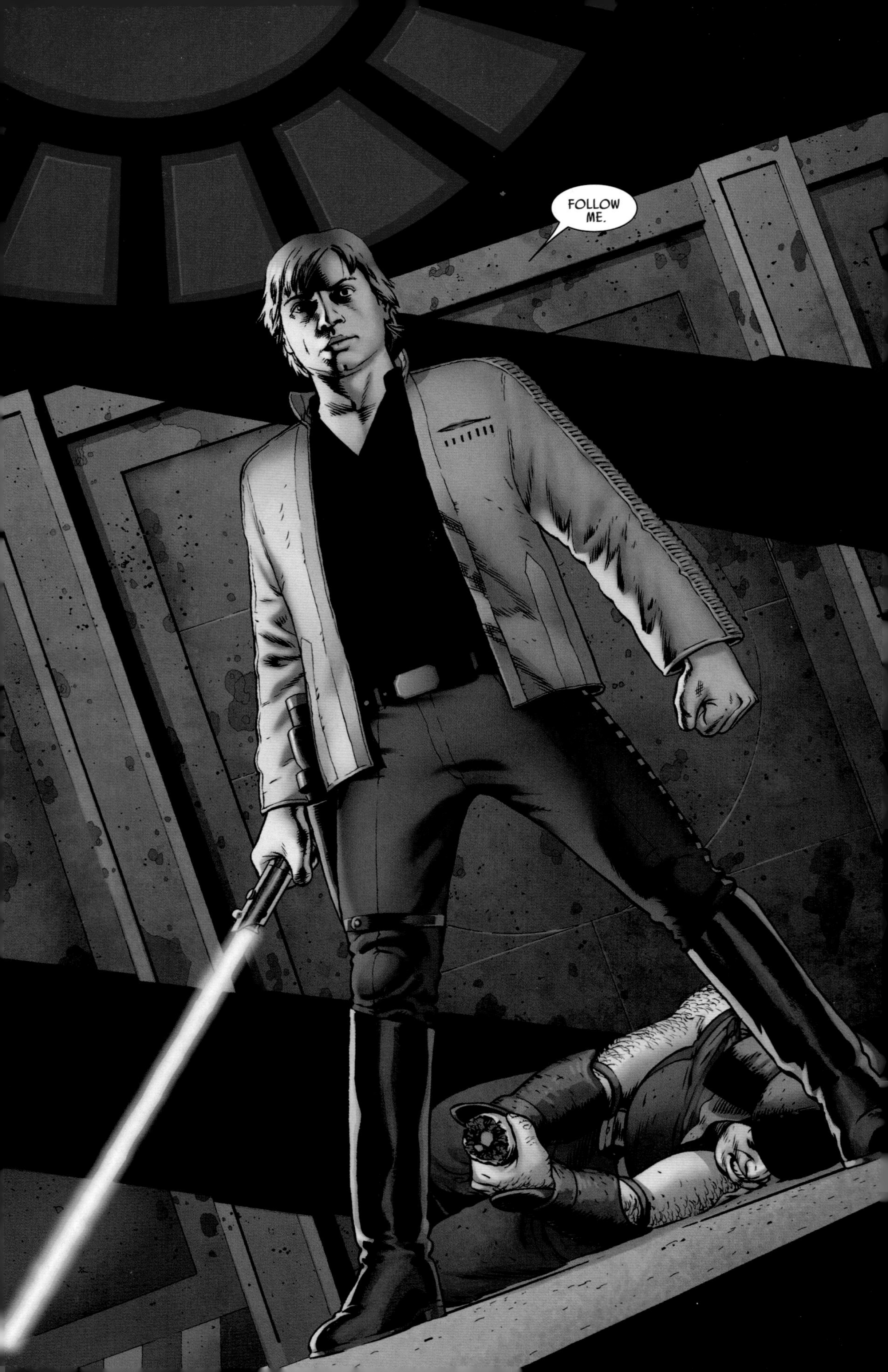
FOLLOW ME.

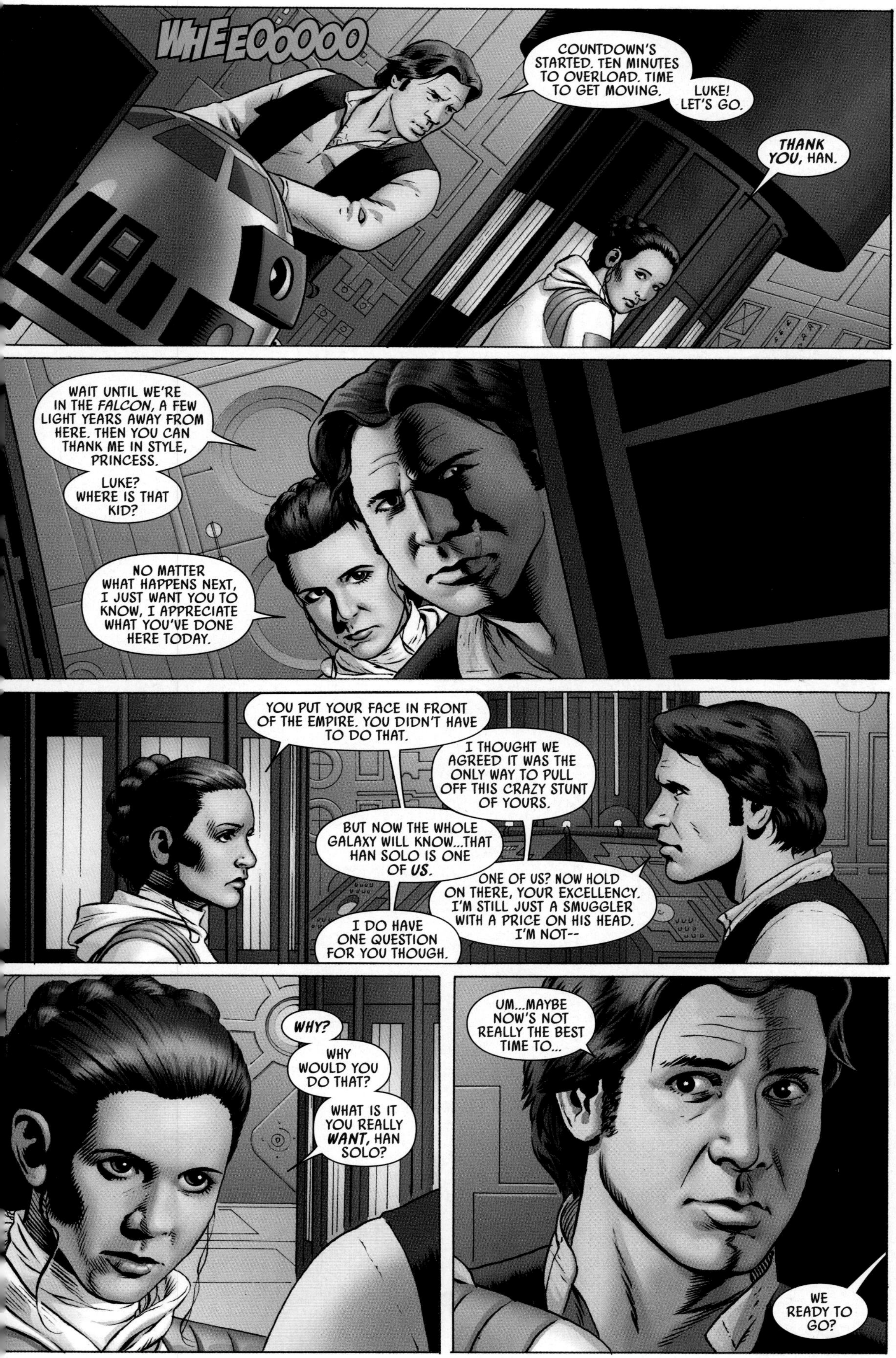
WHEEOOOOO
COUNTDOWN'S STARTED. TEN MINUTES TO OVERLOAD. TIME TO GET MOVING.
LUKE! LET'S GO.
THANK YOU, HAN.
WAIT UNTIL WE'RE IN THE FALCON, A FEW LIGHT YEARS AWAY FROM HERE. THEN YOU CAN THANK ME IN STYLE, PRINCESS.
LUKE? WHERE IS THAT KID?
NO MATTER WHAT HAPPENS NEXT, I JUST WANT YOU TO KNOW, I APPRECIATE WHAT YOU'VE DONE HERE TODAY.
YOU PUT YOUR FACE IN FRONT OF THE EMPIRE. YOU DIDN'T HAVE TO DO THAT.
I THOUGHT WE AGREED IT WAS THE ONLY WAY TO PULL OFF THIS CRAZY STUNT OF YOURS.
BUT NOW THE WHOLE GALAXY WILL KNOW...THAT HAN SOLO IS ONE OF US.
ONE OF US? NOW HOLD ON THERE, YOUR EXCELLENCY. I'M STILL JUST A SMUGGLER WITH A PRICE ON HIS HEAD. I'M NOT--
I DO HAVE ONE QUESTION FOR YOU THOUGH.
WHY?
WHY WOULD YOU DO THAT?
WHAT IS IT YOU REALLY WANT, HAN SOLO?
UM...MAYBE NOW'S NOT REALLY THE BEST TIME TO...
WE READY TO GO?

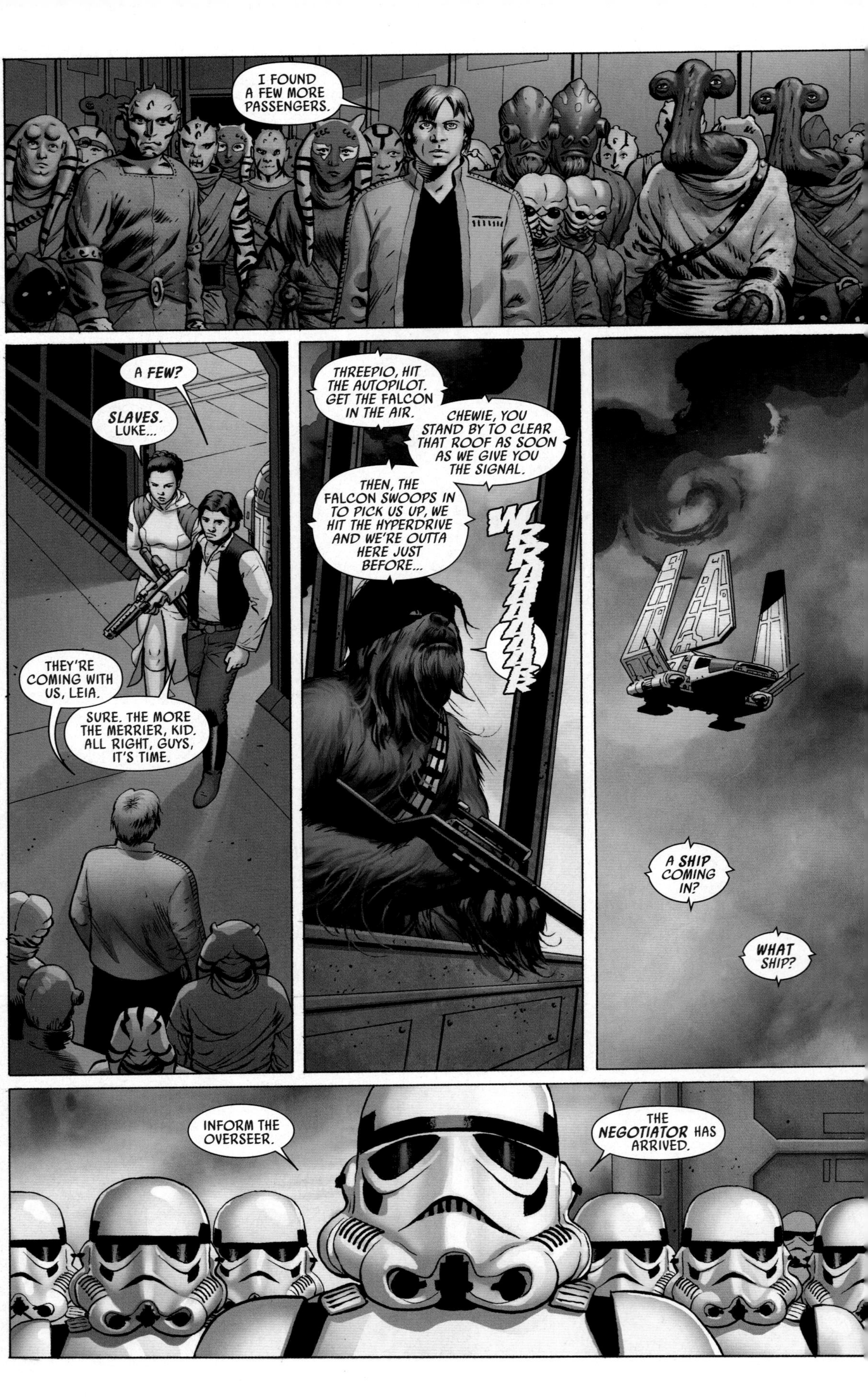

I FOUND A FEW MORE PASSENGERS.
A FEW?
SLAVES. LUKE...
THEY'RE COMING WITH US, LEIA.
SURE. THE MORE THE MERRIER, KID. ALL RIGHT, GUYS, IT'S TIME.
THREEPIO, HIT THE AUTOPILOT. GET THE FALCON IN THE AIR.
CHEWIE, YOU STAND BY TO CLEAR THAT ROOF AS SOON AS WE GIVE YOU THE SIGNAL.
THEN, THE FALCON SWOOPS IN TO PICK US UP, WE HIT THE HYPERDRIVE AND WE'RE OUTTA HERE JUST BEFORE...
WRAAAAAR
A SHIP COMING IN?
WHAT SHIP?
INFORM THE OVERSEER.
THE NEGOTIATOR HAS ARRIVED.

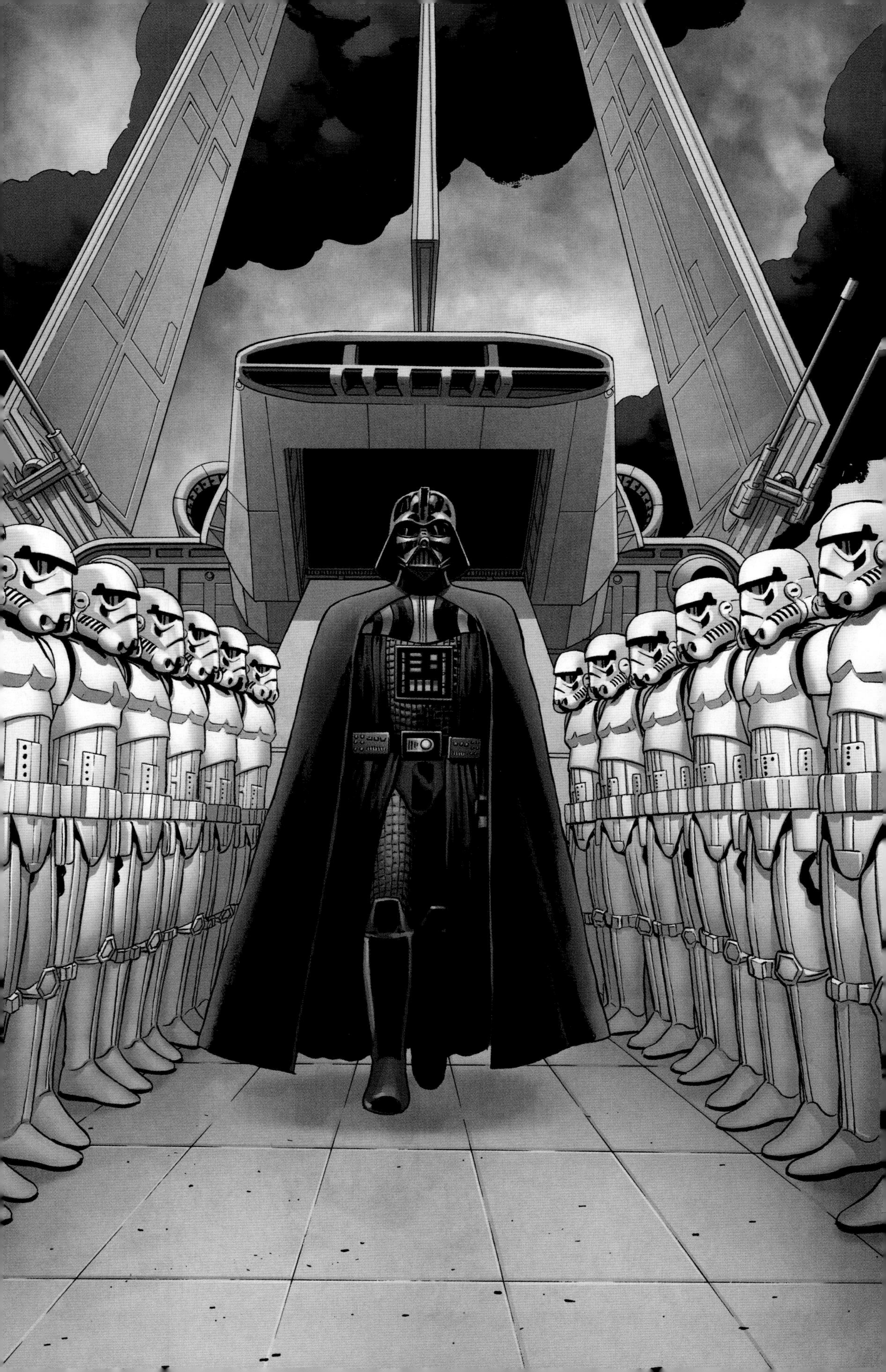

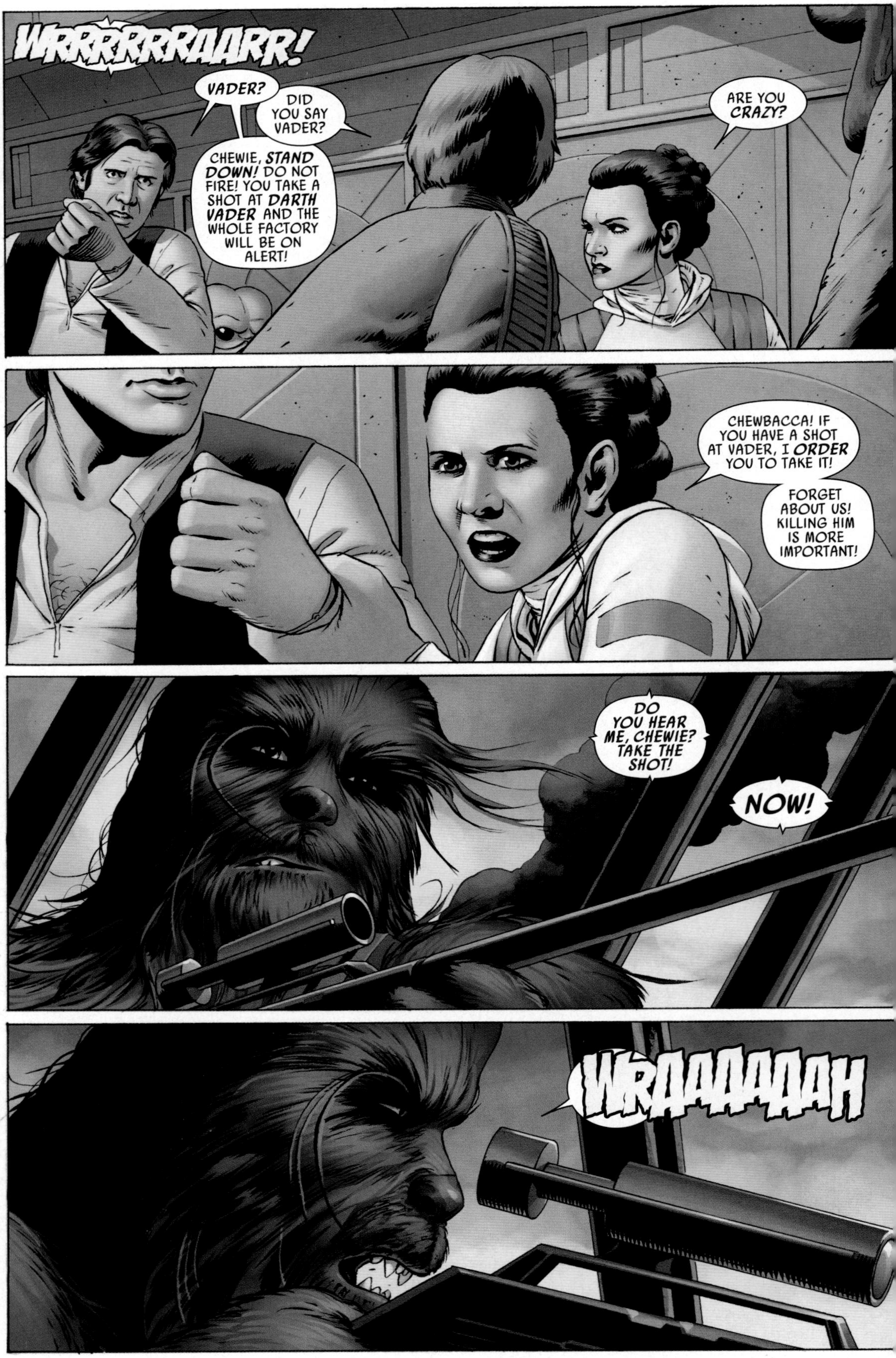
WRRRRRRAARR!
VADER?
DID YOU SAY VADER?
CHEWIE, STAND DOWN! DO NOT FIRE! YOU TAKE A SHOT AT DARTH VADER AND THE WHOLE FACTORY WILL BE ON ALERT!
ARE YOU CRAZY?
CHEWBACCA! IF YOU HAVE A SHOT AT VADER, I ORDER YOU TO TAKE IT!
FORGET ABOUT US! KILLING HIM IS MORE IMPORTANT!
DO YOU HEAR ME, CHEWIE? TAKE THE SHOT!
NOW!
WRAAAAAAH

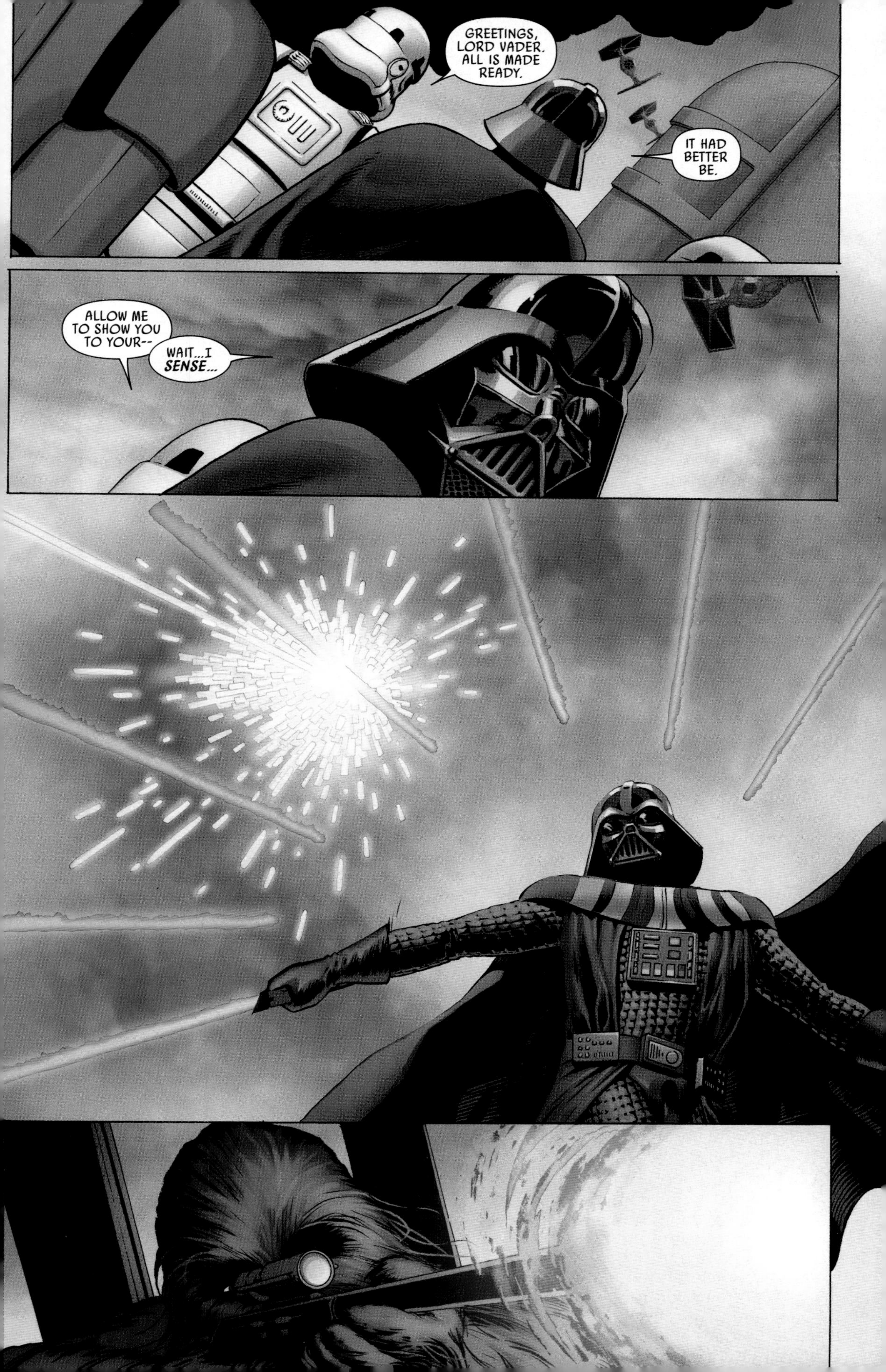
GREETINGS, LORD VADER. ALL IS MADE READY.
IT HAD BETTER BE.
ALLOW ME TO SHOW YOU TO YOUR--
WAIT...I SENSE...

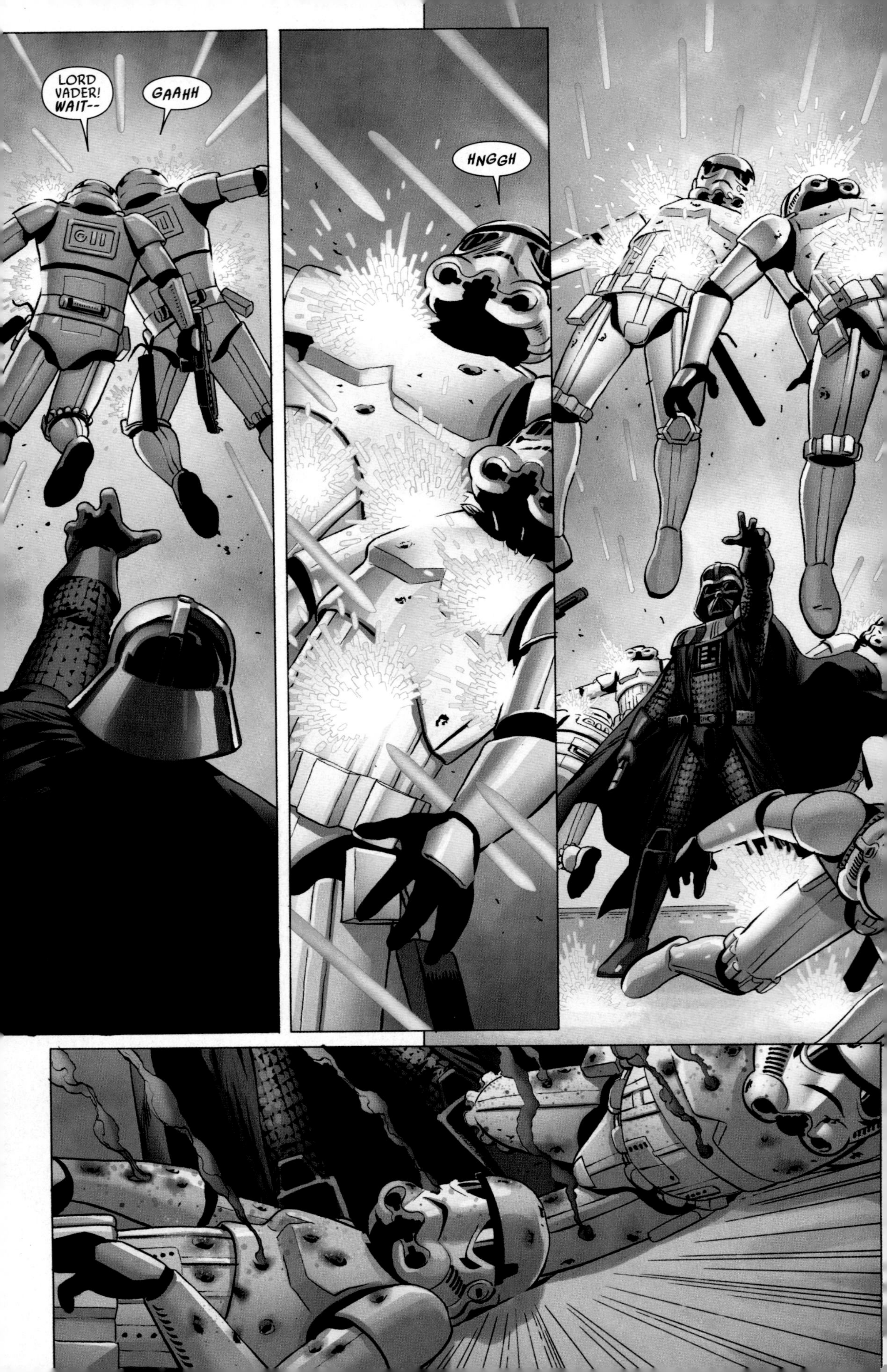
LORD VADER! WAIT--
GAAHH
HNGGH

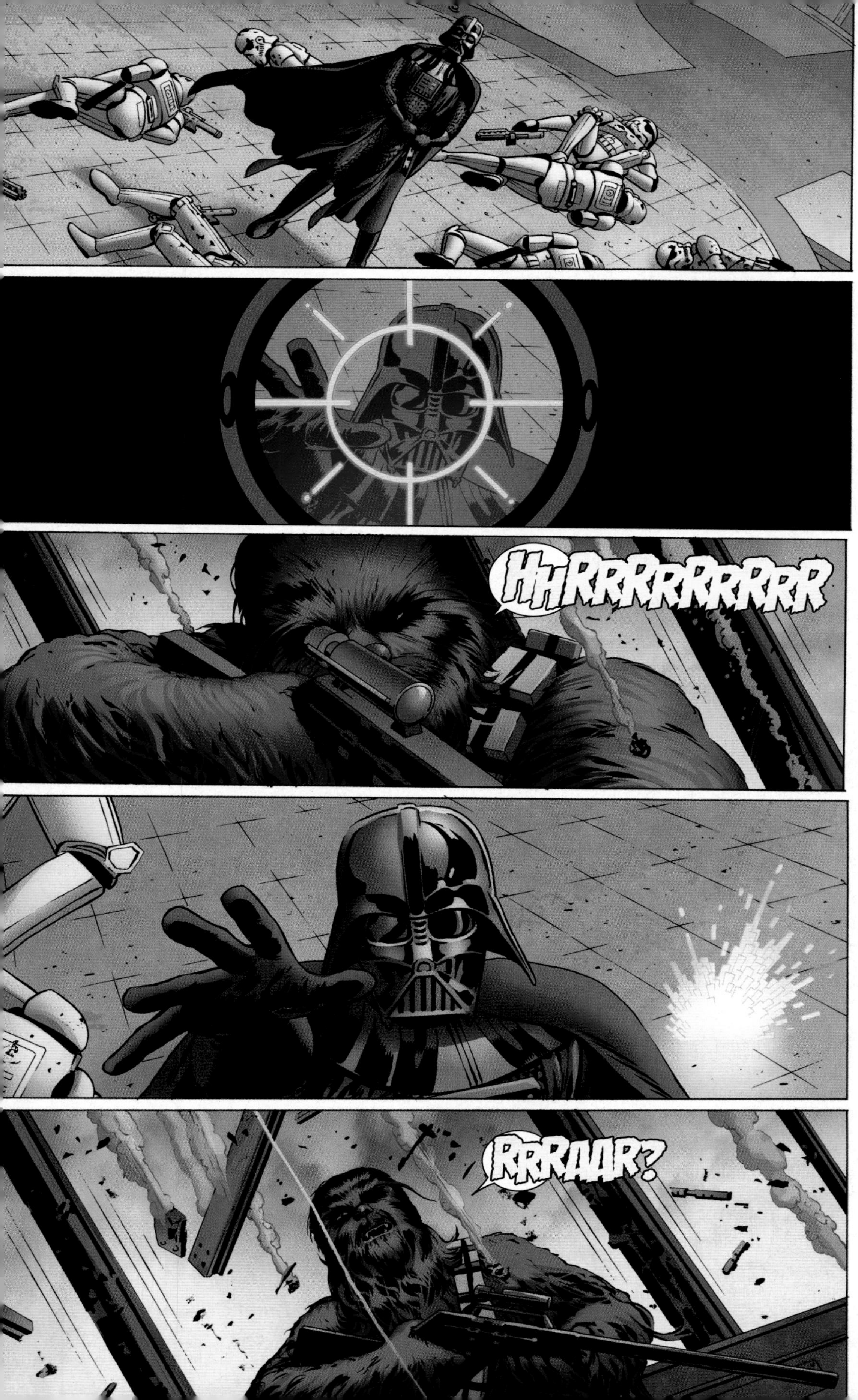
HHRRRRRRRRRR
RRRAAR?

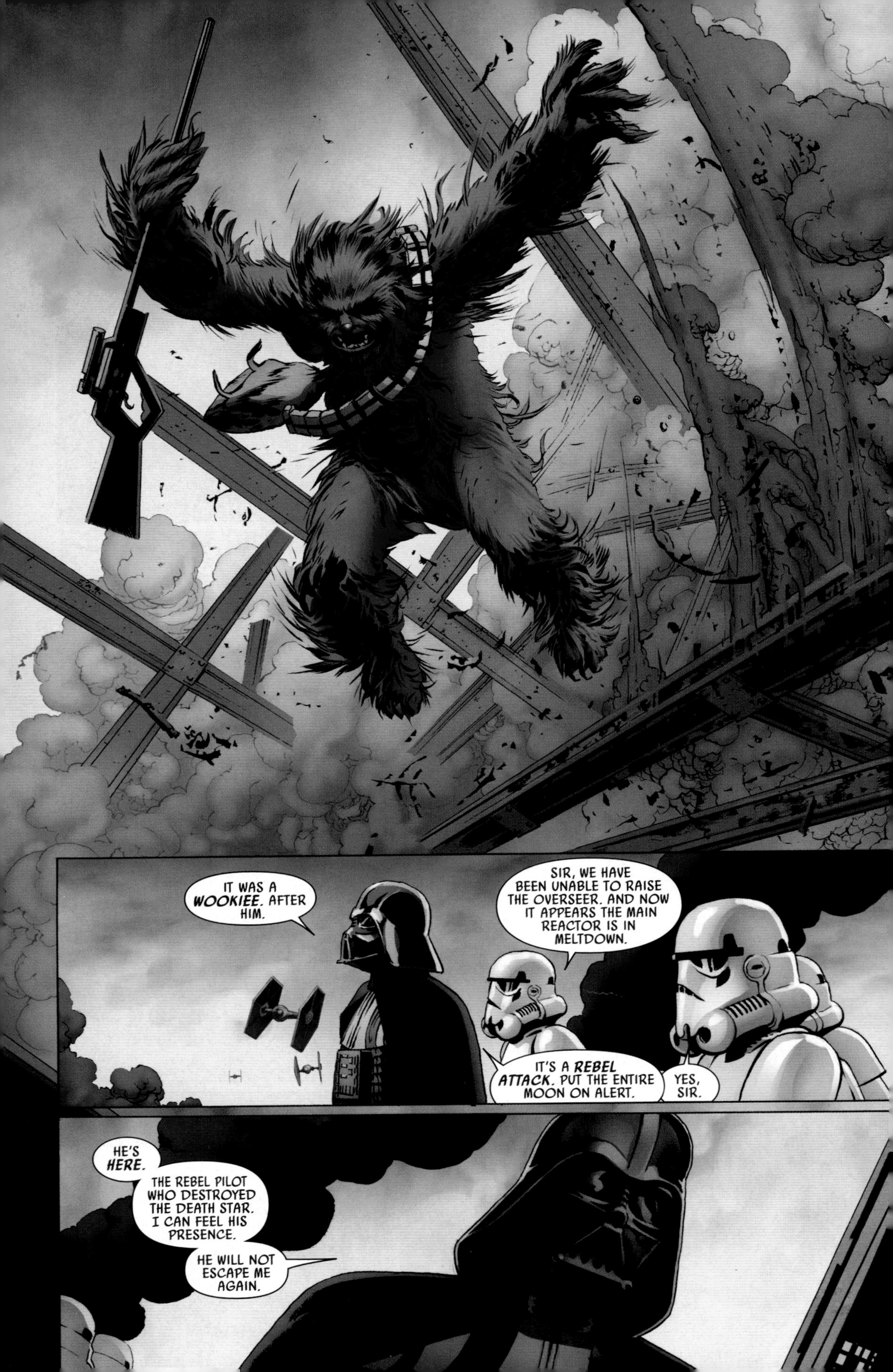

IT WAS A WOOKIEE. AFTER HIM.
SIR, WE HAVE BEEN UNABLE TO RAISE THE OVERSEER. AND NOW IT APPEARS THE MAIN REACTOR IS IN MELTDOWN.
IT'S A REBEL ATTACK. PUT THE ENTIRE MOON ON ALERT.
YES, SIR.
HE'S HERE.
THE REBEL PILOT WHO DESTROYED THE DEATH STAR. I CAN FEEL HIS PRESENCE.
HE WILL NOT ESCAPE ME AGAIN.

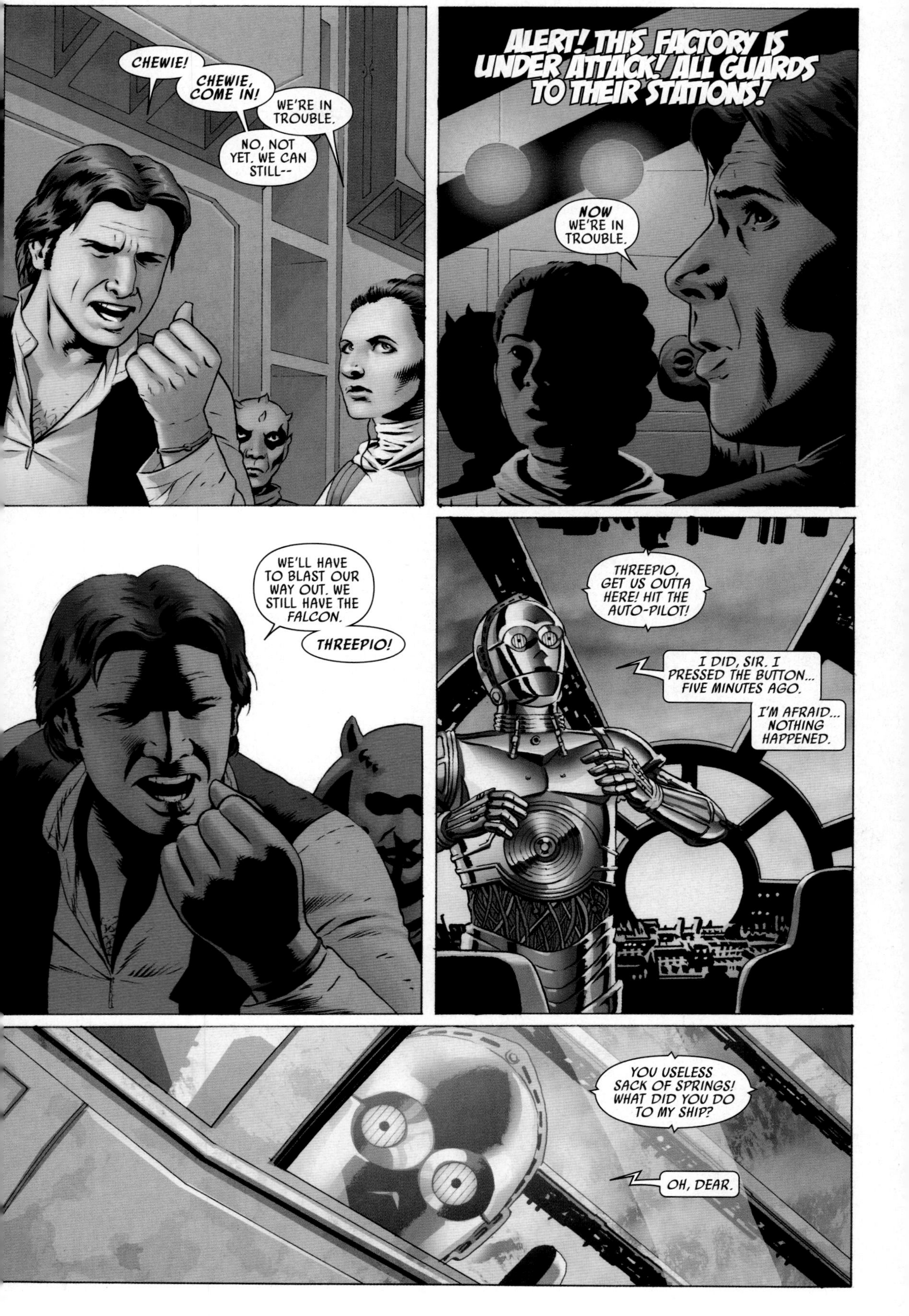
CHEWIE!
CHEWIE, COME IN!
WE'RE IN TROUBLE.
NO, NOT YET. WE CAN STILL--
ALERT! THIS FACTORY IS UNDER ATTACK! ALL GUARDS TO THEIR STATIONS!
NOW WE'RE IN TROUBLE.
WE'LL HAVE TO BLAST OUR WAY OUT. WE STILL HAVE THE FALCON.
THREEPIO!
THREEPIO, GET US OUTTA HERE! HIT THE AUTO-PILOT!
I DID, SIR. I PRESSED THE BUTTON... FIVE MINUTES AGO.
I'M AFRAID... NOTHING HAPPENED.
YOU USELESS SACK OF SPRINGS! WHAT DID YOU DO TO MY SHIP?
OH, DEAR.

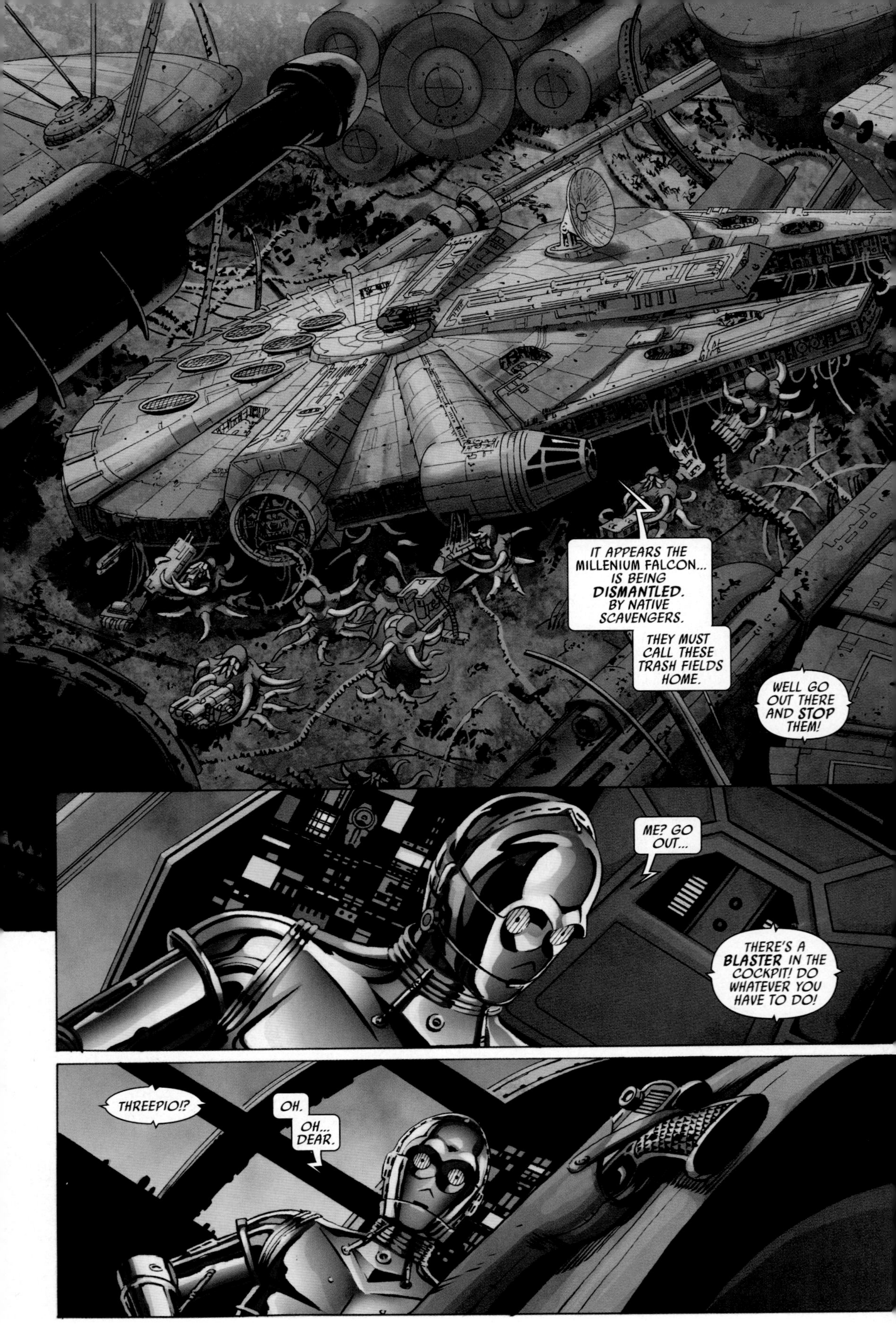
IT APPEARS THE MILLENIUM FALCON... IS BEING DISMANTLED. BY NATIVE SCAVENGERS.
THEY MUST CALL THESE TRASH FIELDS HOME.
WELL GO OUT THERE AND STOP THEM!
ME? GO OUT...
THERE'S A BLASTER IN THE COCKPIT! DO WHATEVER YOU HAVE TO DO!
THREEPIO!?
OH.
OH... DEAR.

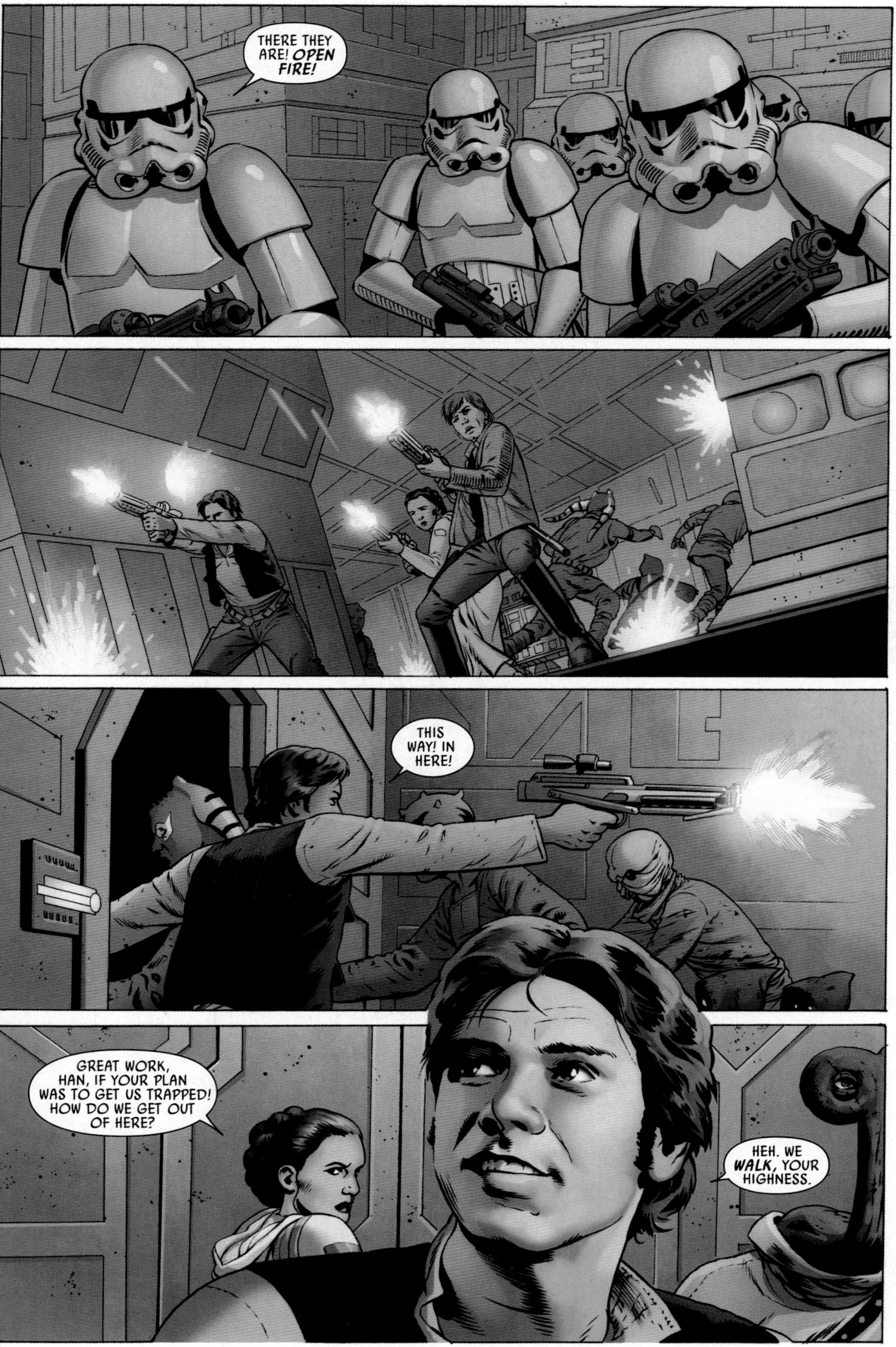
THERE THEY ARE! OPEN FIRE!
THIS WAY! IN HERE!
GREAT WORK, HAN, IF YOUR PLAN WAS TO GET US TRAPPED! HOW DO WE GET OUT OF HERE?
HEH. WE WALK, YOUR HIGHNESS.

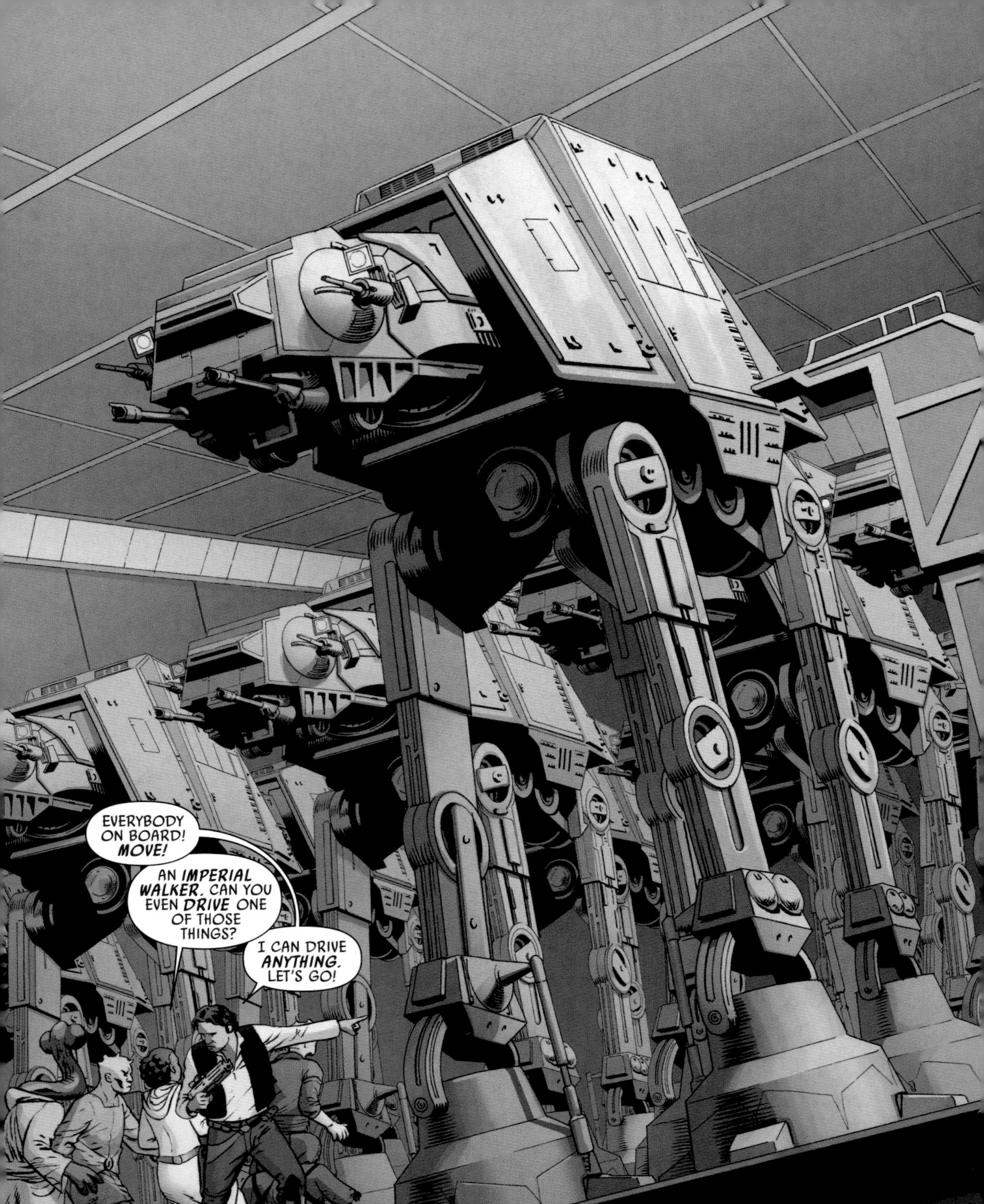
EVERYBODY ON BOARD! MOVE!
AN IMPERIAL WALKER. CAN YOU EVEN DRIVE ONE OF THOSE THINGS?
I CAN DRIVE ANYTHING. LET'S GO!

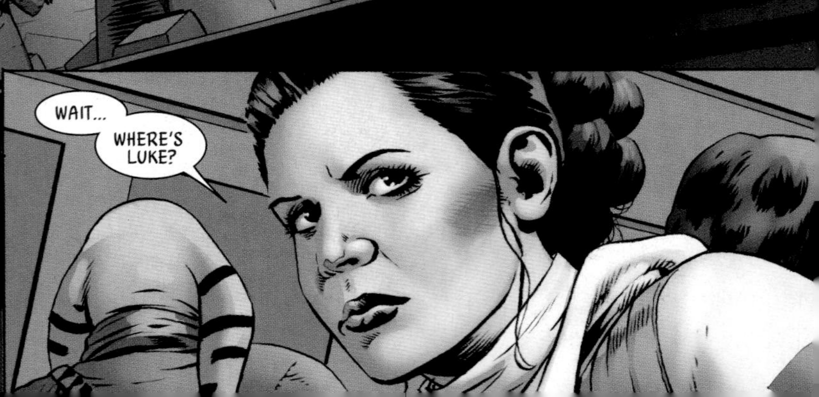
WAIT...
WHERE'S LUKE?

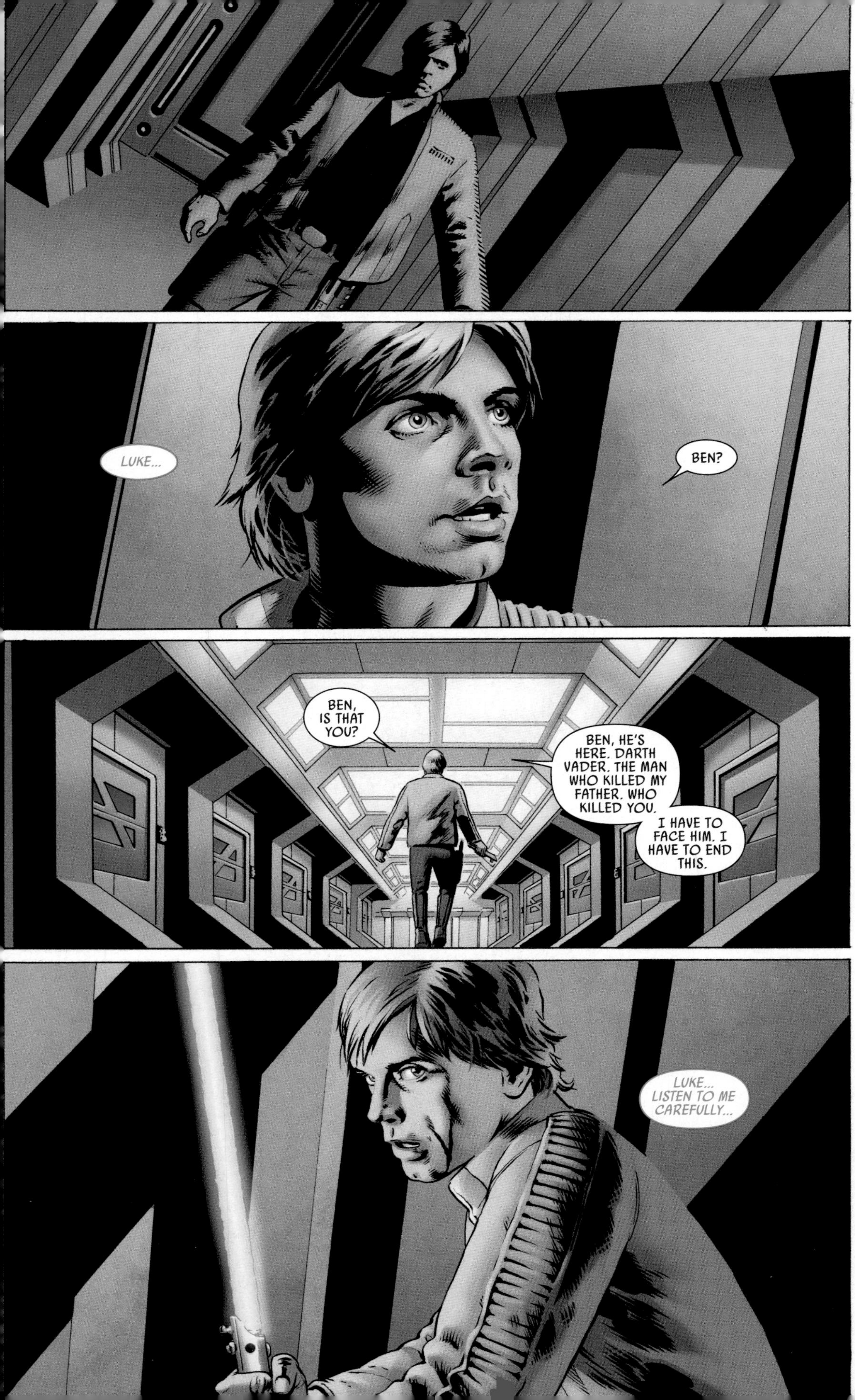

LUKE...
BEN?
BEN, IS THAT YOU?
BEN, HE'S HERE. DARTH VADER. THE MAN WHO KILLED MY FATHER. WHO KILLED YOU.
I HAVE TO FACE HIM. I HAVE TO END THIS.
LUKE... LISTEN TO ME CAREFULLY...

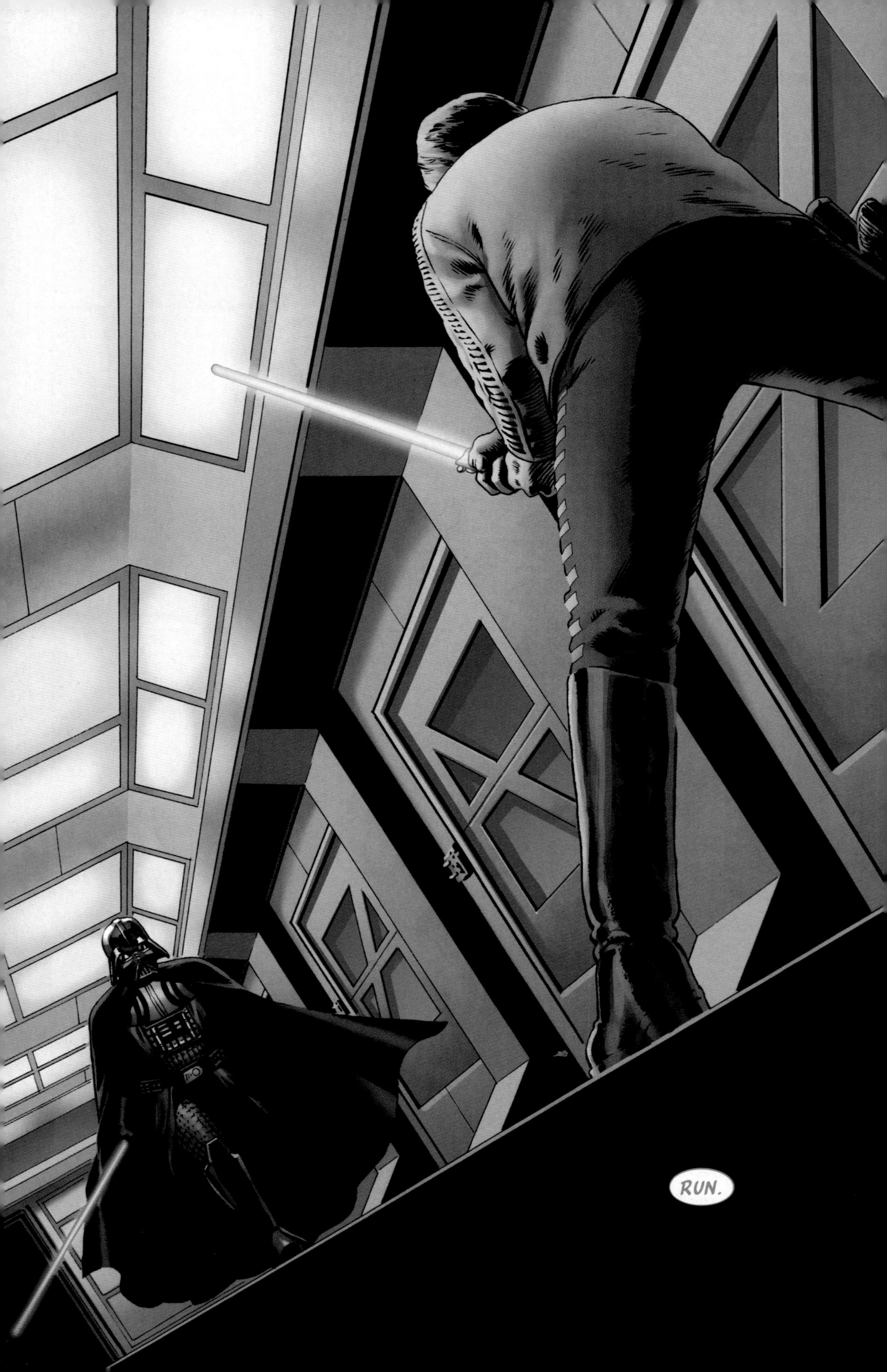
RUN.

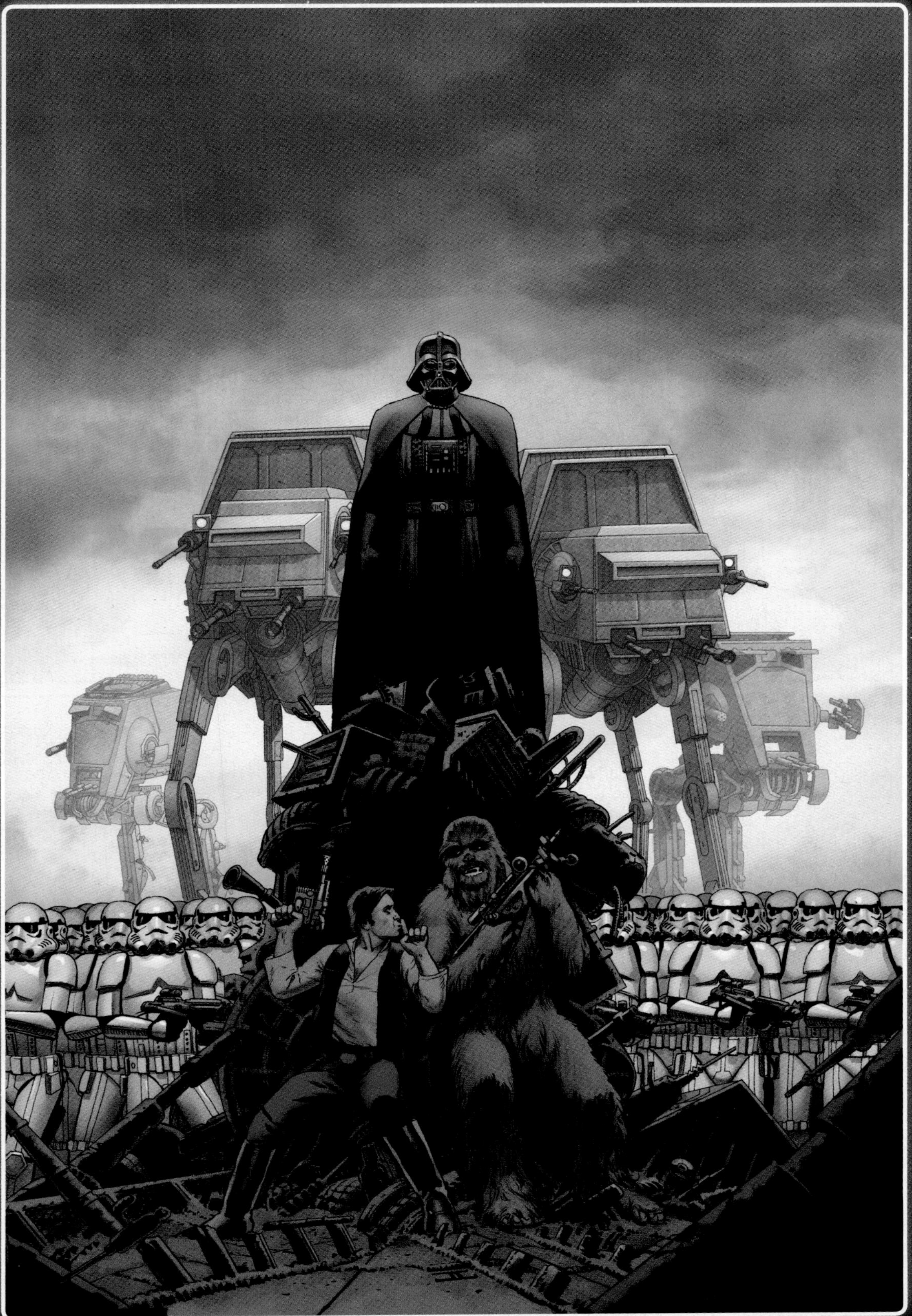

2

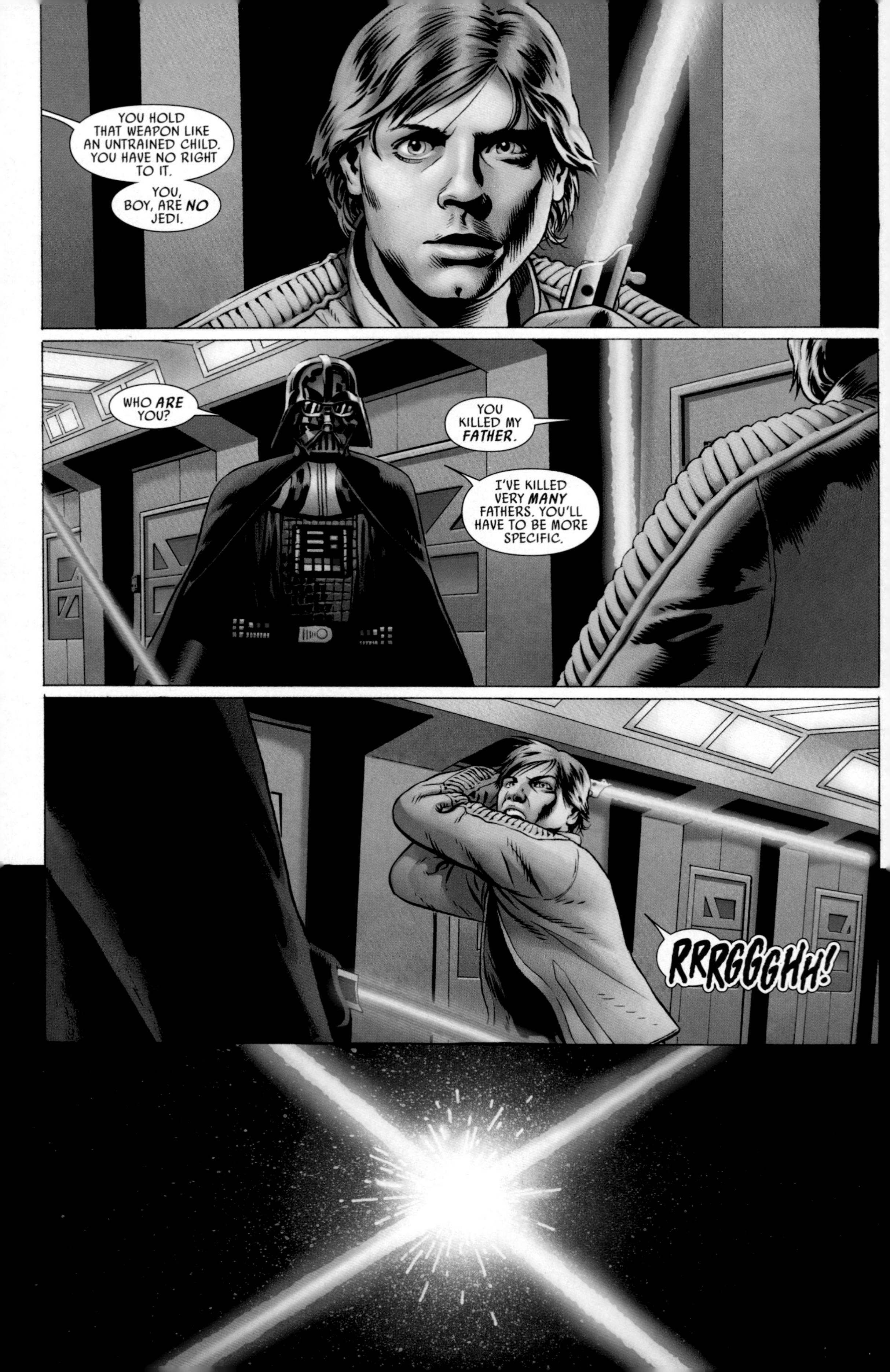
YOU HOLD THAT WEAPON LIKE AN UNTRAINED CHILD. YOU HAVE NO RIGHT TO IT.
YOU, BOY, ARE NO JEDI.
WHO ARE YOU?
YOU KILLED MY FATHER.
I'VE KILLED VERY MANY FATHERS. YOU'LL HAVE TO BE MORE SPECIFIC.
RRRGGGHH!

UGGH!

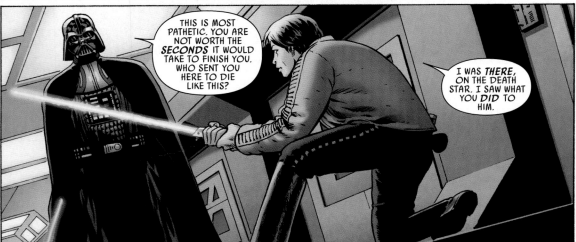

THIS IS MOST PATHETIC. YOU ARE NOT WORTH THE *SECONDS* IT WOULD TAKE TO FINISH YOU. WHO SENT YOU HERE TO DIE LIKE THIS?

I WAS *THERE*, ON THE DEATH STAR. I SAW WHAT YOU *DID* TO HIM.

YOU KILLED *MASTER KENOBI!*

AND NOW I'M HERE TO MAKE SURE YOU--

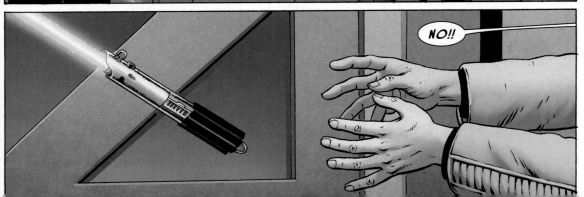

NO!!

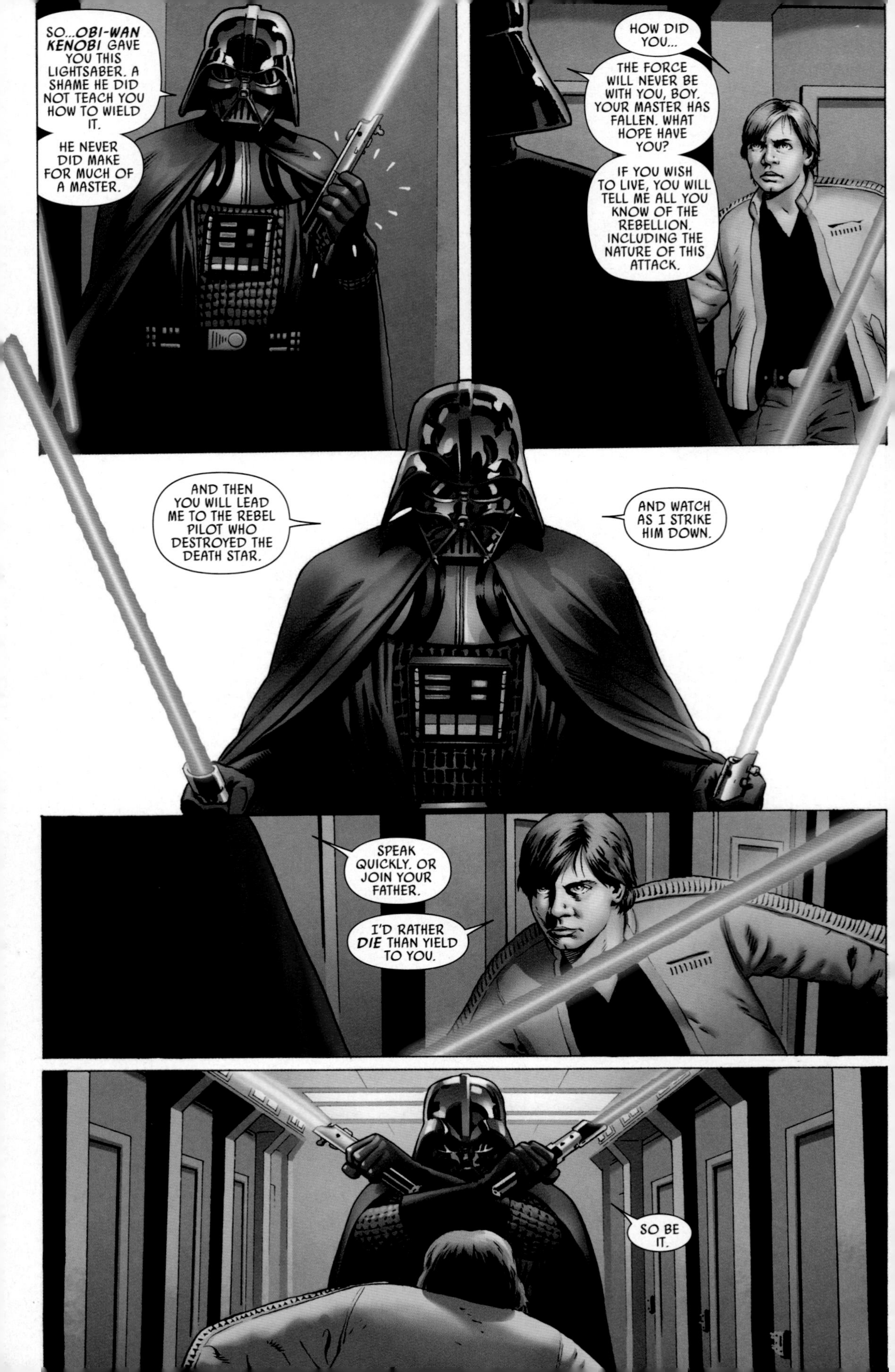
SO...*OBI-WAN KENOBI* GAVE YOU THIS LIGHTSABER. A SHAME HE DID NOT TEACH YOU HOW TO WIELD IT.
HE NEVER DID MAKE FOR MUCH OF A MASTER.
HOW DID YOU...
THE FORCE WILL NEVER BE WITH YOU, BOY. YOUR MASTER HAS FALLEN. WHAT HOPE HAVE YOU?
IF YOU WISH TO LIVE, YOU WILL TELL ME ALL YOU KNOW OF THE REBELLION. INCLUDING THE NATURE OF THIS ATTACK.
AND THEN YOU WILL LEAD ME TO THE REBEL PILOT WHO DESTROYED THE DEATH STAR.
AND WATCH AS I STRIKE HIM DOWN.
SPEAK QUICKLY, OR JOIN YOUR FATHER.
I'D RATHER *DIE* THAN YIELD TO YOU.
SO BE IT.

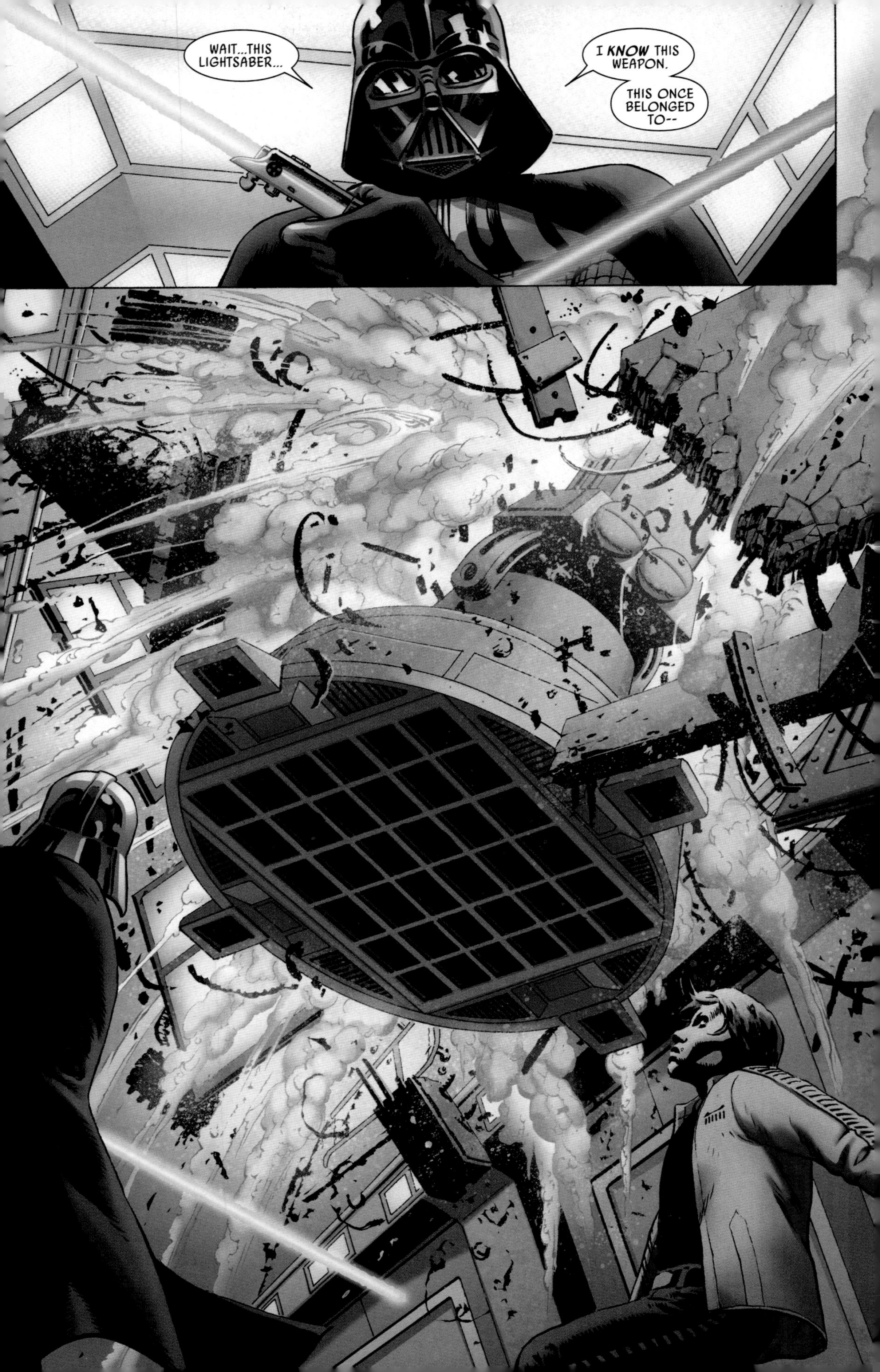
WAIT...THIS LIGHTSABER...
I KNOW THIS WEAPON.
THIS ONCE BELONGED TO--

WATCH OUT, KID. THIS THING HANDLES LIKE A *DRUNKEN BANTHA.*

HAN?!

I'M CLEARING US A PATH *OUTTA HERE,* LUKE. YOU AND THE REST OF YOUR FRIENDS FOLLOW ME.

OH, CHEWIE WOULD *LOVE* THIS.

THERE'S *VADER!* LET'S RAM THIS THING RIGHT DOWN HIS THROAT!

AYE-AYE, PRINCESS.

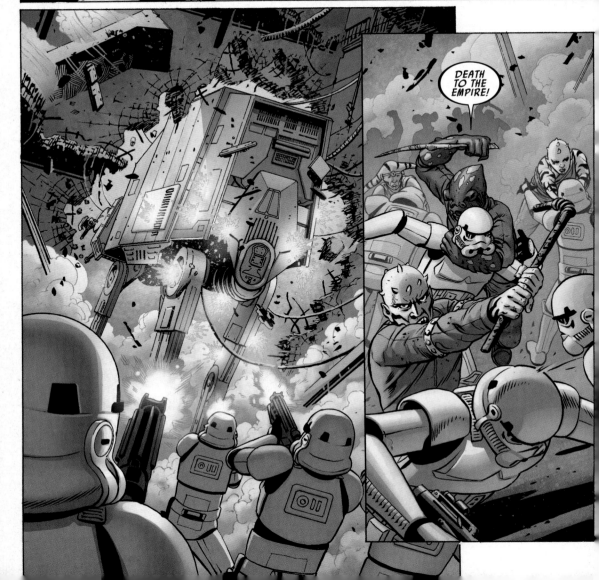

DEATH TO THE EMPIRE!

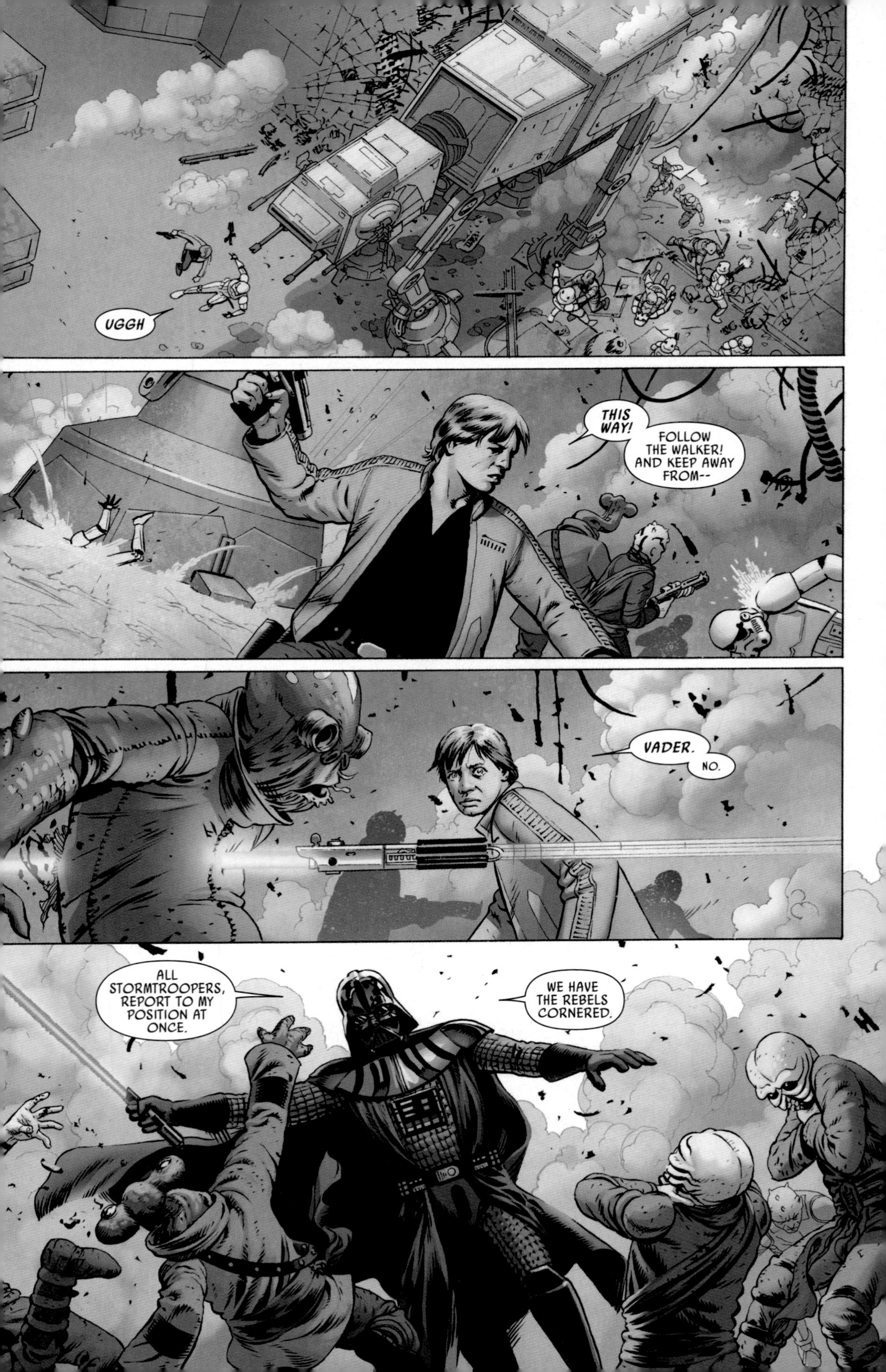
UGGH
THIS WAY!
FOLLOW THE WALKER! AND KEEP AWAY FROM--
VADER.
NO.
ALL STORMTROOPERS, REPORT TO MY POSITION AT ONCE.
WE HAVE THE REBELS CORNERED.

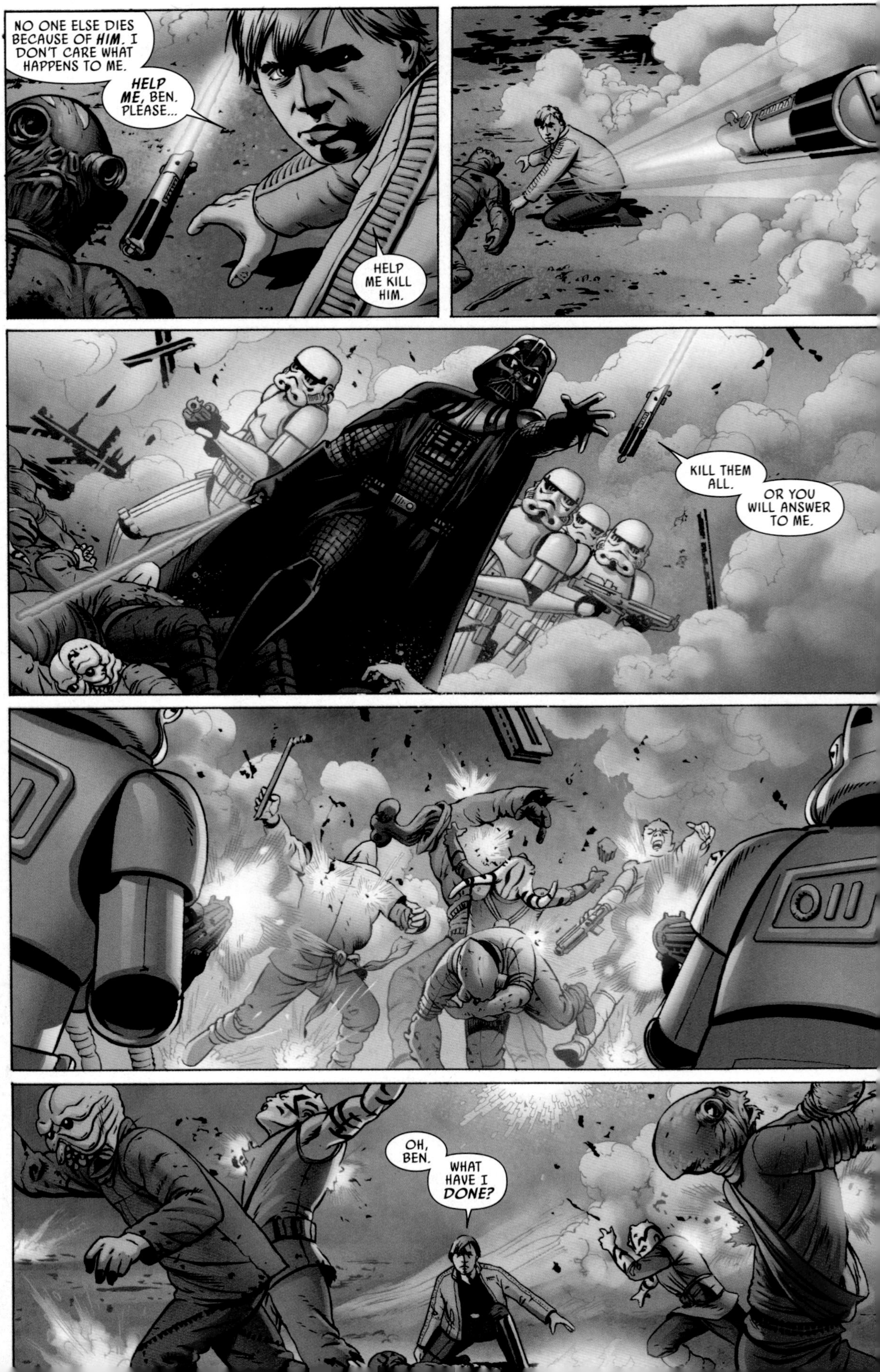
NO ONE ELSE DIES BECAUSE OF HIM. I DON'T CARE WHAT HAPPENS TO ME.
HELP ME, BEN. PLEASE...
HELP ME KILL HIM.
KILL THEM ALL.
OR YOU WILL ANSWER TO ME.
OH, BEN.
WHAT HAVE I DONE?

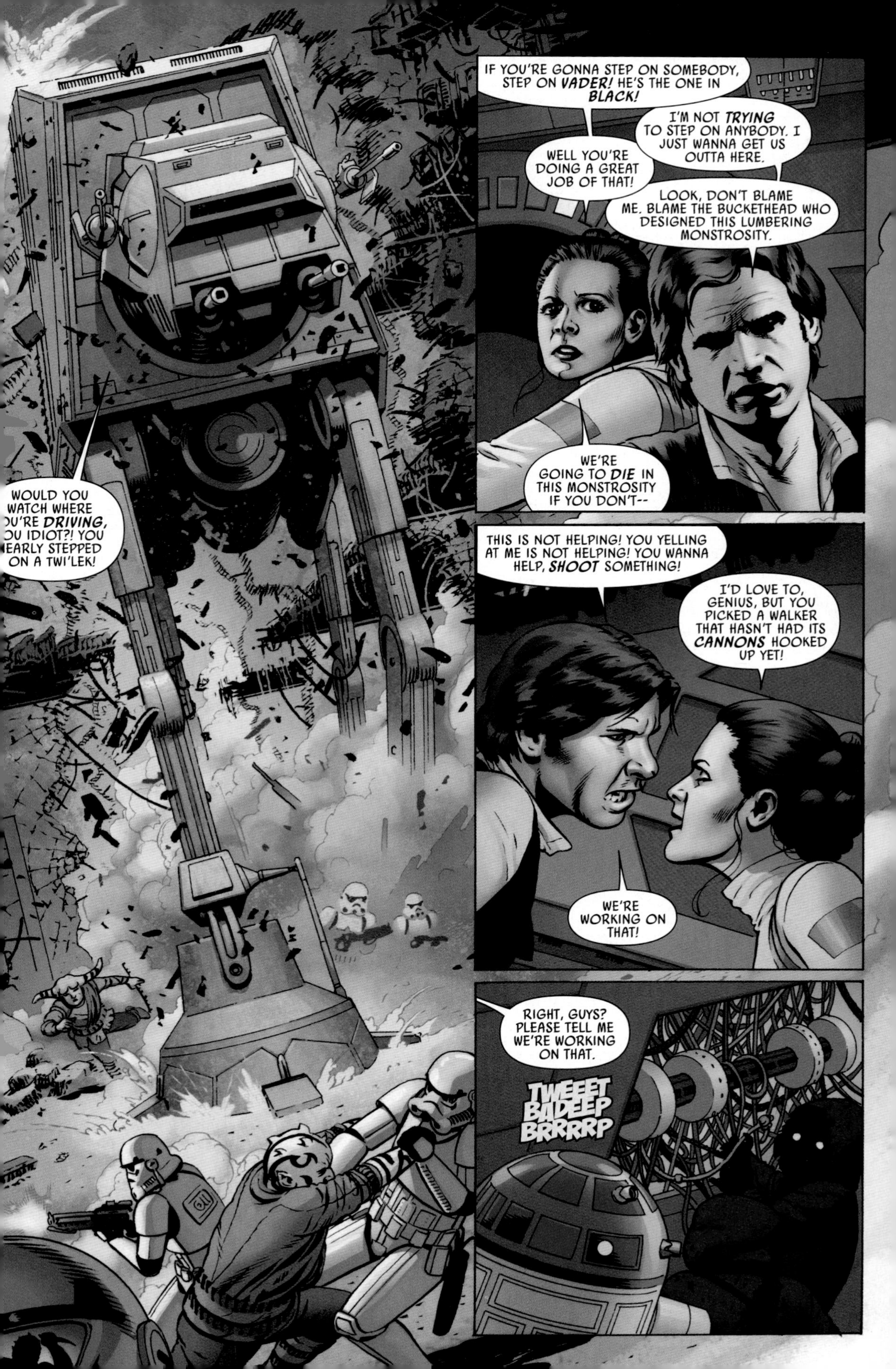
WOULD YOU WATCH WHERE OU'RE DRIVING, OU IDIOT?! YOU EARLY STEPPED ON A TWI'LEK!
IF YOU'RE GONNA STEP ON SOMEBODY, STEP ON VADER! HE'S THE ONE IN BLACK!
I'M NOT TRYING TO STEP ON ANYBODY. I JUST WANNA GET US OUTTA HERE.
WELL YOU'RE DOING A GREAT JOB OF THAT!
LOOK, DON'T BLAME ME. BLAME THE BUCKETHEAD WHO DESIGNED THIS LUMBERING MONSTROSITY.
WE'RE GOING TO DIE IN THIS MONSTROSITY IF YOU DON'T--
THIS IS NOT HELPING! YOU YELLING AT ME IS NOT HELPING! YOU WANNA HELP, SHOOT SOMETHING!
I'D LOVE TO, GENIUS, BUT YOU PICKED A WALKER THAT HASN'T HAD ITS CANNONS HOOKED UP YET!
WE'RE WORKING ON THAT!
RIGHT, GUYS? PLEASE TELL ME WE'RE WORKING ON THAT.
TWEEET BADEEP BRRRRP

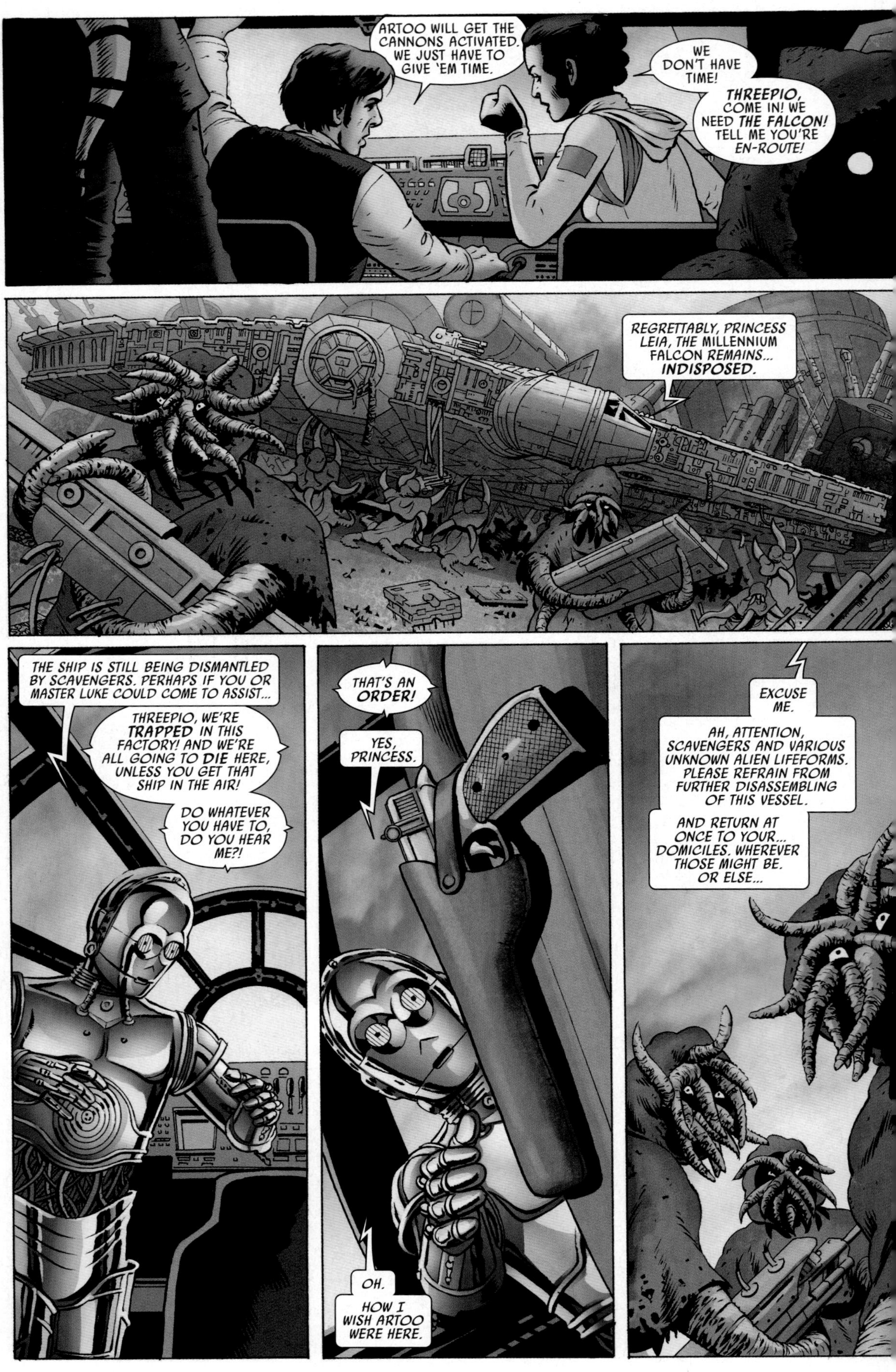
ARTOO WILL GET THE CANNONS ACTIVATED. WE JUST HAVE TO GIVE 'EM TIME.
WE DON'T HAVE TIME!
THREEPIO, COME IN! WE NEED THE FALCON! TELL ME YOU'RE EN-ROUTE!
REGRETTABLY, PRINCESS LEIA, THE MILLENNIUM FALCON REMAINS... INDISPOSED.
THE SHIP IS STILL BEING DISMANTLED BY SCAVENGERS. PERHAPS IF YOU OR MASTER LUKE COULD COME TO ASSIST...
THREEPIO, WE'RE TRAPPED IN THIS FACTORY! AND WE'RE ALL GOING TO DIE HERE, UNLESS YOU GET THAT SHIP IN THE AIR!
DO WHATEVER YOU HAVE TO, DO YOU HEAR ME?!
THAT'S AN ORDER!
YES, PRINCESS.
OH.
HOW I WISH ARTOO WERE HERE.
EXCUSE ME.
AH, ATTENTION, SCAVENGERS AND VARIOUS UNKNOWN ALIEN LIFEFORMS. PLEASE REFRAIN FROM FURTHER DISASSEMBLING OF THIS VESSEL.
AND RETURN AT ONCE TO YOUR... DOMICILES. WHEREVER THOSE MIGHT BE. OR ELSE...

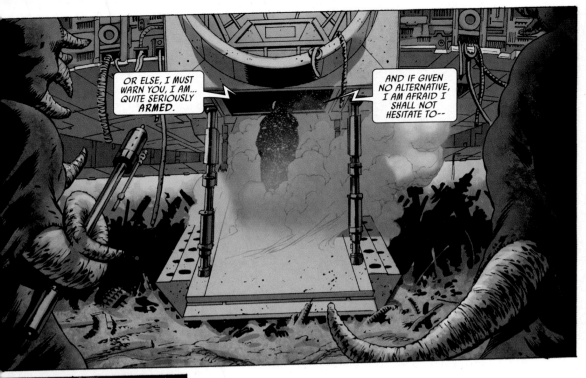

OR ELSE, I MUST WARN YOU, I AM... QUITE SERIOUSLY ARMED.

AND IF GIVEN NO ALTERNATIVE, I AM AFRAID I SHALL NOT HESITATE TO--

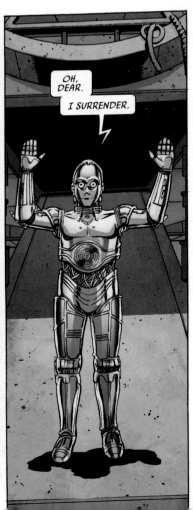

OH, DEAR.

I SURRENDER.

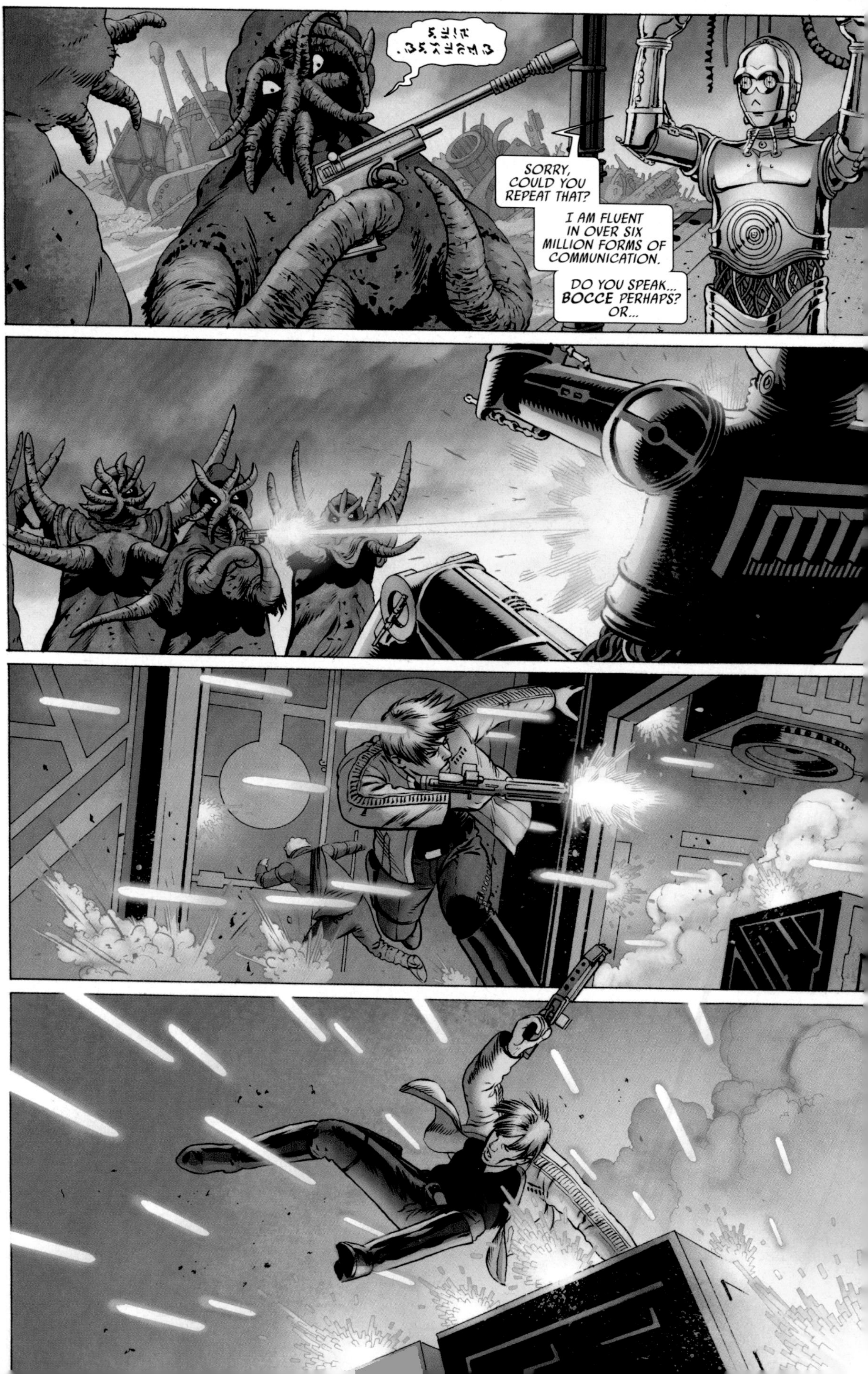
SORRY, COULD YOU REPEAT THAT?
I AM FLUENT IN OVER SIX MILLION FORMS OF COMMUNICATION.
DO YOU SPEAK... BOCCE PERHAPS? OR...

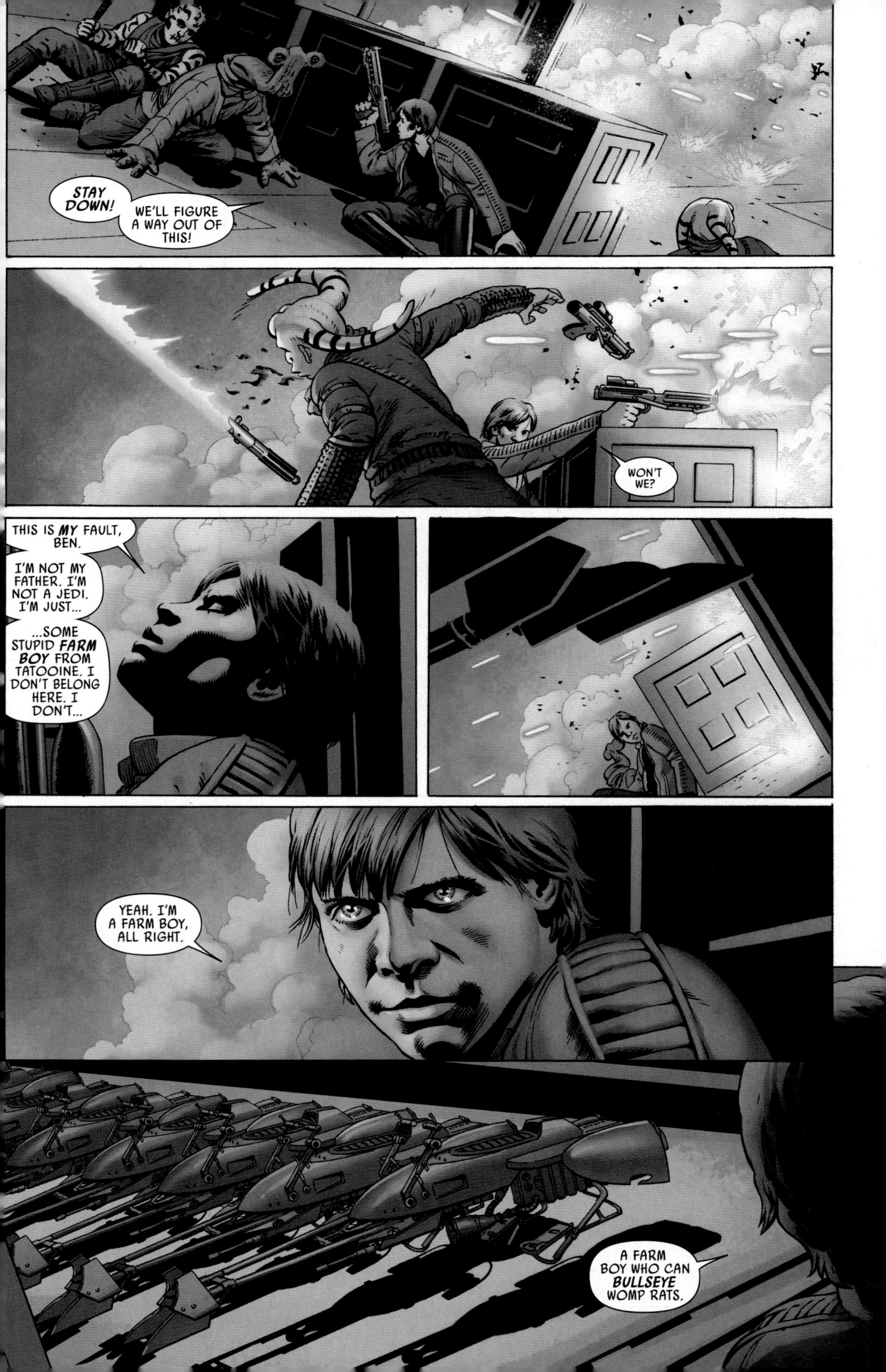
STAY DOWN!
WE'LL FIGURE A WAY OUT OF THIS!
WON'T WE?
THIS IS MY FAULT, BEN.
I'M NOT MY FATHER. I'M NOT A JEDI. I'M JUST...
...SOME STUPID FARM BOY FROM TATOOINE. I DON'T BELONG HERE. I DON'T...
YEAH. I'M A FARM BOY, ALL RIGHT.
A FARM BOY WHO CAN BULLSEYE WOMP RATS.

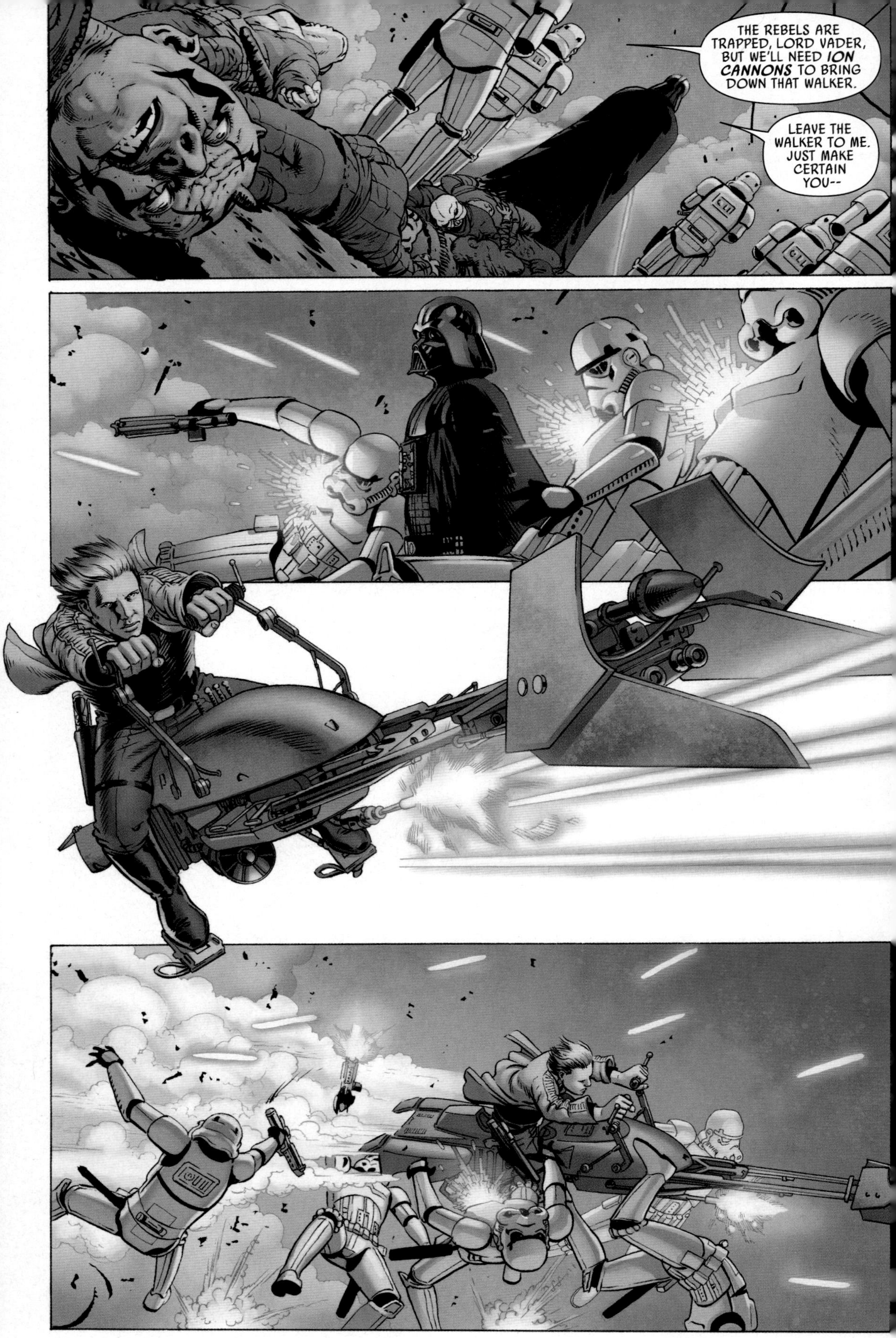
THE REBELS ARE TRAPPED, LORD VADER, BUT WE'LL NEED ION CANNONS TO BRING DOWN THAT WALKER.
LEAVE THE WALKER TO ME. JUST MAKE CERTAIN YOU--

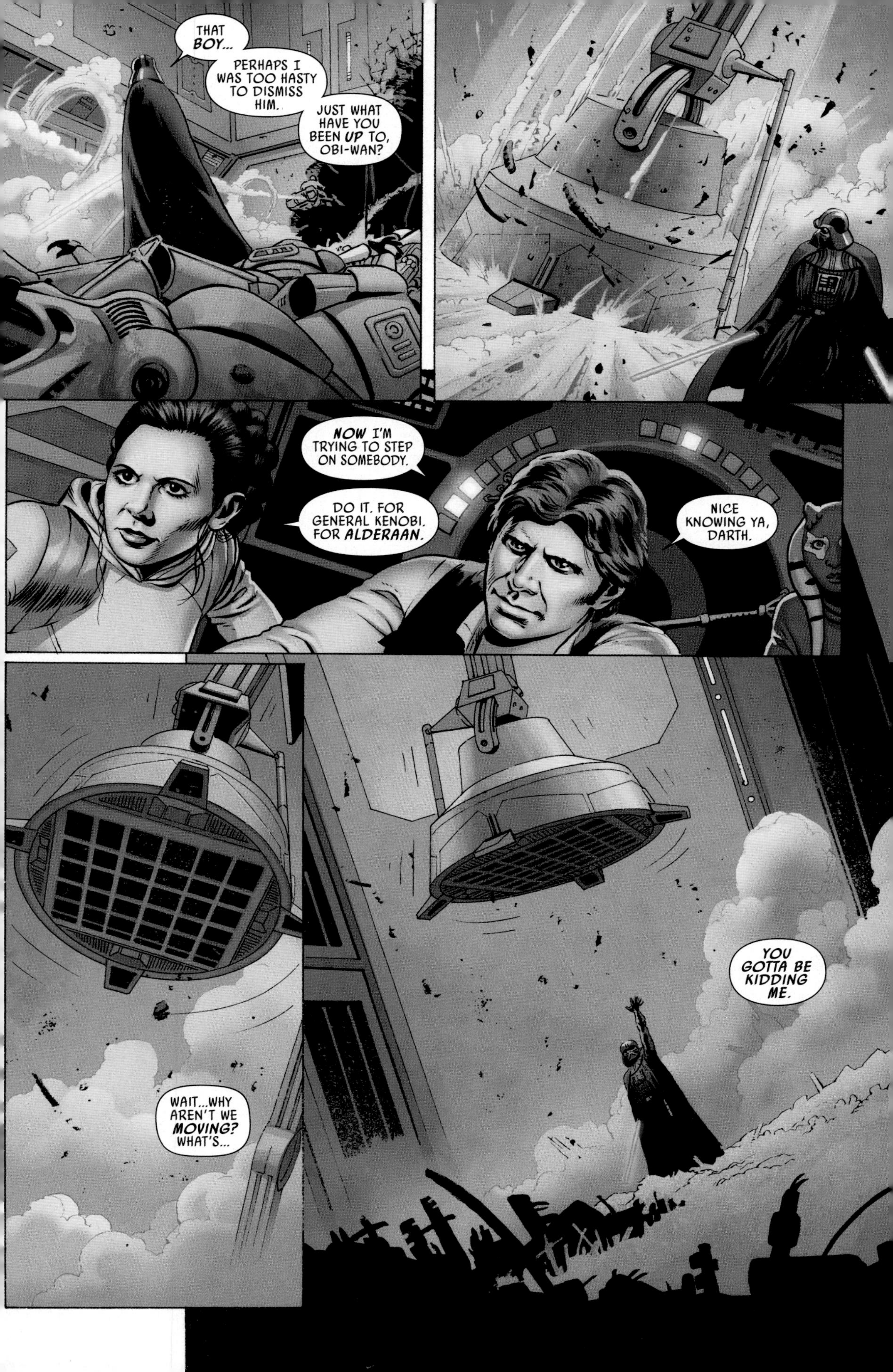
THAT BOY...
PERHAPS I WAS TOO HASTY TO DISMISS HIM.
JUST WHAT HAVE YOU BEEN UP TO, OBI-WAN?
NOW I'M TRYING TO STEP ON SOMEBODY.
DO IT. FOR GENERAL KENOBI. FOR ALDERAAN.
NICE KNOWING YA, DARTH.
WAIT...WHY AREN'T WE MOVING? WHAT'S...
YOU GOTTA BE KIDDING ME.

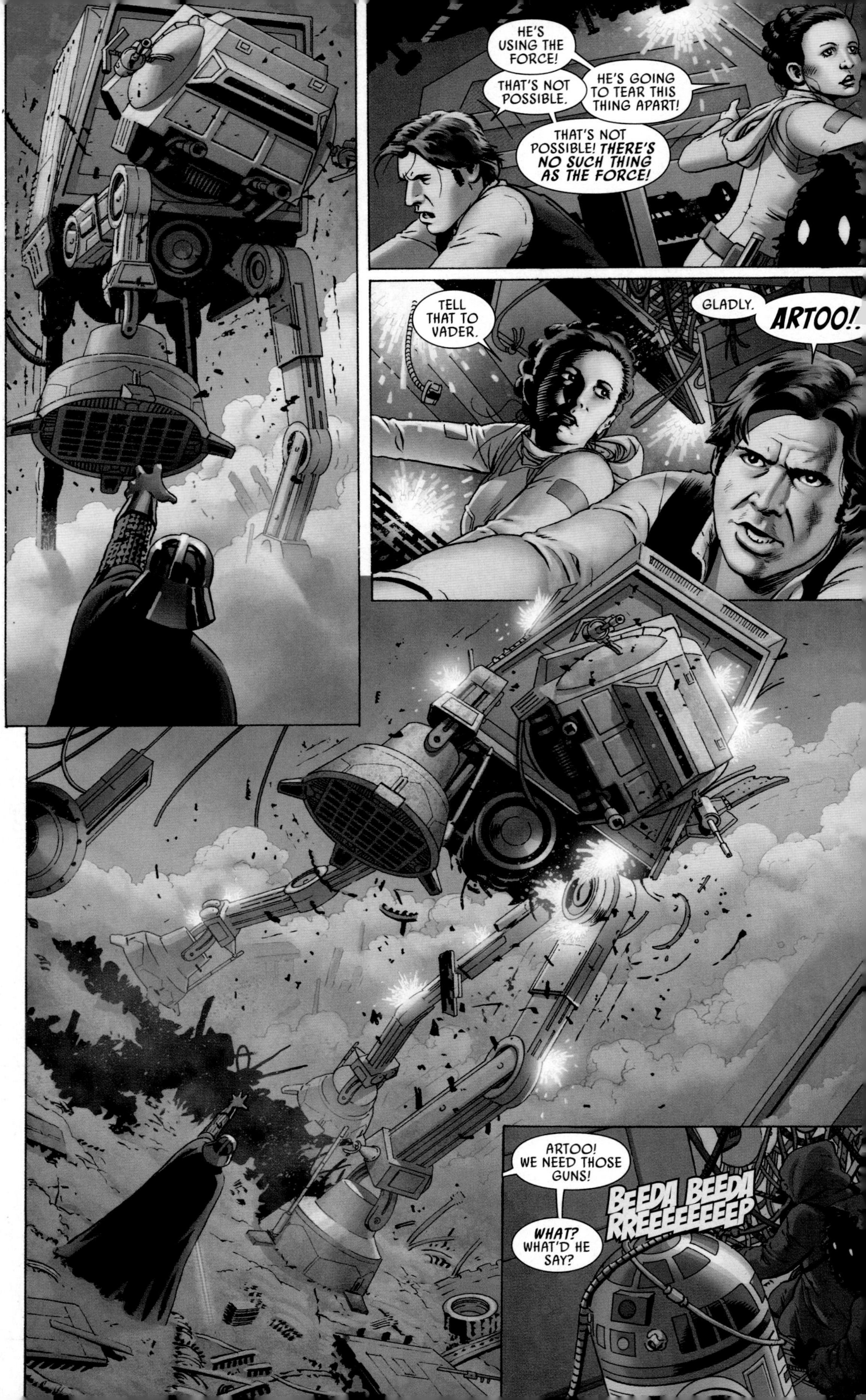
HE'S USING THE FORCE!
THAT'S NOT POSSIBLE.
HE'S GOING TO TEAR THIS THING APART!
THAT'S NOT POSSIBLE! THERE'S NO SUCH THING AS THE FORCE!
TELL THAT TO VADER.
GLADLY.
ARTOO!
ARTOO! WE NEED THOSE GUNS!
BEEDA BEEDA RREEEEEEEEP
WHAT? WHAT'D HE SAY?

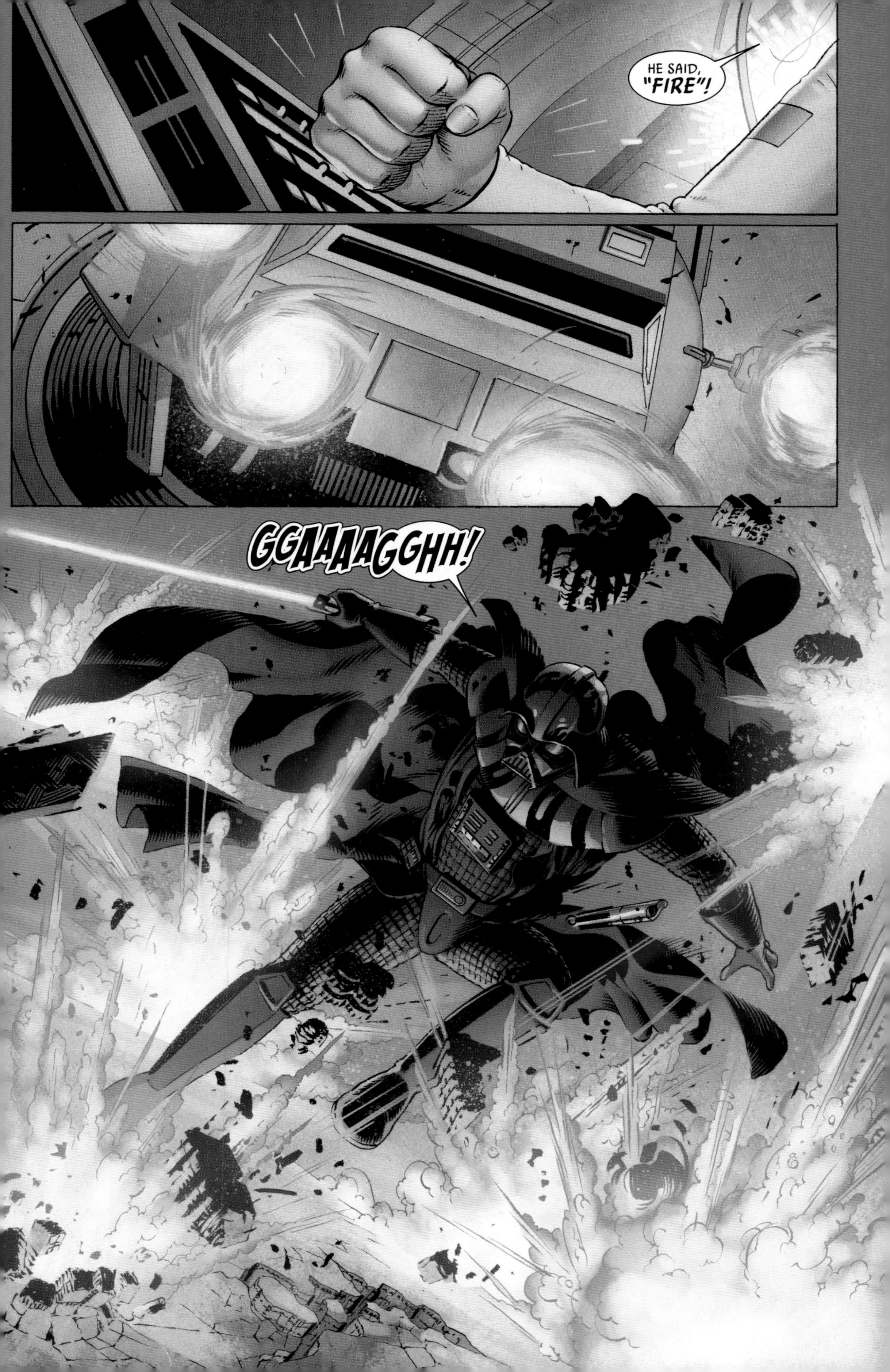
HE SAID, "FIRE"!
GGAAAAGGHH!

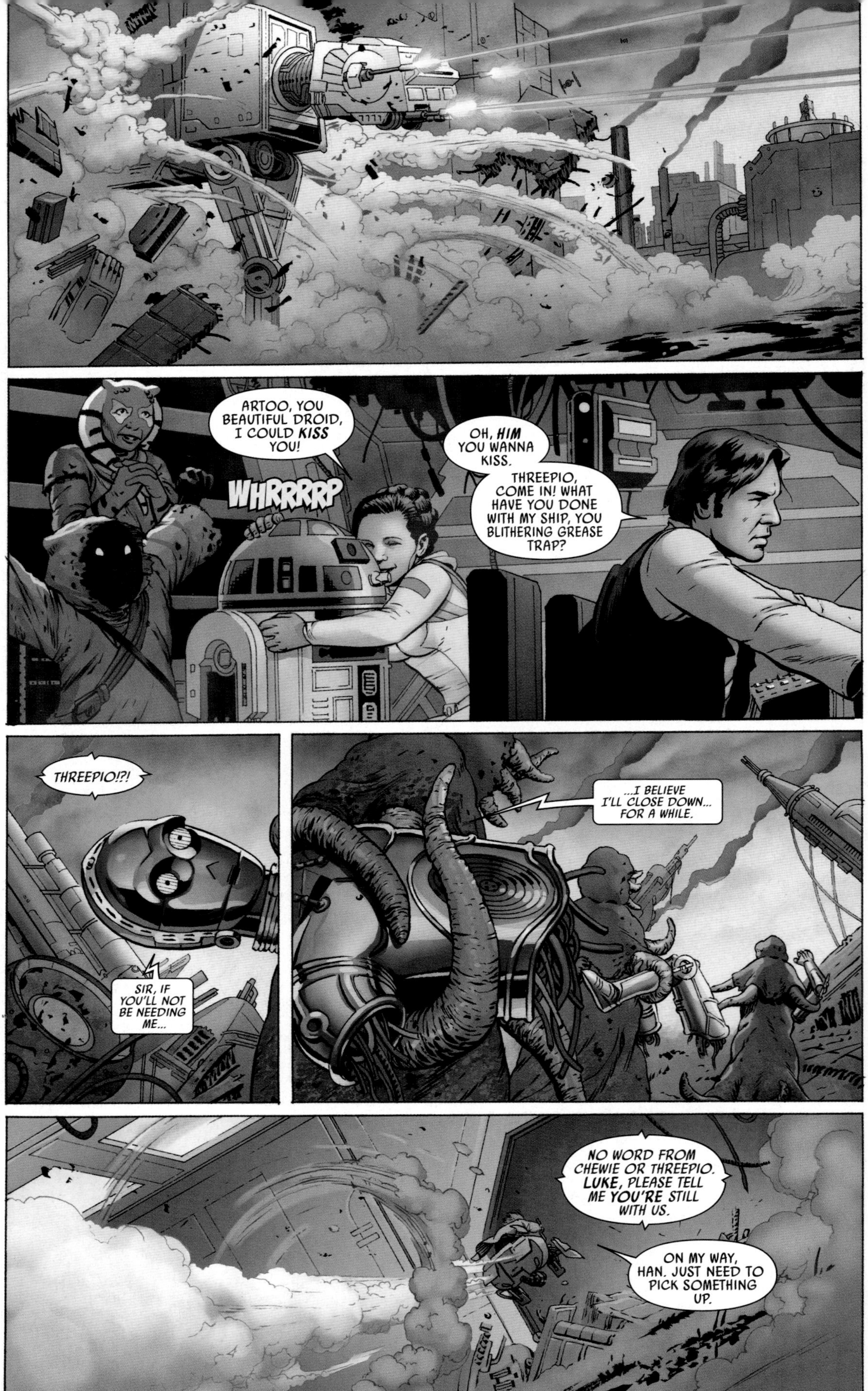
ARTOO, YOU BEAUTIFUL DROID, I COULD KISS YOU!
WHRRRRP
OH, HIM YOU WANNA KISS.
THREEPIO, COME IN! WHAT HAVE YOU DONE WITH MY SHIP, YOU BLITHERING GREASE TRAP?
THREEPIO!?!
SIR, IF YOU'LL NOT BE NEEDING ME...
...I BELIEVE I'LL CLOSE DOWN... FOR A WHILE.
NO WORD FROM CHEWIE OR THREEPIO. LUKE, PLEASE TELL ME YOU'RE STILL WITH US.
ON MY WAY, HAN. JUST NEED TO PICK SOMETHING UP.

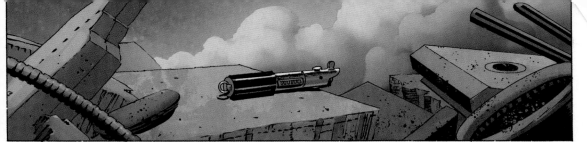

AARRGGHH!

NO SIGN OF VADER. LET'S MOVE OUT.

I DON'T THINK WE'LL BE SEEING ANY MORE OF VADER, KID. NOT AFTER WHAT WE JUST DID TO HIM.

I WISH I COULD BELIEVE THAT...

"...BUT YOU DON'T KNOW THE *POWER* OF THE FORCE."

LORD VADER, WE HAVE...

HGGGK =WHEEZE=

MOTHER OF MOONS.

I'M...I'M SORRY, MY LORD. I DIDN'T REALIZE...

GRRK

LORD VADER, THIS IS OVERSEER AGGADEEN.

SIR, I'M AFRAID WE ARE...UNABLE TO HALT THE POWER CORE'S MELTDOWN. REQUEST PERMISSION TO EVACUATE THE FACILITY.

PERMISSION DENIED, OVERSEER. IF THIS FACTORY EXPLODES, YOU HAD BEST EXPLODE WITH IT.

FURTHE WILL B HARSH INVA

Y-YES, MY LORD.

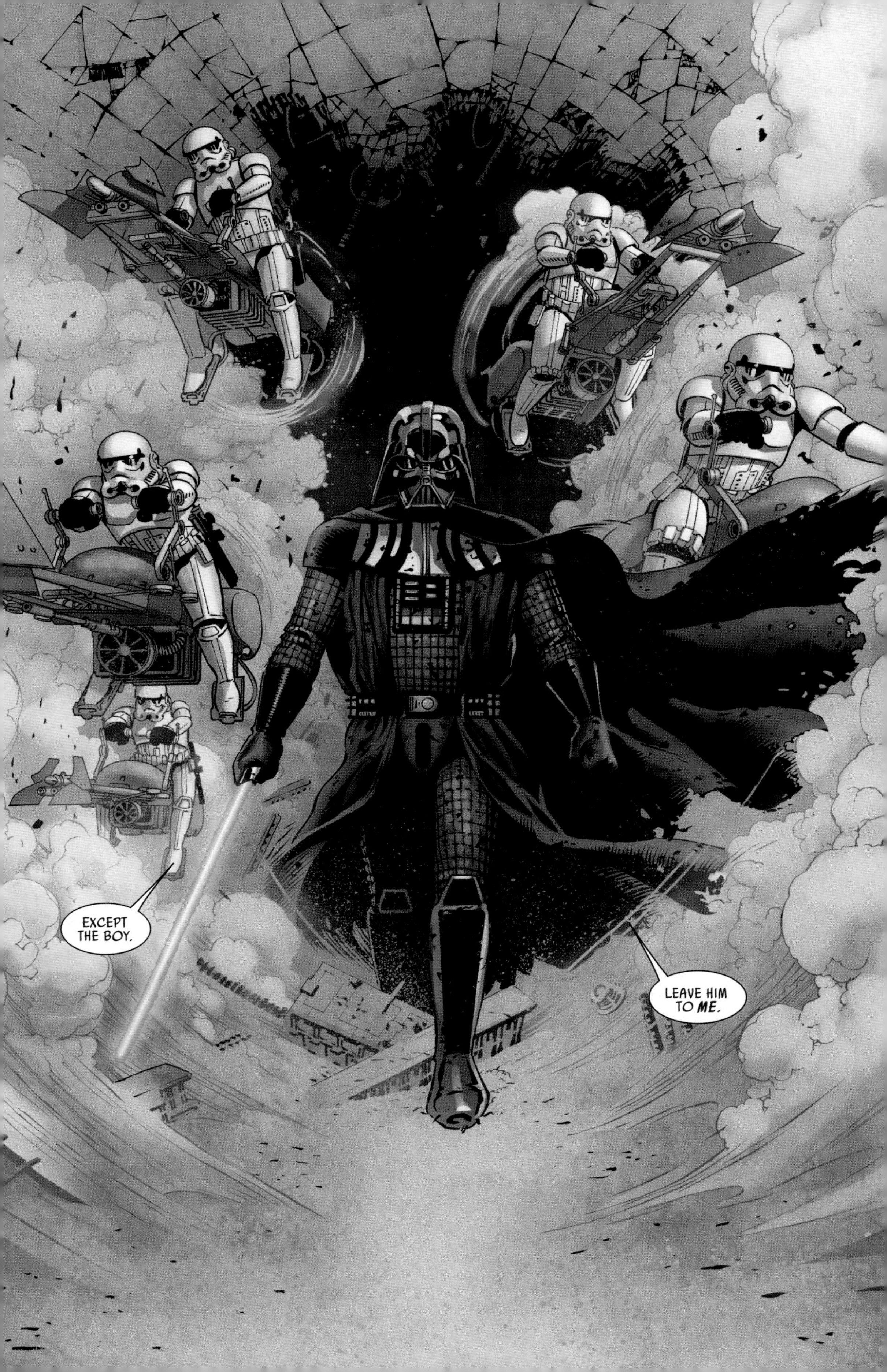
EXCEPT THE BOY.
LEAVE HIM TO ME.

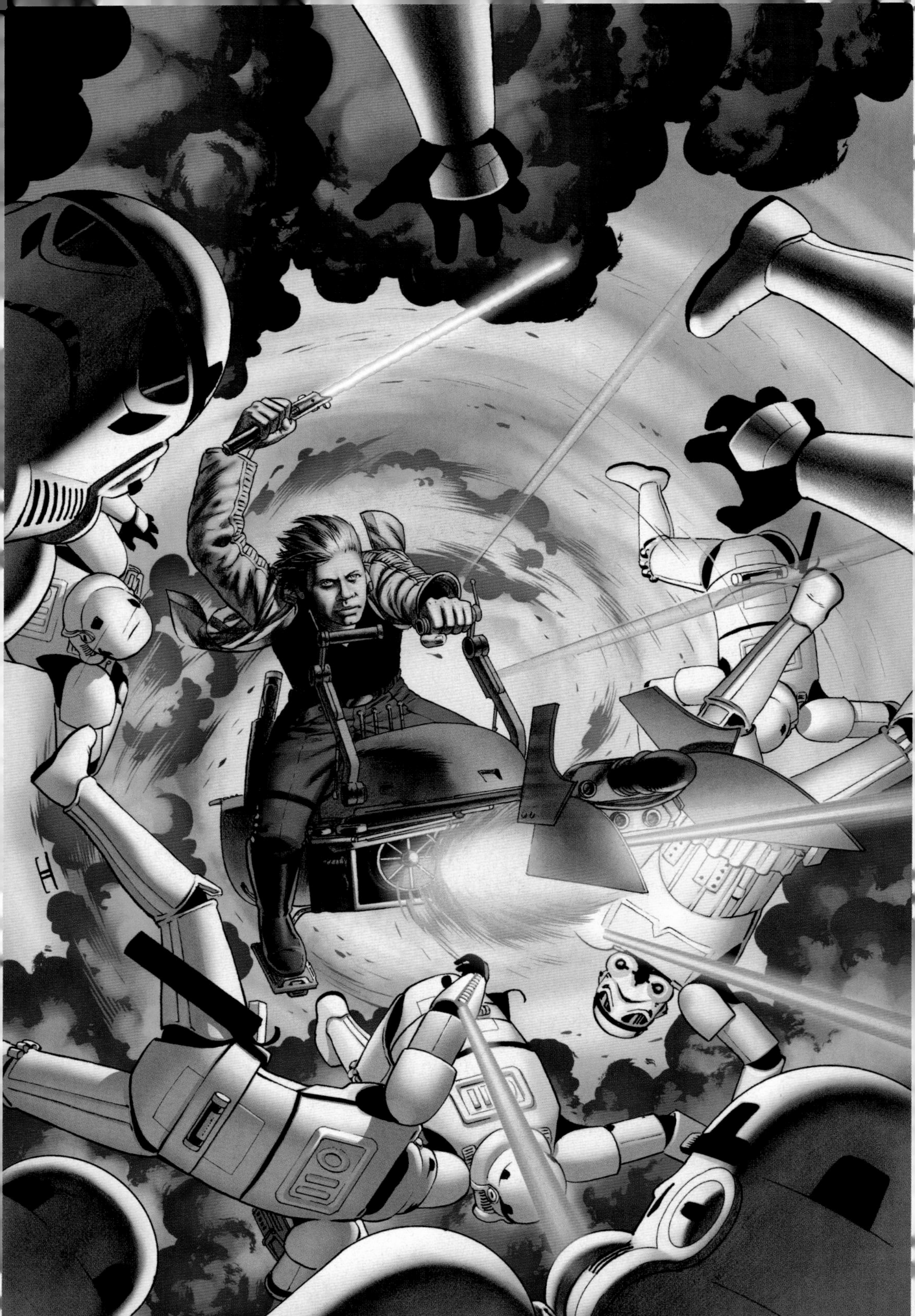

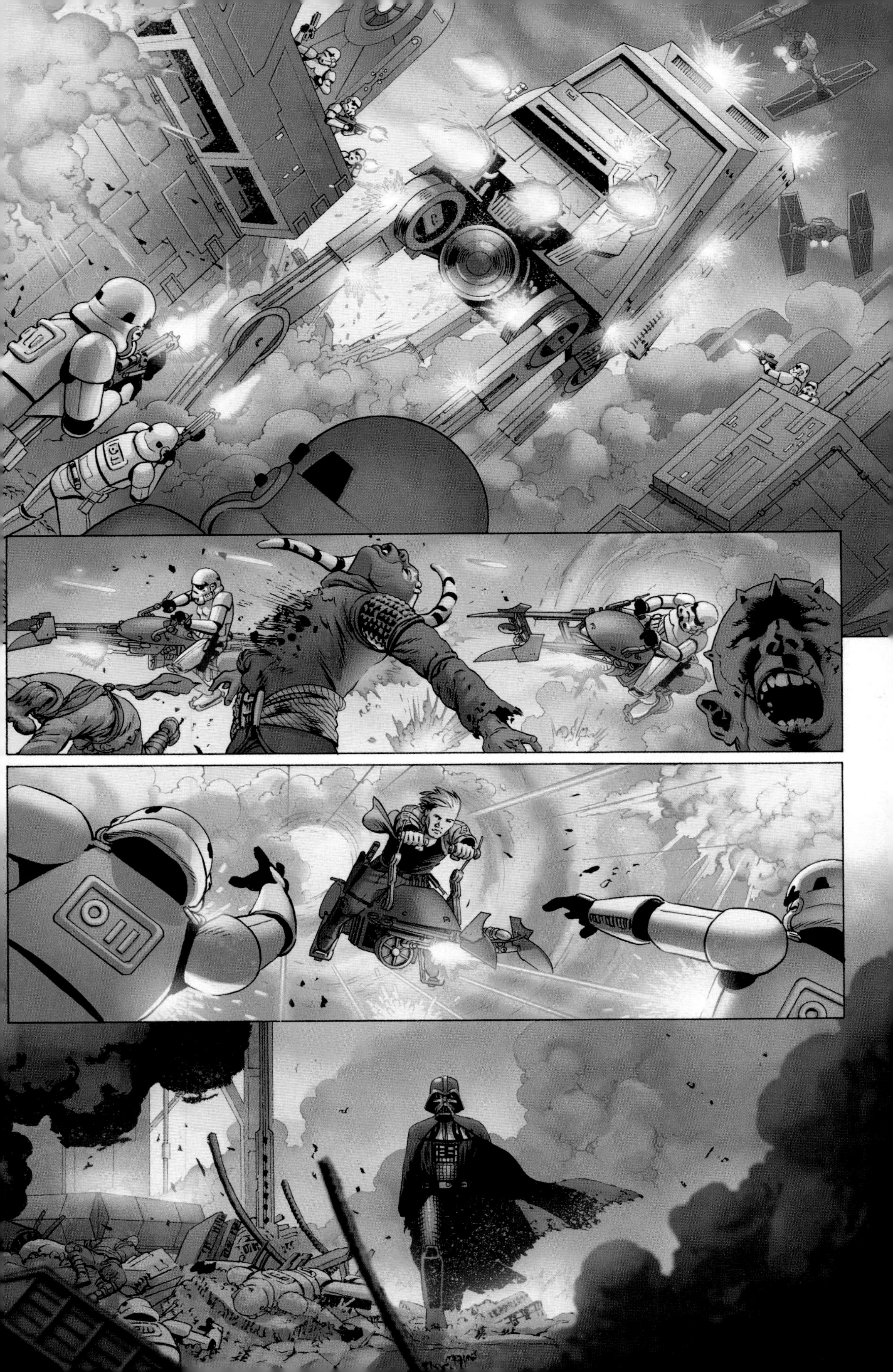

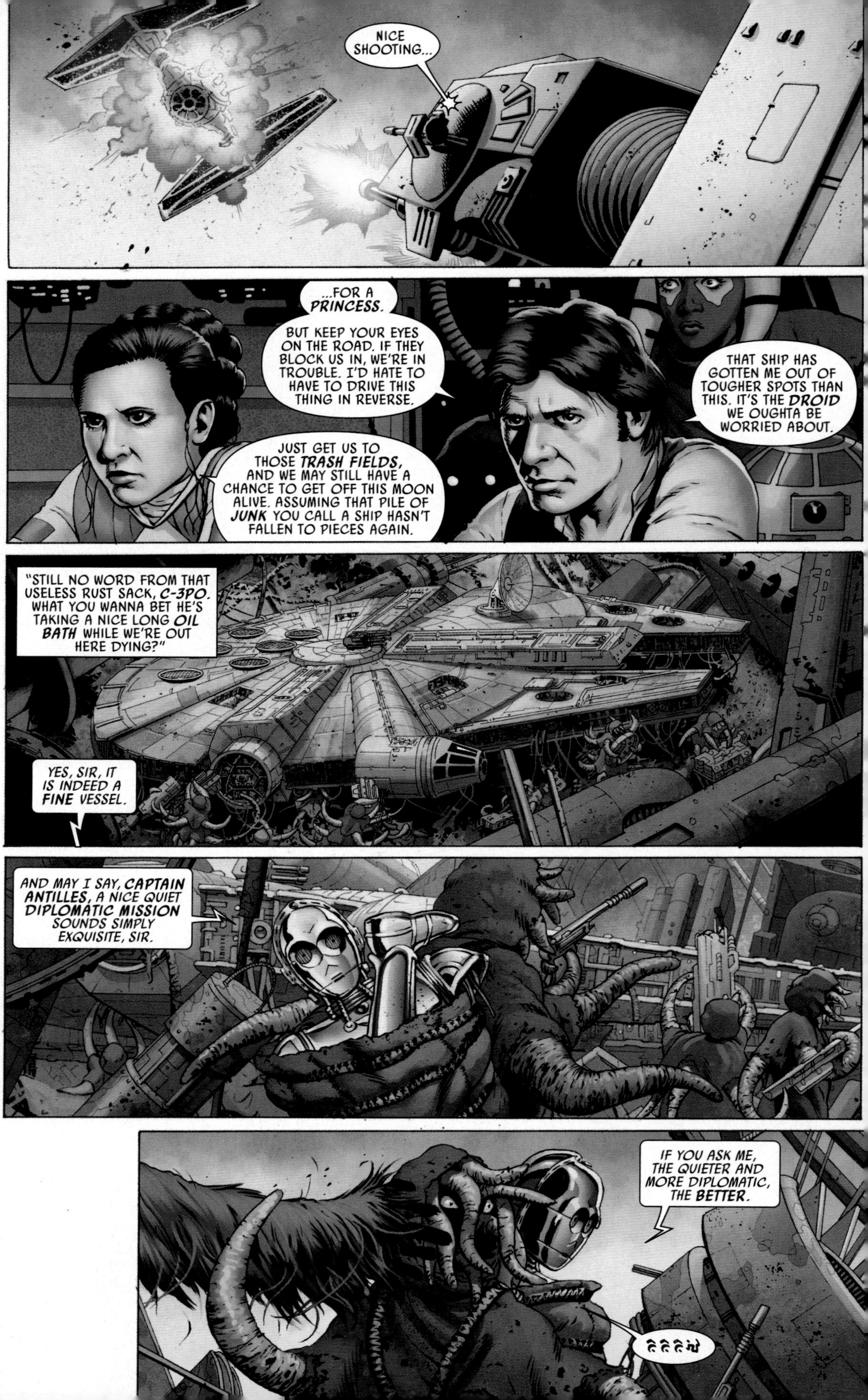
NICE SHOOTING...
...FOR A PRINCESS.
BUT KEEP YOUR EYES ON THE ROAD. IF THEY BLOCK US IN, WE'RE IN TROUBLE. I'D HATE TO HAVE TO DRIVE THIS THING IN REVERSE.
JUST GET US TO THOSE TRASH FIELDS, AND WE MAY STILL HAVE A CHANCE TO GET OFF THIS MOON ALIVE. ASSUMING THAT PILE OF JUNK YOU CALL A SHIP HASN'T FALLEN TO PIECES AGAIN.
THAT SHIP HAS GOTTEN ME OUT OF TOUGHER SPOTS THAN THIS. IT'S THE DROID WE OUGHTA BE WORRIED ABOUT.
"STILL NO WORD FROM THAT USELESS RUST SACK, C-3PO. WHAT YOU WANNA BET HE'S TAKING A NICE LONG OIL BATH WHILE WE'RE OUT HERE DYING?"
YES, SIR, IT IS INDEED A FINE VESSEL.
AND MAY I SAY, CAPTAIN ANTILLES, A NICE QUIET DIPLOMATIC MISSION SOUNDS SIMPLY EXQUISITE, SIR.
IF YOU ASK ME, THE QUIETER AND MORE DIPLOMATIC, THE BETTER.

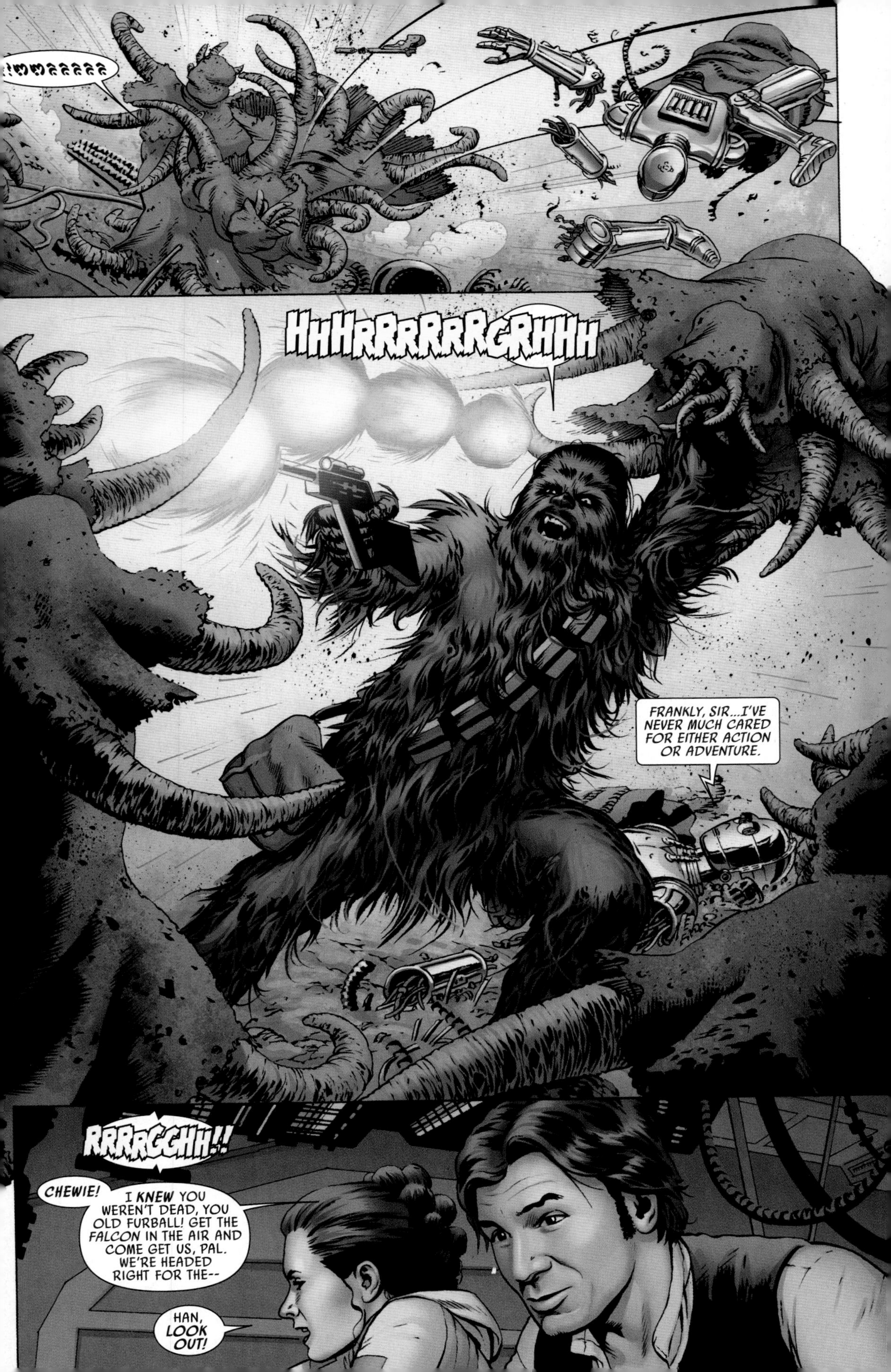

HHHRRRRRRRGRHHH
FRANKLY, SIR...I'VE NEVER MUCH CARED FOR EITHER ACTION OR ADVENTURE.
RRRRGGHH!!
CHEWIE!
I KNEW YOU WEREN'T DEAD, YOU OLD FURBALL! GET THE FALCON IN THE AIR AND COME GET US, PAL. WE'RE HEADED RIGHT FOR THE--
HAN, LOOK OUT!

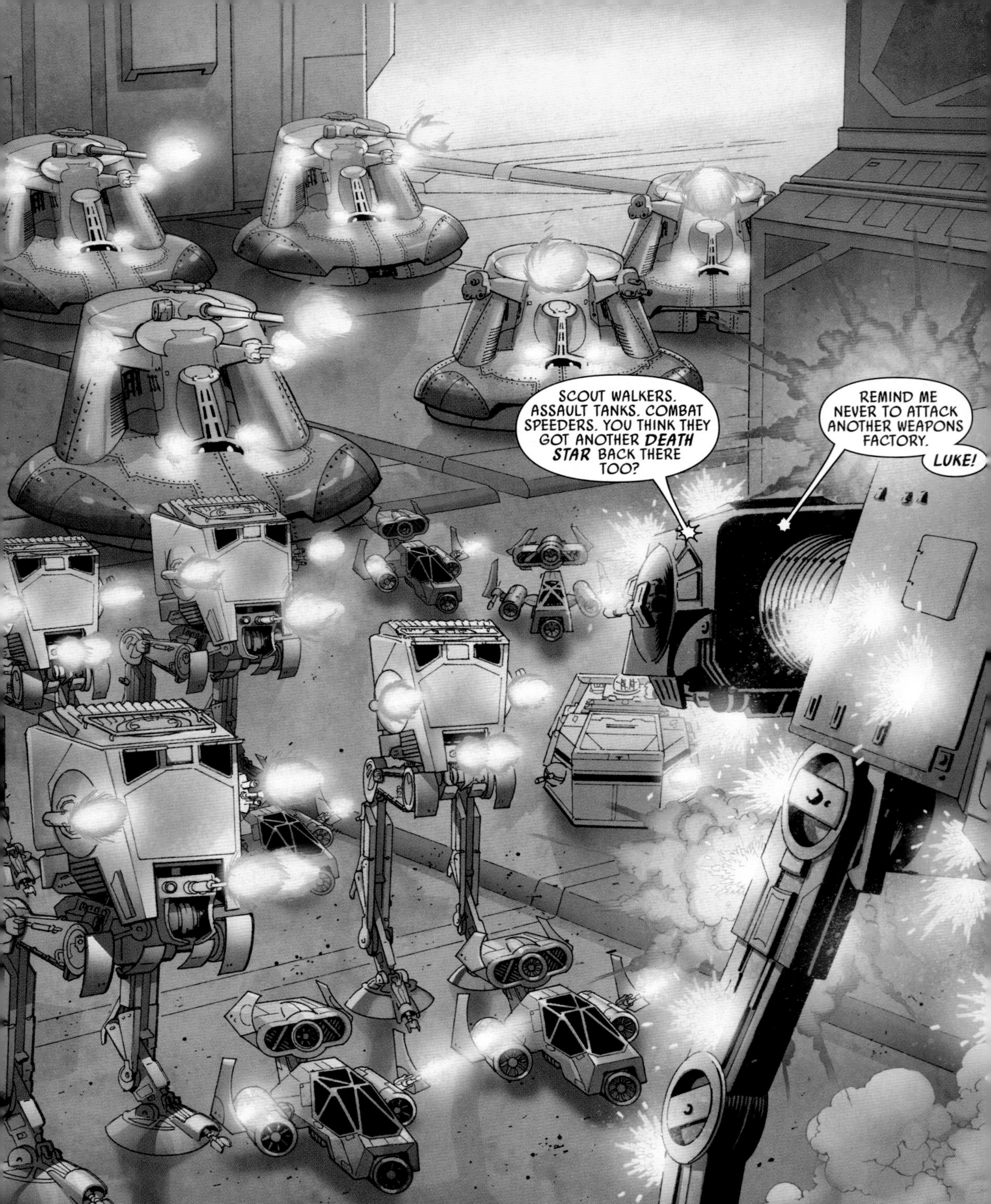
SCOUT WALKERS. ASSAULT TANKS. COMBAT SPEEDERS. YOU THINK THEY GOT ANOTHER DEATH STAR BACK THERE TOO?
REMIND ME NEVER TO ATTACK ANOTHER WEAPONS FACTORY.
LUKE!

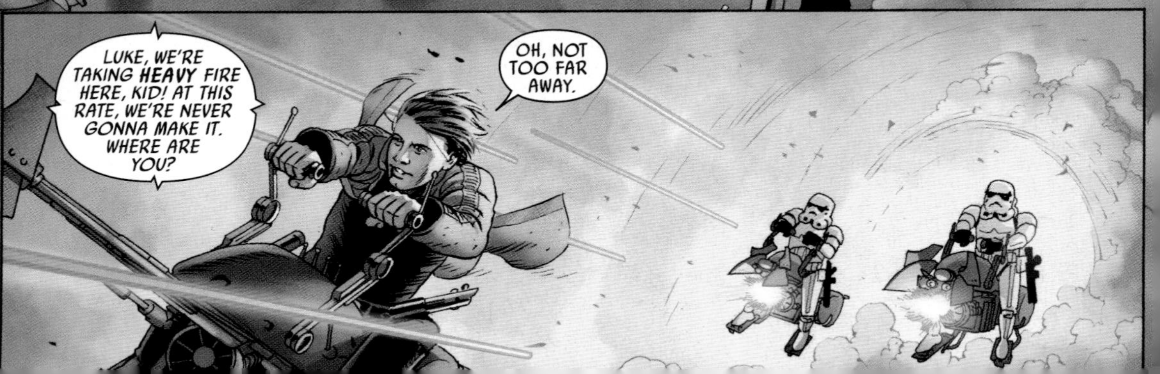
LUKE, WE'RE TAKING HEAVY FIRE HERE, KID! AT THIS RATE, WE'RE NEVER GONNA MAKE IT. WHERE ARE YOU?
OH, NOT TOO FAR AWAY.

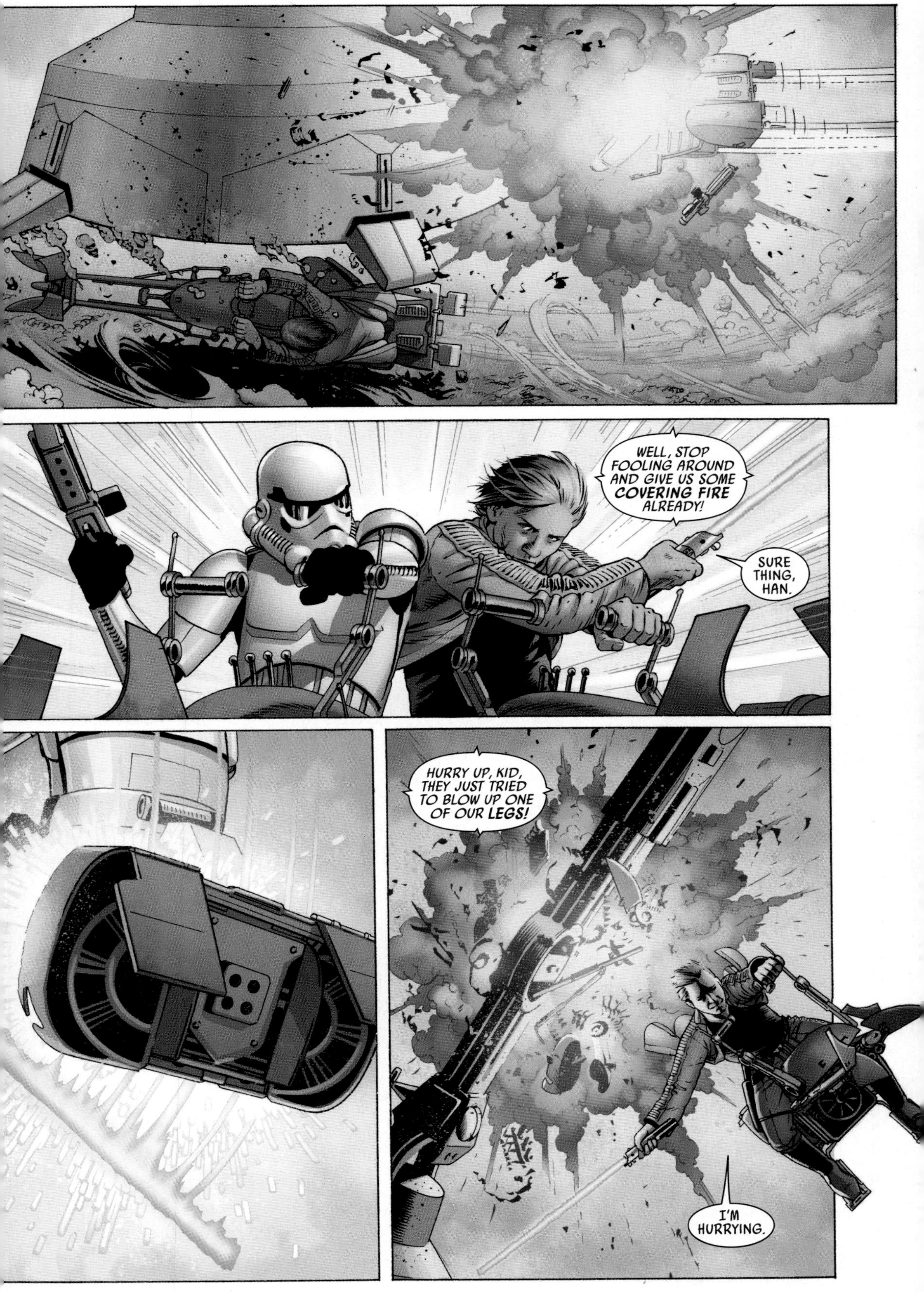
WELL, STOP FOOLING AROUND AND GIVE US SOME COVERING FIRE ALREADY!
SURE THING, HAN.
HURRY UP, KID, THEY JUST TRIED TO BLOW UP ONE OF OUR LEGS!
I'M HURRYING.

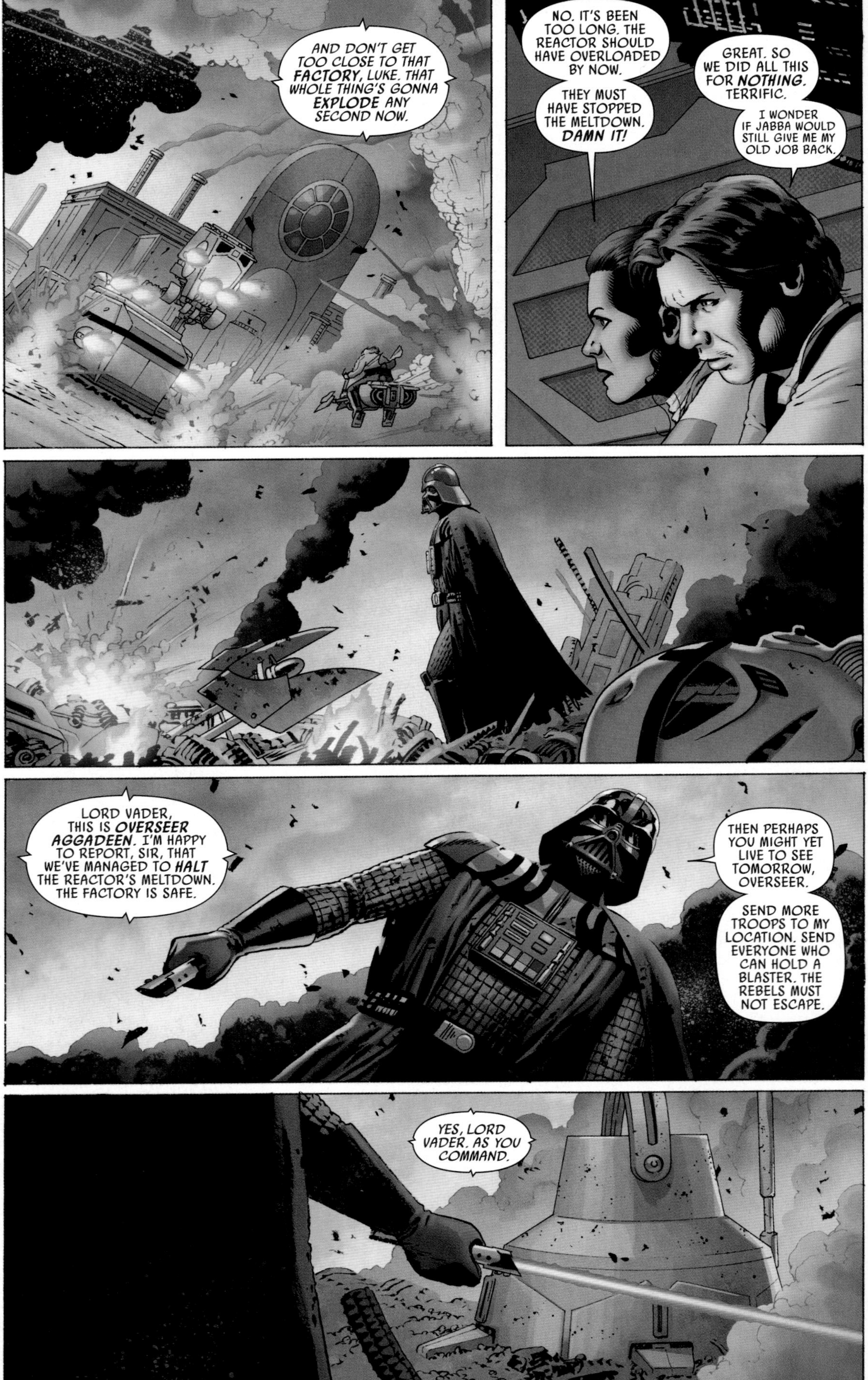
AND DON'T GET TOO CLOSE TO THAT FACTORY, LUKE. THAT WHOLE THING'S GONNA EXPLODE ANY SECOND NOW.
NO. IT'S BEEN TOO LONG. THE REACTOR SHOULD HAVE OVERLOADED BY NOW.
THEY MUST HAVE STOPPED THE MELTDOWN. DAMN IT!
GREAT. SO WE DID ALL THIS FOR NOTHING. TERRIFIC.
I WONDER IF JABBA WOULD STILL GIVE ME MY OLD JOB BACK.
LORD VADER, THIS IS OVERSEER AGGADEEN. I'M HAPPY TO REPORT, SIR, THAT WE'VE MANAGED TO HALT THE REACTOR'S MELTDOWN. THE FACTORY IS SAFE.
THEN PERHAPS YOU MIGHT YET LIVE TO SEE TOMORROW, OVERSEER.
SEND MORE TROOPS TO MY LOCATION. SEND EVERYONE WHO CAN HOLD A BLASTER. THE REBELS MUST NOT ESCAPE.
YES, LORD VADER. AS YOU COMMAND.

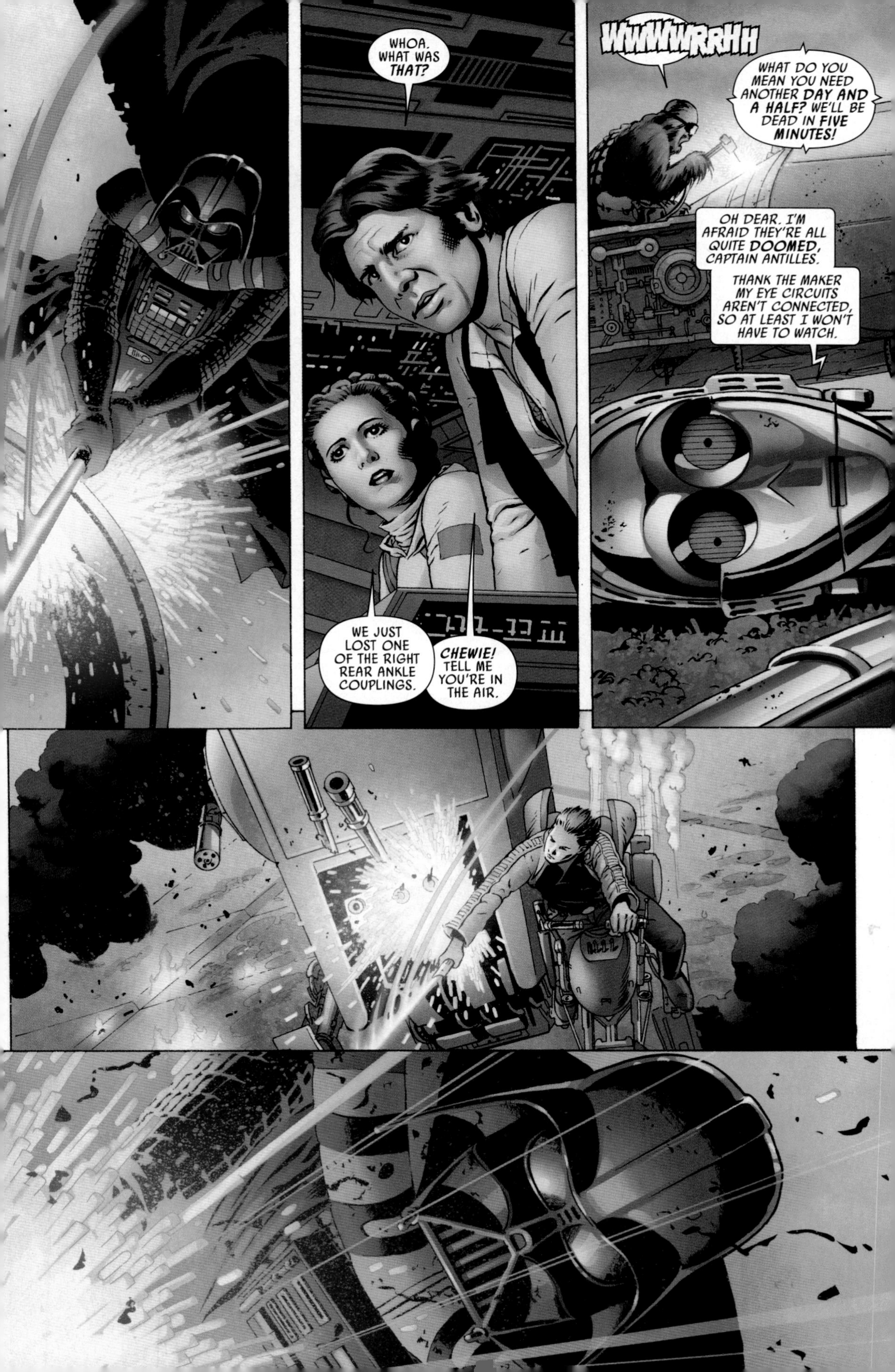
WHOA. WHAT WAS THAT?
WE JUST LOST ONE OF THE RIGHT REAR ANKLE COUPLINGS.
CHEWIE! TELL ME YOU'RE IN THE AIR.
WWWWRRHH
WHAT DO YOU MEAN YOU NEED ANOTHER DAY AND A HALF? WE'LL BE DEAD IN FIVE MINUTES!
OH DEAR. I'M AFRAID THEY'RE ALL QUITE DOOMED, CAPTAIN ANTILLES.
THANK THE MAKER MY EYE CIRCUITS AREN'T CONNECTED, SO AT LEAST I WON'T HAVE TO WATCH.

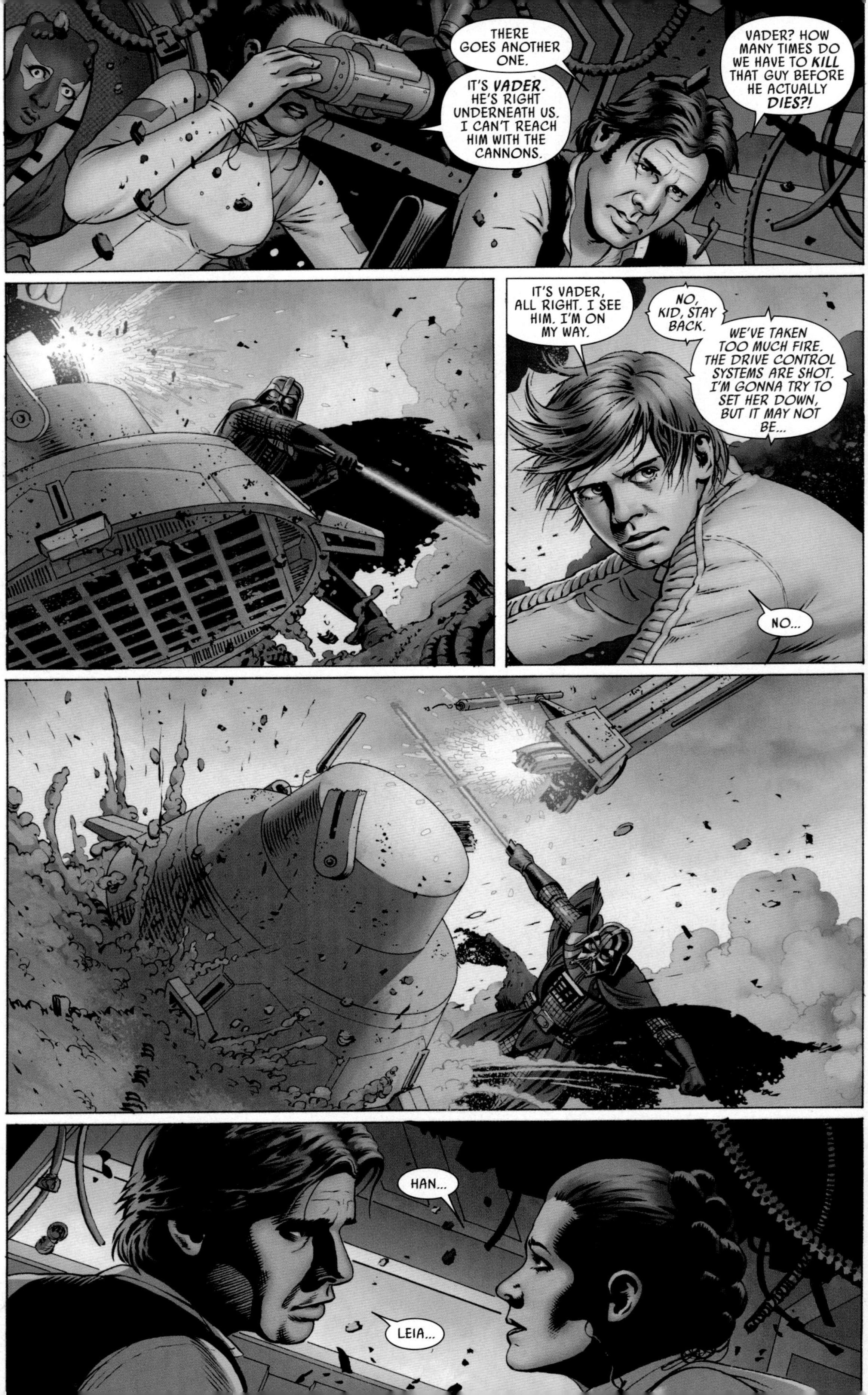
THERE GOES ANOTHER ONE.
IT'S VADER. HE'S RIGHT UNDERNEATH US. I CAN'T REACH HIM WITH THE CANNONS.
VADER? HOW MANY TIMES DO WE HAVE TO KILL THAT GUY BEFORE HE ACTUALLY DIES?!
IT'S VADER, ALL RIGHT. I SEE HIM. I'M ON MY WAY.
NO, KID, STAY BACK.
WE'VE TAKEN TOO MUCH FIRE. THE DRIVE CONTROL SYSTEMS ARE SHOT. I'M GONNA TRY TO SET HER DOWN, BUT IT MAY NOT BE...
NO...
HAN...
LEIA...

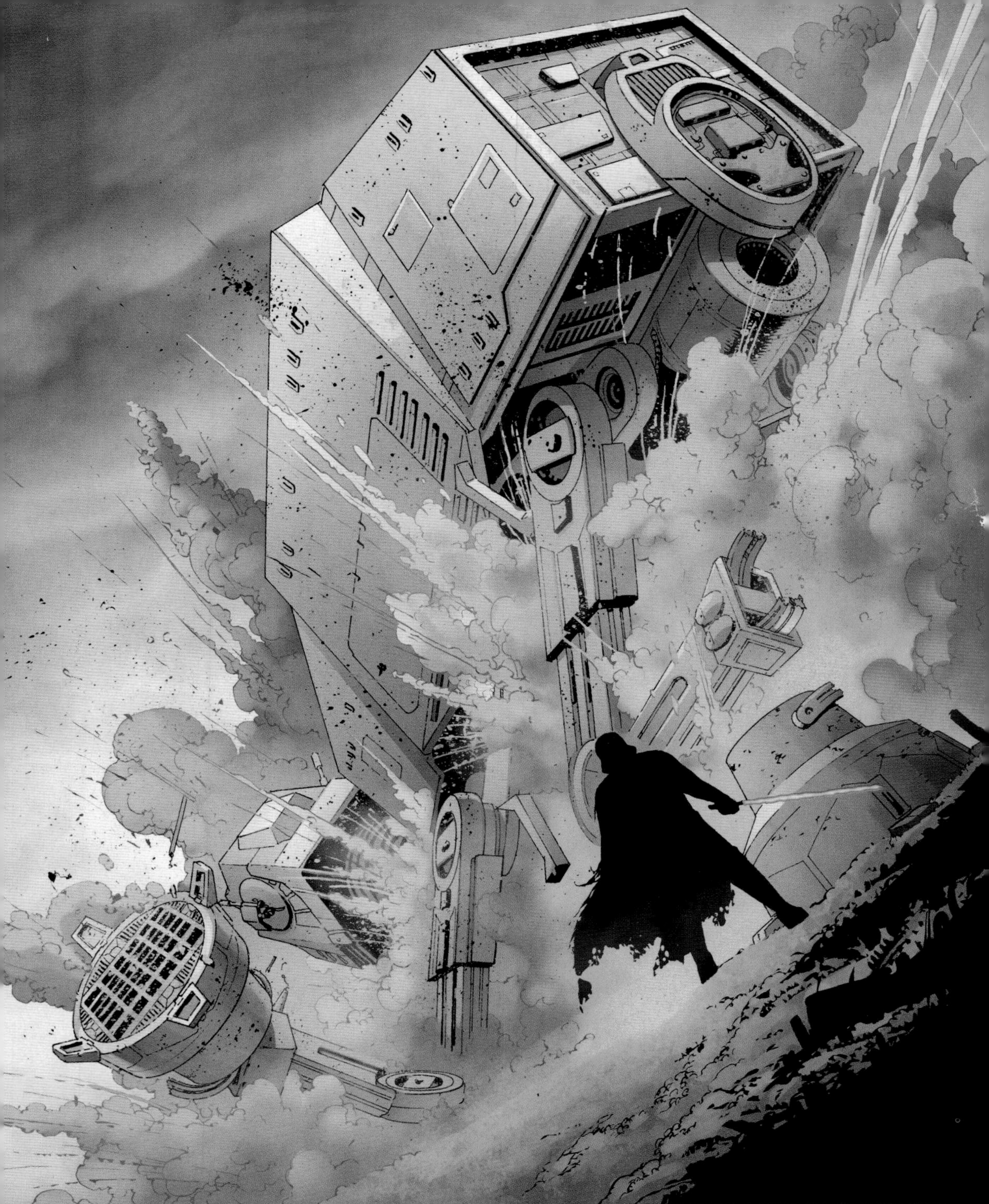

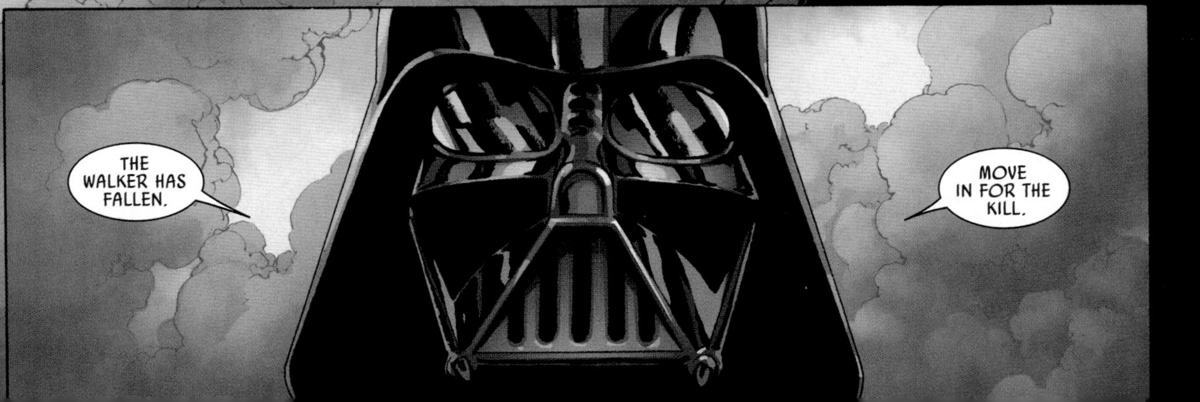
THE WALKER HAS FALLEN.
MOVE IN FOR THE KILL.

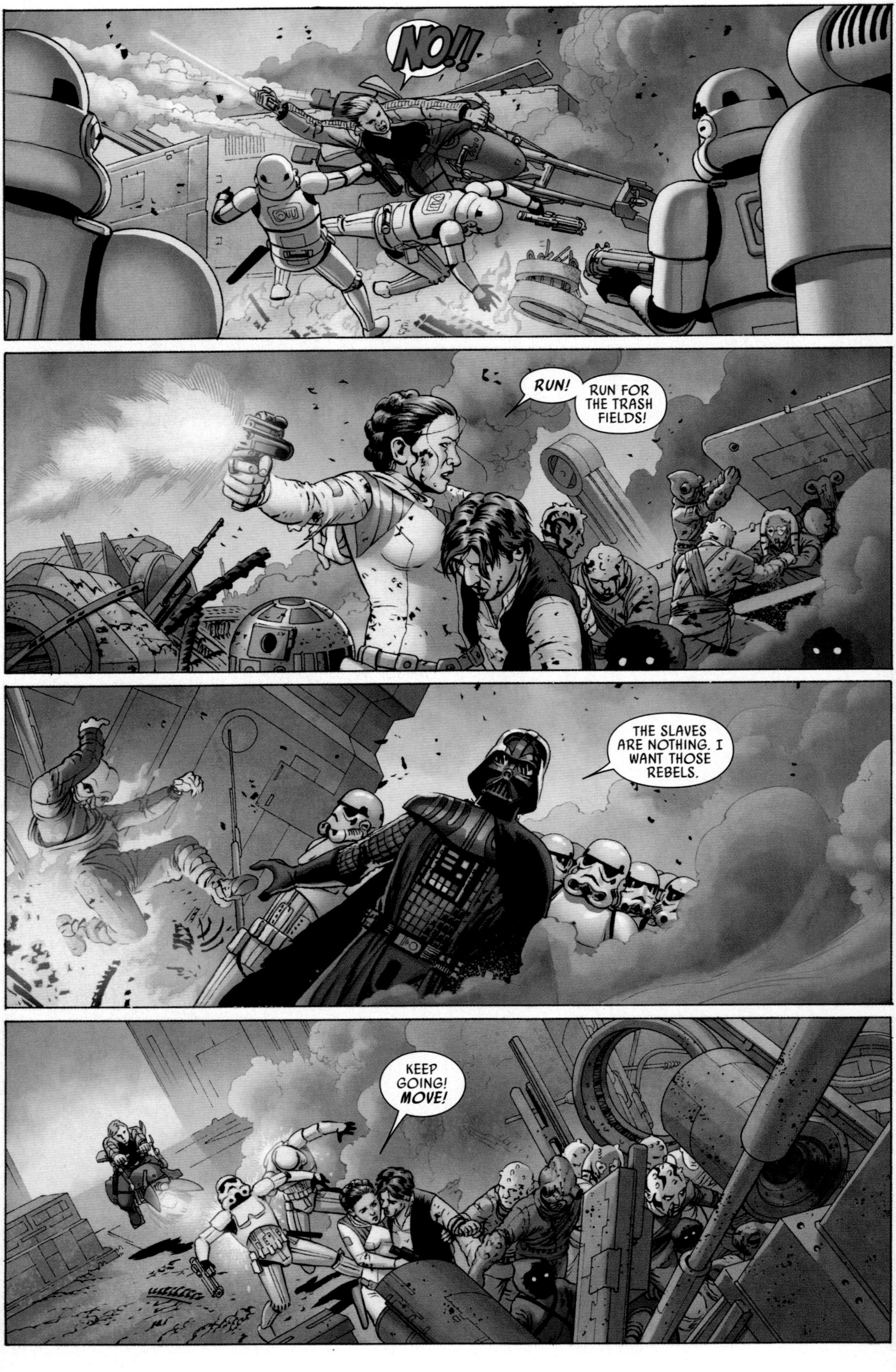
NO!!
RUN!
RUN FOR THE TRASH FIELDS!
THE SLAVES ARE NOTHING. I WANT THOSE REBELS.
KEEP GOING! MOVE!

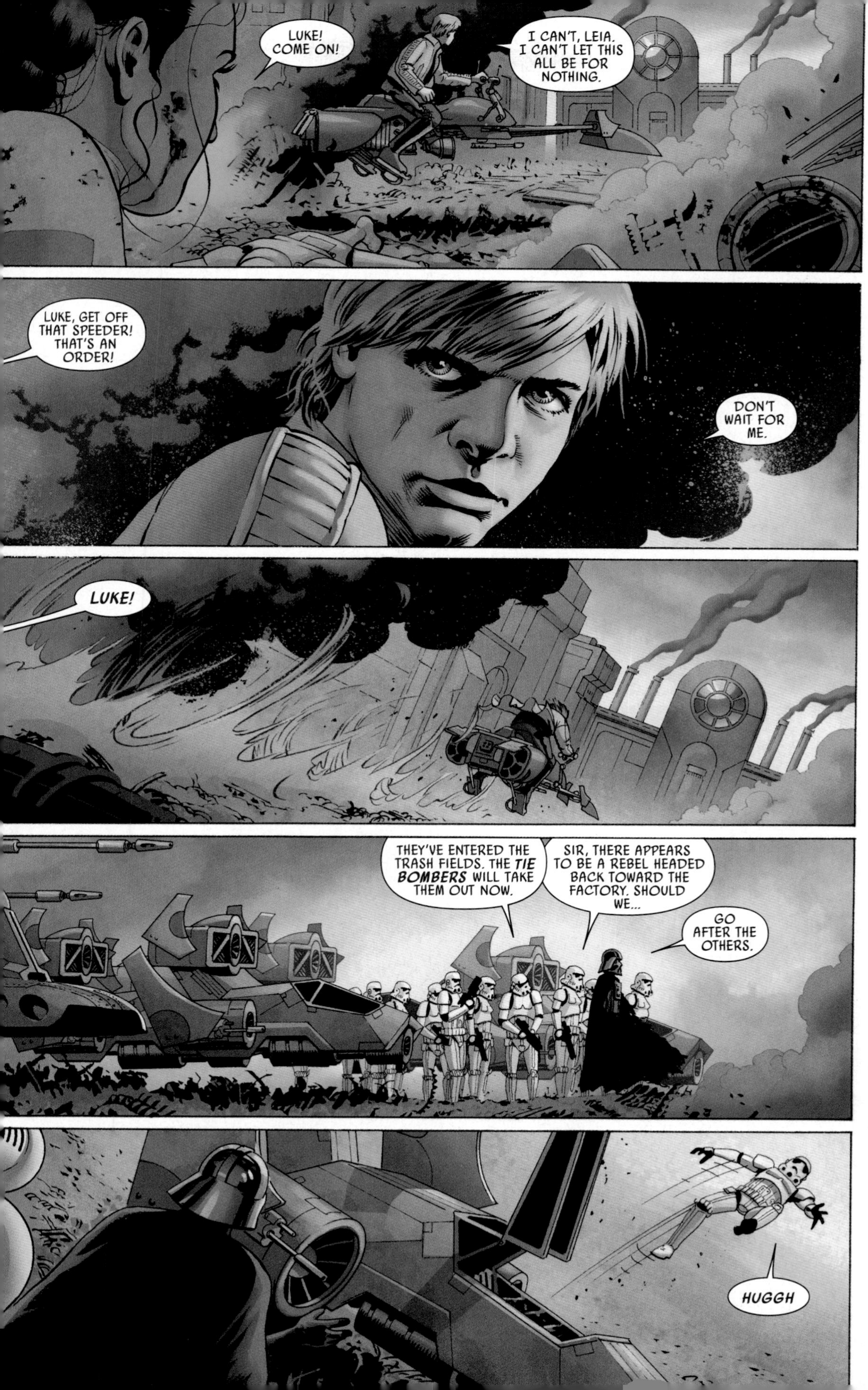
LUKE! COME ON!
I CAN'T, LEIA. I CAN'T LET THIS ALL BE FOR NOTHING.
LUKE, GET OFF THAT SPEEDER! THAT'S AN ORDER!
DON'T WAIT FOR ME.
LUKE!
THEY'VE ENTERED THE TRASH FIELDS. THE TIE BOMBERS WILL TAKE THEM OUT NOW.
SIR, THERE APPEARS TO BE A REBEL HEADED BACK TOWARD THE FACTORY. SHOULD WE...
GO AFTER THE OTHERS.
HUGGH

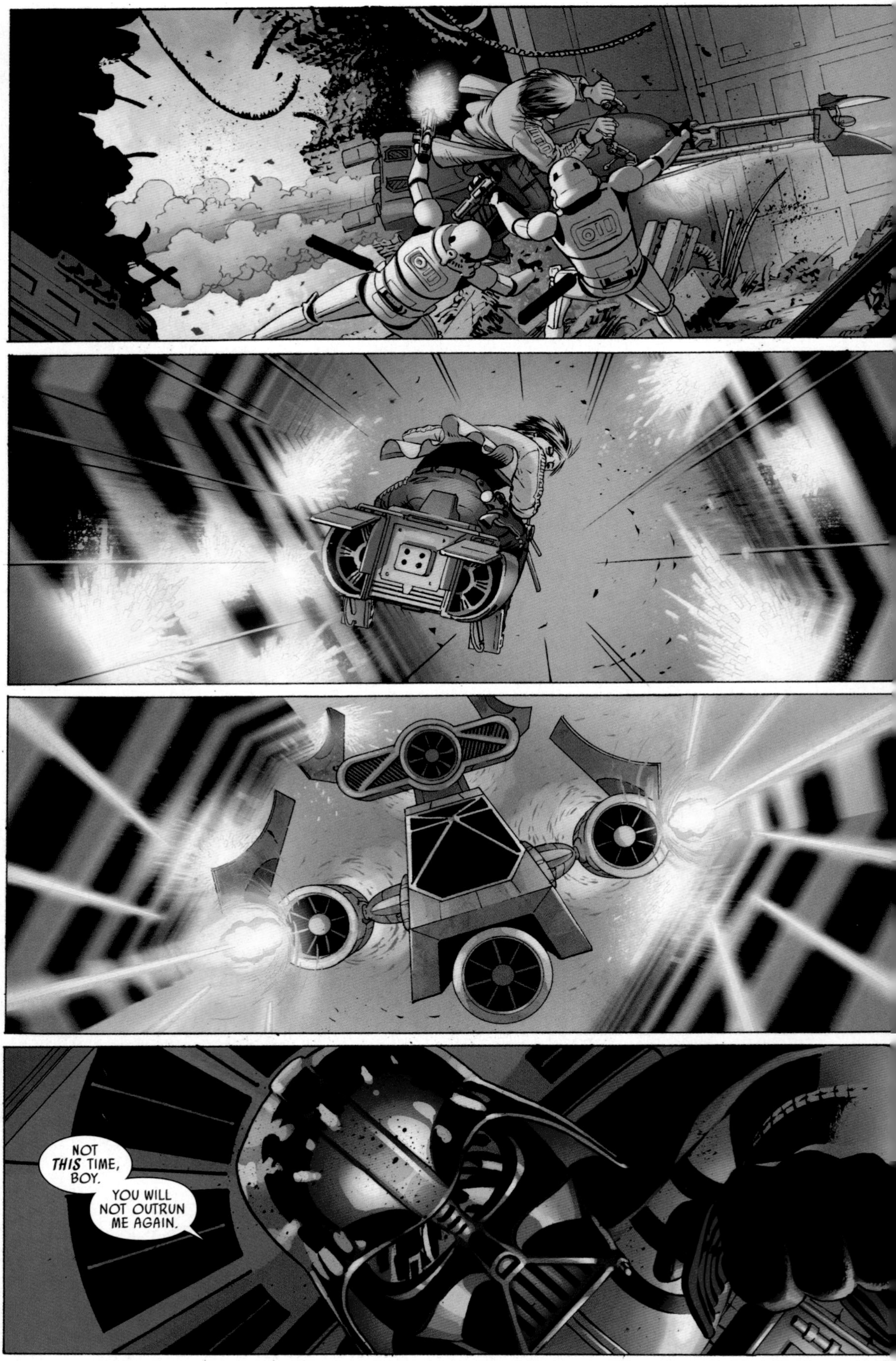
NOT THIS TIME, BOY.
YOU WILL NOT OUTRUN ME AGAIN.

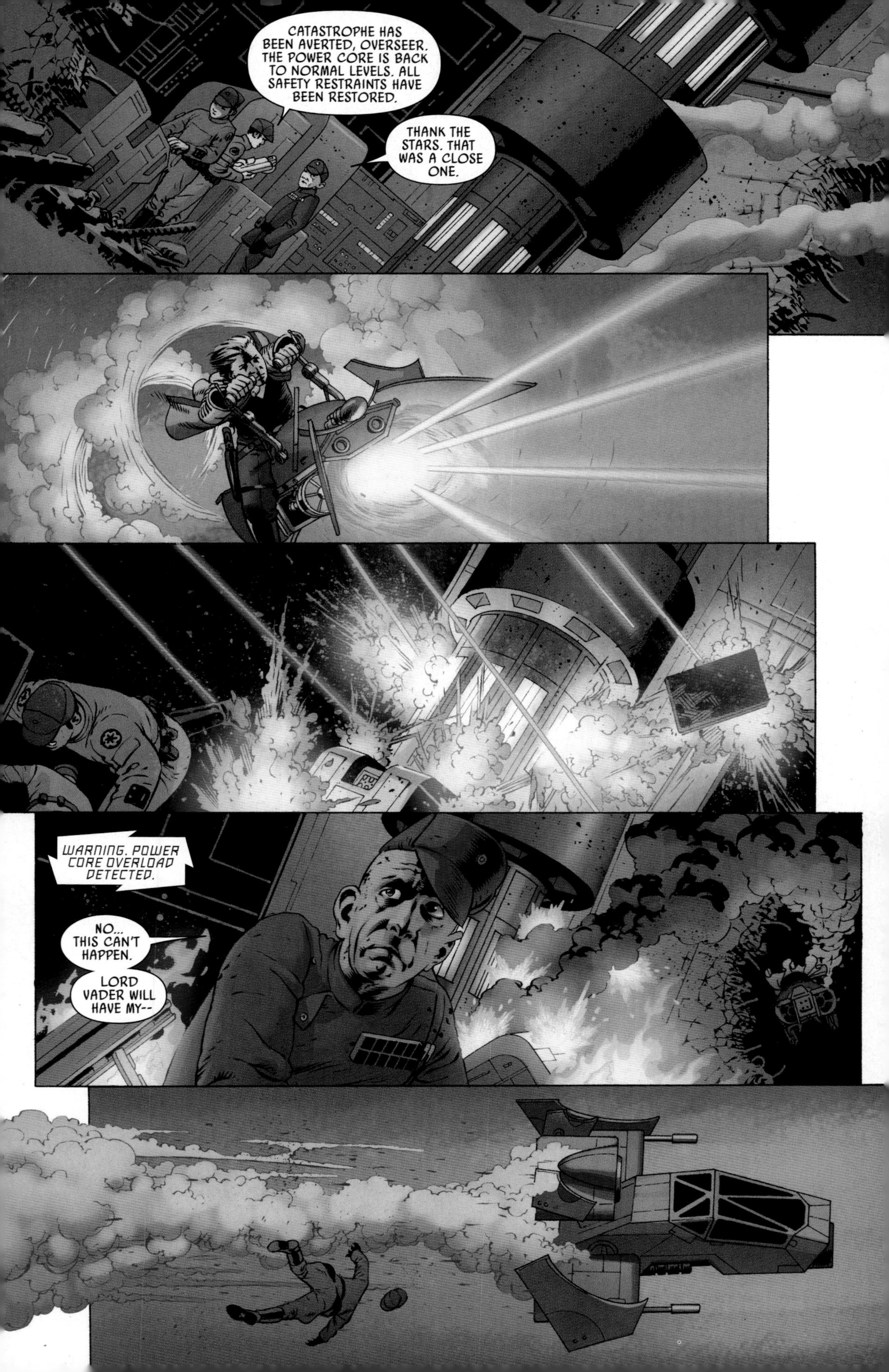
CATASTROPHE HAS BEEN AVERTED, OVERSEER. THE POWER CORE IS BACK TO NORMAL LEVELS. ALL SAFETY RESTRAINTS HAVE BEEN RESTORED.
THANK THE STARS. THAT WAS A CLOSE ONE.
WARNING. POWER CORE OVERLOAD DETECTED.
NO... THIS CAN'T HAPPEN.
LORD VADER WILL HAVE MY--

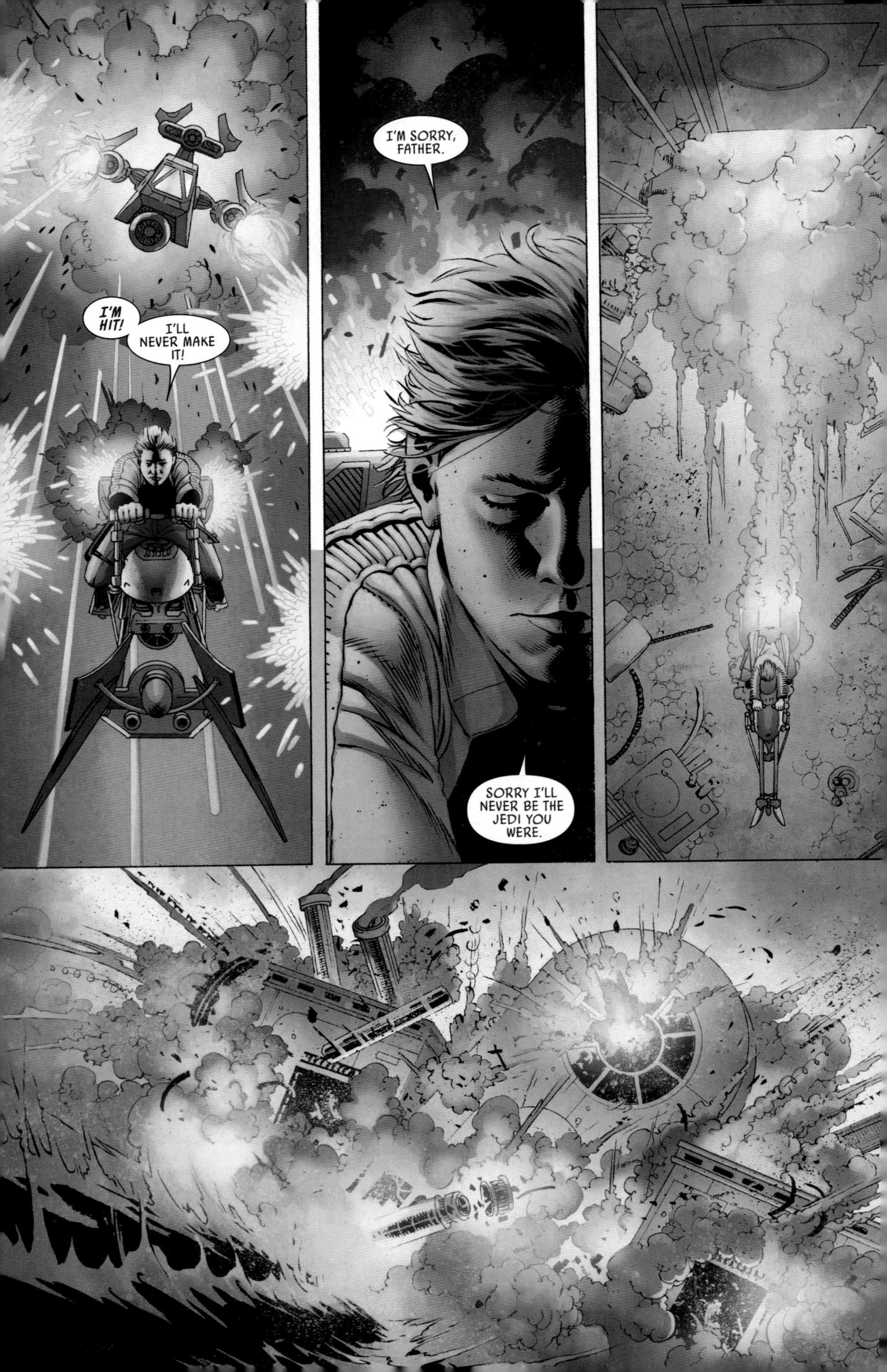
I'M HIT!
I'LL NEVER MAKE IT!
I'M SORRY, FATHER.
SORRY I'LL NEVER BE THE JEDI YOU WERE.

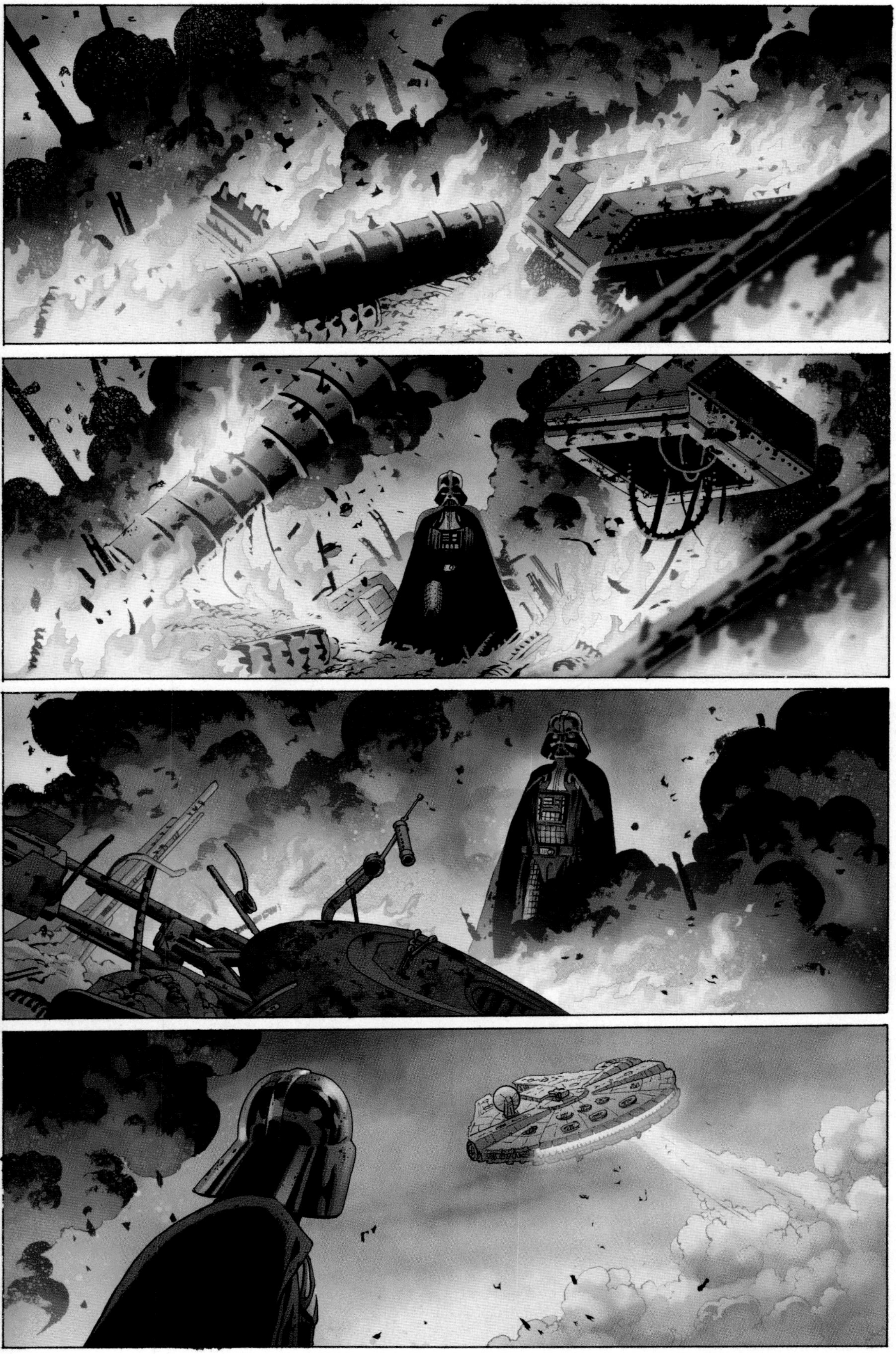

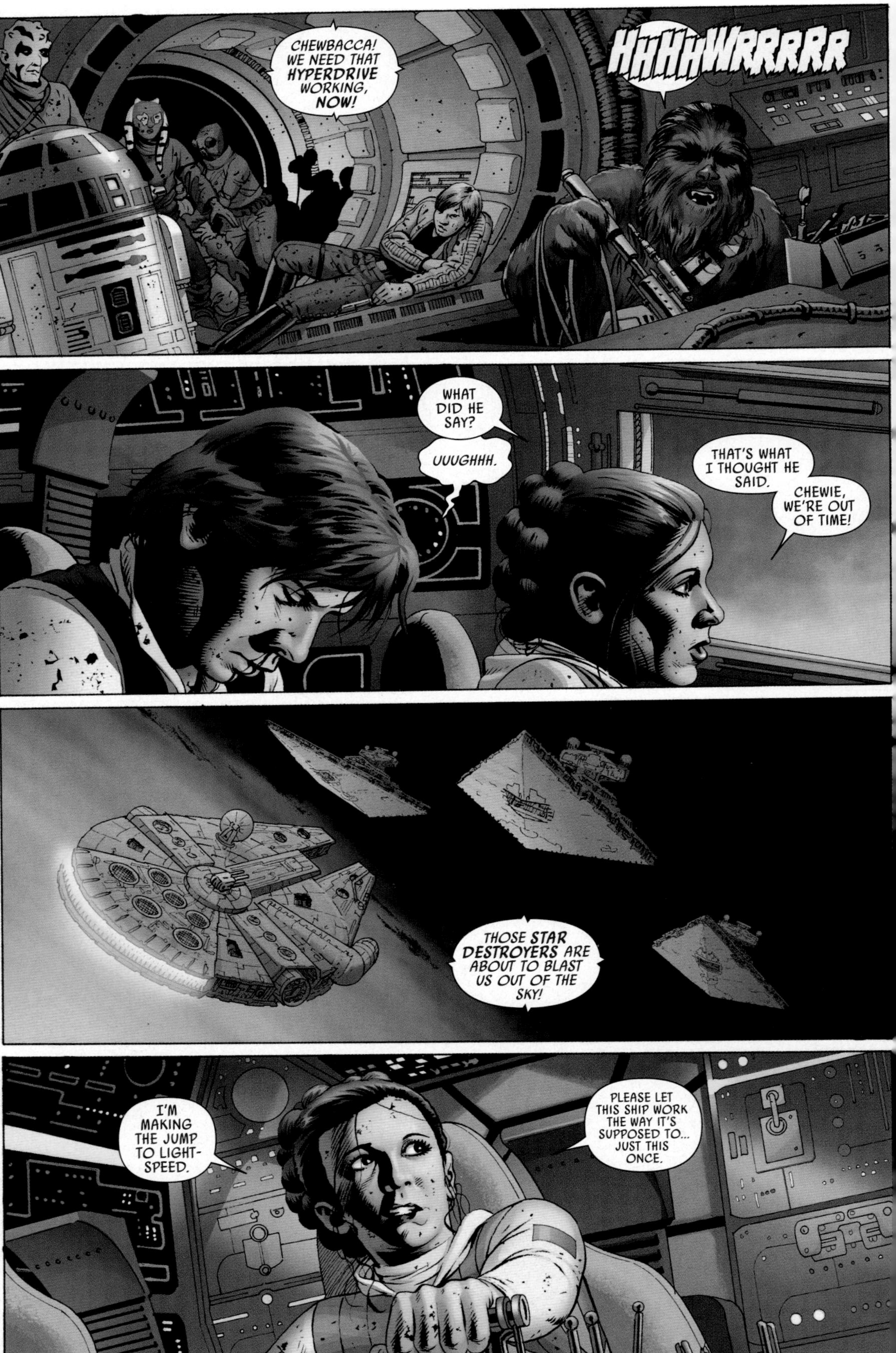
CHEWBACCA! WE NEED THAT HYPERDRIVE WORKING, NOW!
HHHHWRRRRR
WHAT DID HE SAY?
UUUGHHH.
THAT'S WHAT I THOUGHT HE SAID.
CHEWIE, WE'RE OUT OF TIME!
THOSE STAR DESTROYERS ARE ABOUT TO BLAST US OUT OF THE SKY!
I'M MAKING THE JUMP TO LIGHT-SPEED.
PLEASE LET THIS SHIP WORK THE WAY IT'S SUPPOSED TO... JUST THIS ONCE.

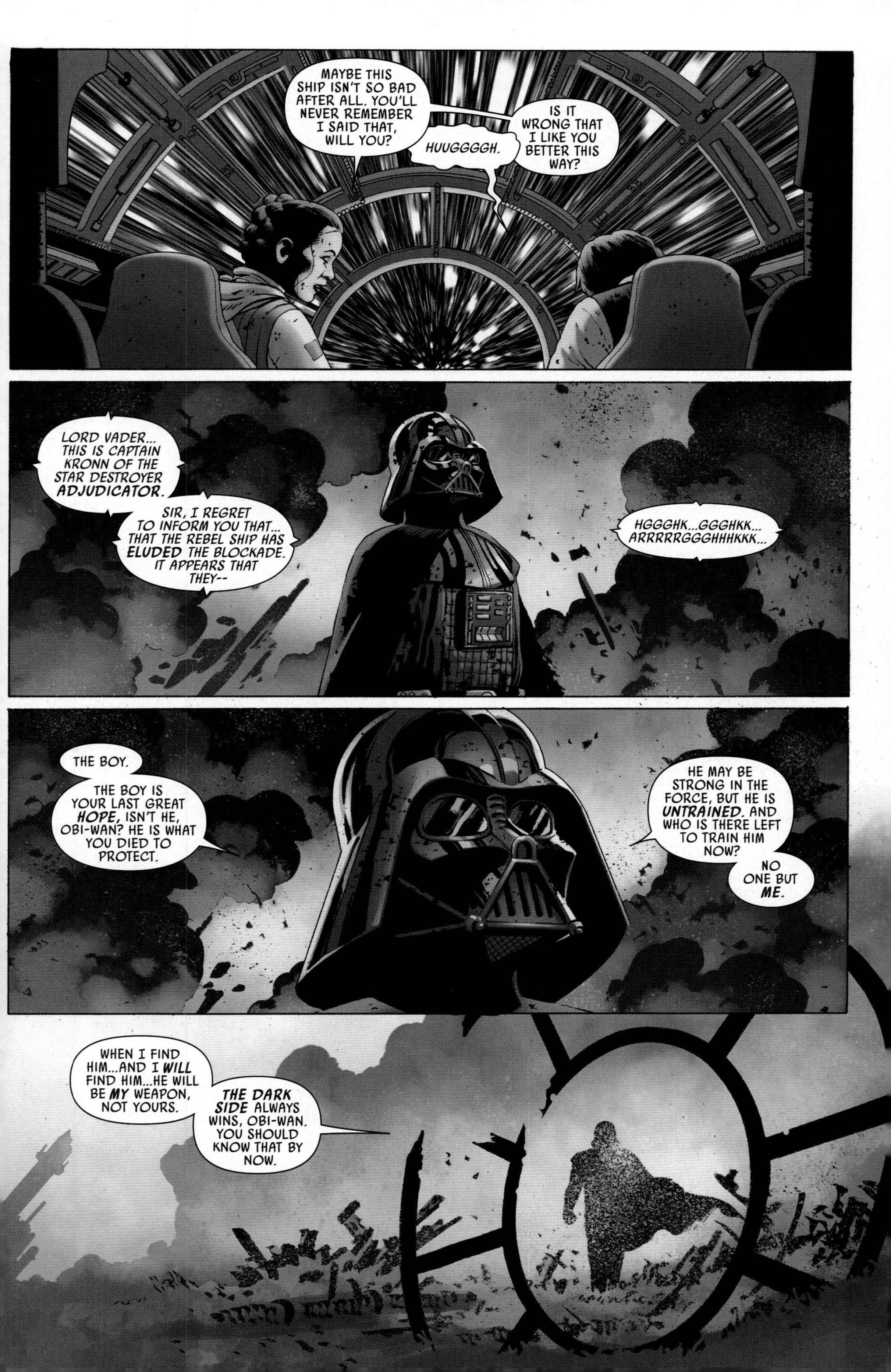
MAYBE THIS SHIP ISN'T SO BAD AFTER ALL. YOU'LL NEVER REMEMBER I SAID THAT, WILL YOU?
HUUGGGGH.
IS IT WRONG THAT I LIKE YOU BETTER THIS WAY?
LORD VADER... THIS IS CAPTAIN KRONN OF THE STAR DESTROYER ADJUDICATOR.
SIR, I REGRET TO INFORM YOU THAT... THAT THE REBEL SHIP HAS ELUDED THE BLOCKADE. IT APPEARS THAT THEY--
HGGGHK...GGGHKK... ARRRRRGGGHHHKKK...
THE BOY.
THE BOY IS YOUR LAST GREAT HOPE, ISN'T HE, OBI-WAN? HE IS WHAT YOU DIED TO PROTECT.
HE MAY BE STRONG IN THE FORCE, BUT HE IS UNTRAINED. AND WHO IS THERE LEFT TO TRAIN HIM NOW?
NO ONE BUT ME.
WHEN I FIND HIM...AND I WILL FIND HIM...HE WILL BE MY WEAPON, NOT YOURS.
THE DARK SIDE ALWAYS WINS, OBI-WAN. YOU SHOULD KNOW THAT BY NOW.

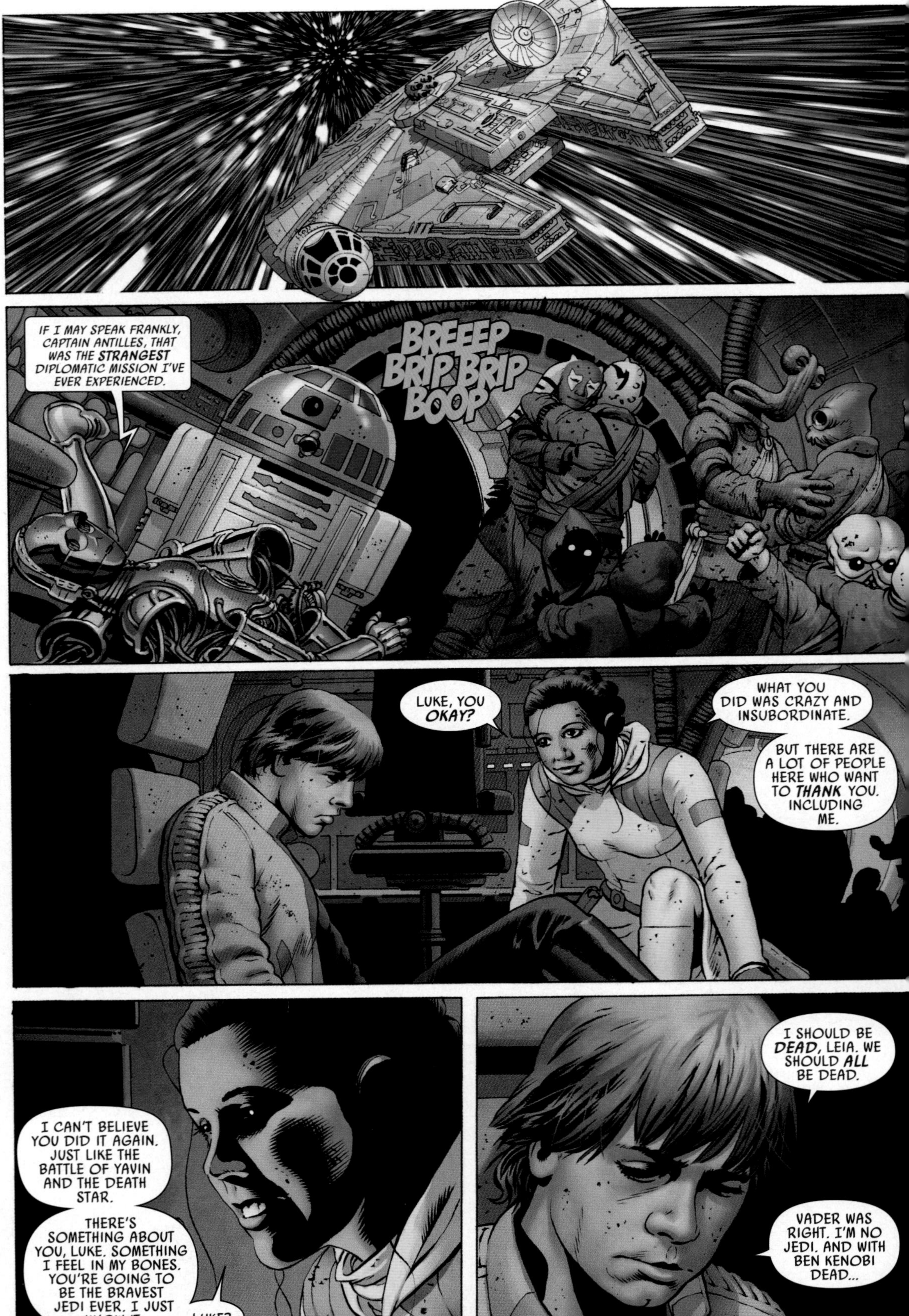
IF I MAY SPEAK FRANKLY, CAPTAIN ANTILLES, THAT WAS THE **STRANGEST** DIPLOMATIC MISSION I'VE EVER EXPERIENCED.
BREEEP BRIP BRIP BOOP
LUKE, YOU ***OKAY?***
WHAT YOU DID WAS CRAZY AND INSUBORDINATE.
BUT THERE ARE A LOT OF PEOPLE HERE WHO WANT TO ***THANK*** YOU. INCLUDING ME.
I CAN'T BELIEVE YOU DID IT AGAIN. JUST LIKE THE BATTLE OF YAVIN AND THE DEATH STAR.
THERE'S SOMETHING ABOUT YOU, LUKE. SOMETHING I FEEL IN MY BONES. YOU'RE GOING TO BE THE BRAVEST JEDI EVER. I JUST KNOW IT.
LUKE?
I SHOULD BE ***DEAD,*** LEIA. WE SHOULD ***ALL*** BE DEAD.
VADER WAS RIGHT. I'M NO JEDI. AND WITH BEN KENOBI DEAD...

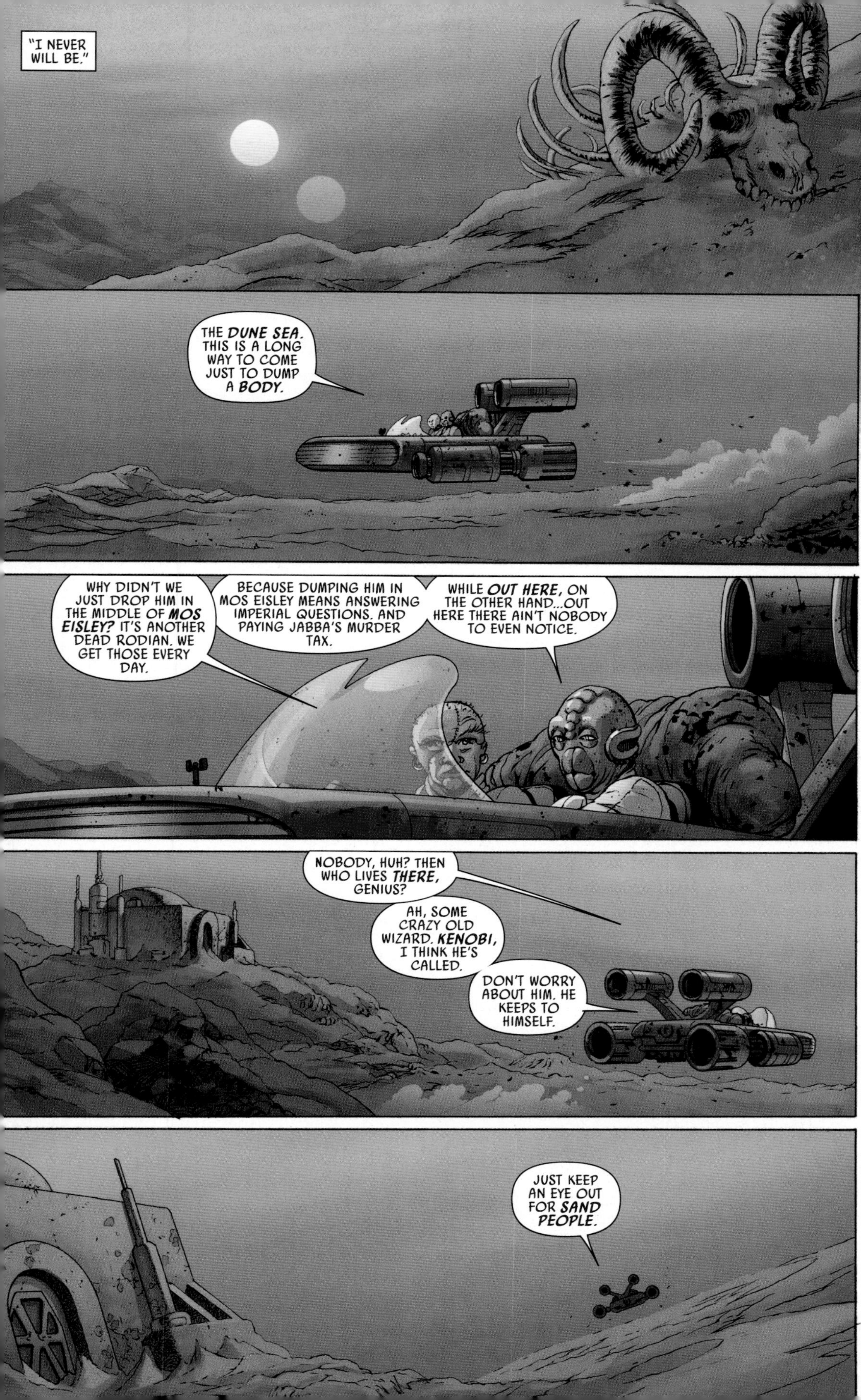
"I NEVER WILL BE."
THE DUNE SEA. THIS IS A LONG WAY TO COME JUST TO DUMP A BODY.
WHY DIDN'T WE JUST DROP HIM IN THE MIDDLE OF MOS EISLEY? IT'S ANOTHER DEAD RODIAN. WE GET THOSE EVERY DAY.
BECAUSE DUMPING HIM IN MOS EISLEY MEANS ANSWERING IMPERIAL QUESTIONS. AND PAYING JABBA'S MURDER TAX.
WHILE OUT HERE, ON THE OTHER HAND...OUT HERE THERE AIN'T NOBODY TO EVEN NOTICE.
NOBODY, HUH? THEN WHO LIVES THERE, GENIUS?
AH, SOME CRAZY OLD WIZARD. KENOBI, I THINK HE'S CALLED.
DON'T WORRY ABOUT HIM. HE KEEPS TO HIMSELF.
JUST KEEP AN EYE OUT FOR SAND PEOPLE.

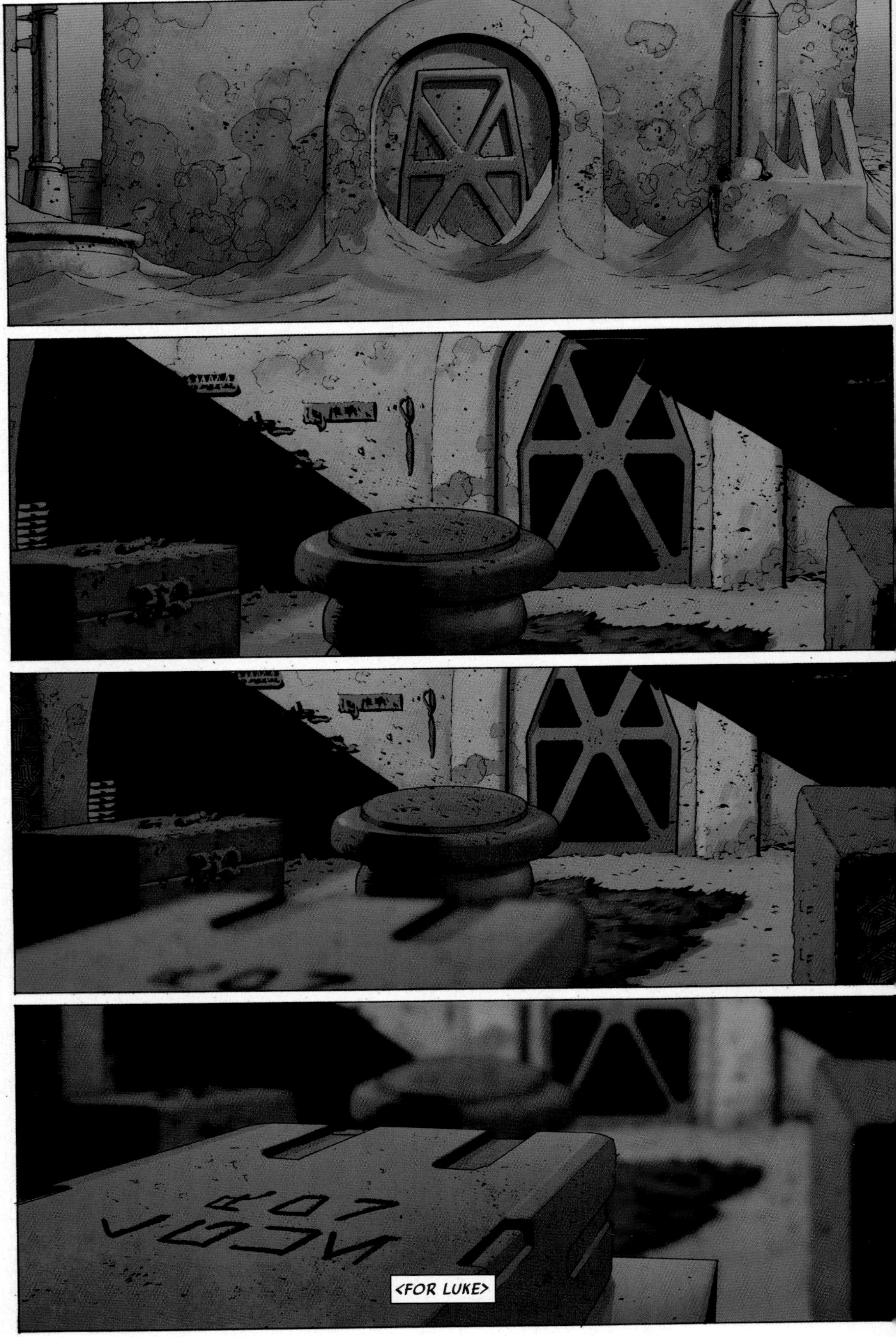
<FOR LUKE>

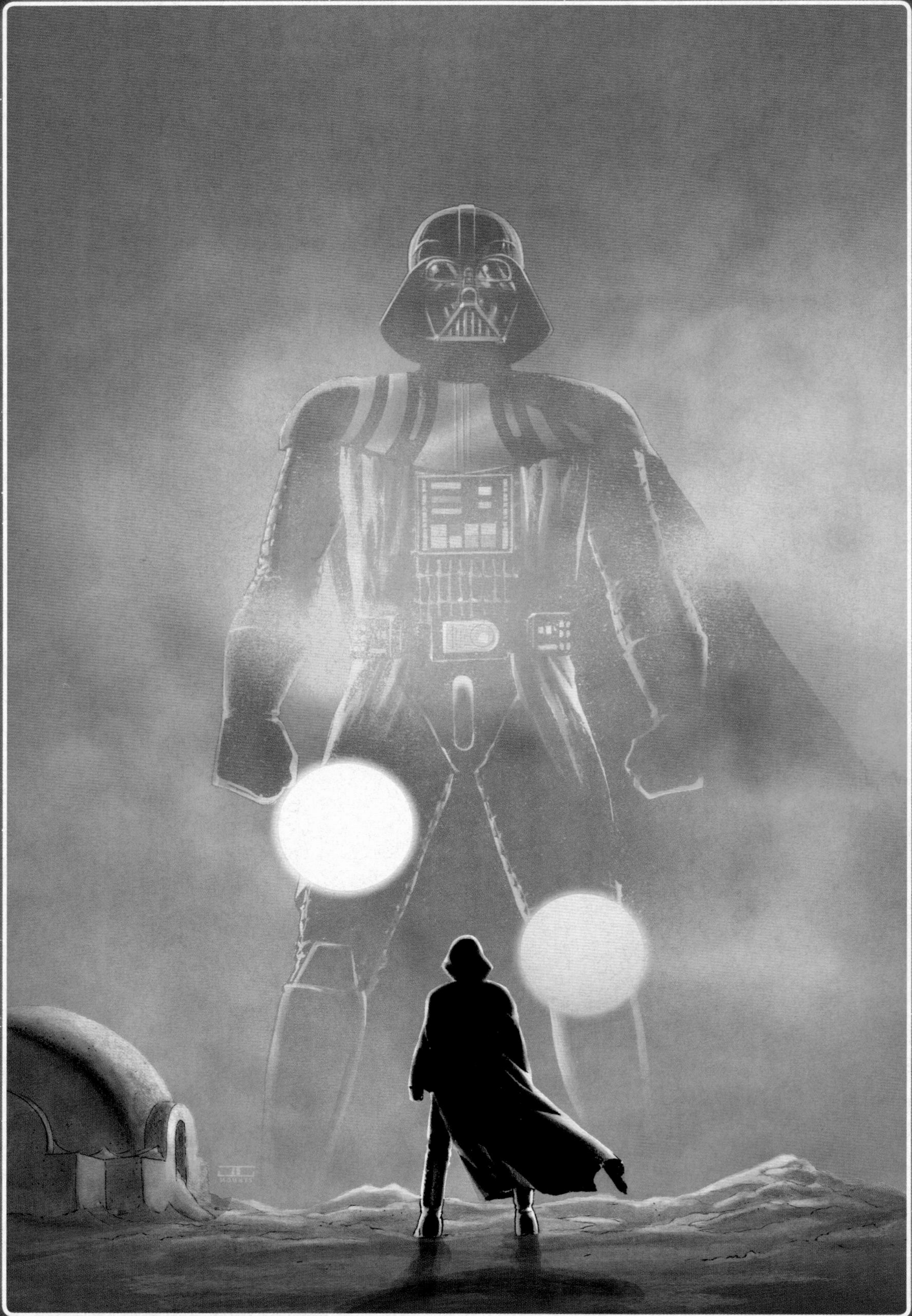

4

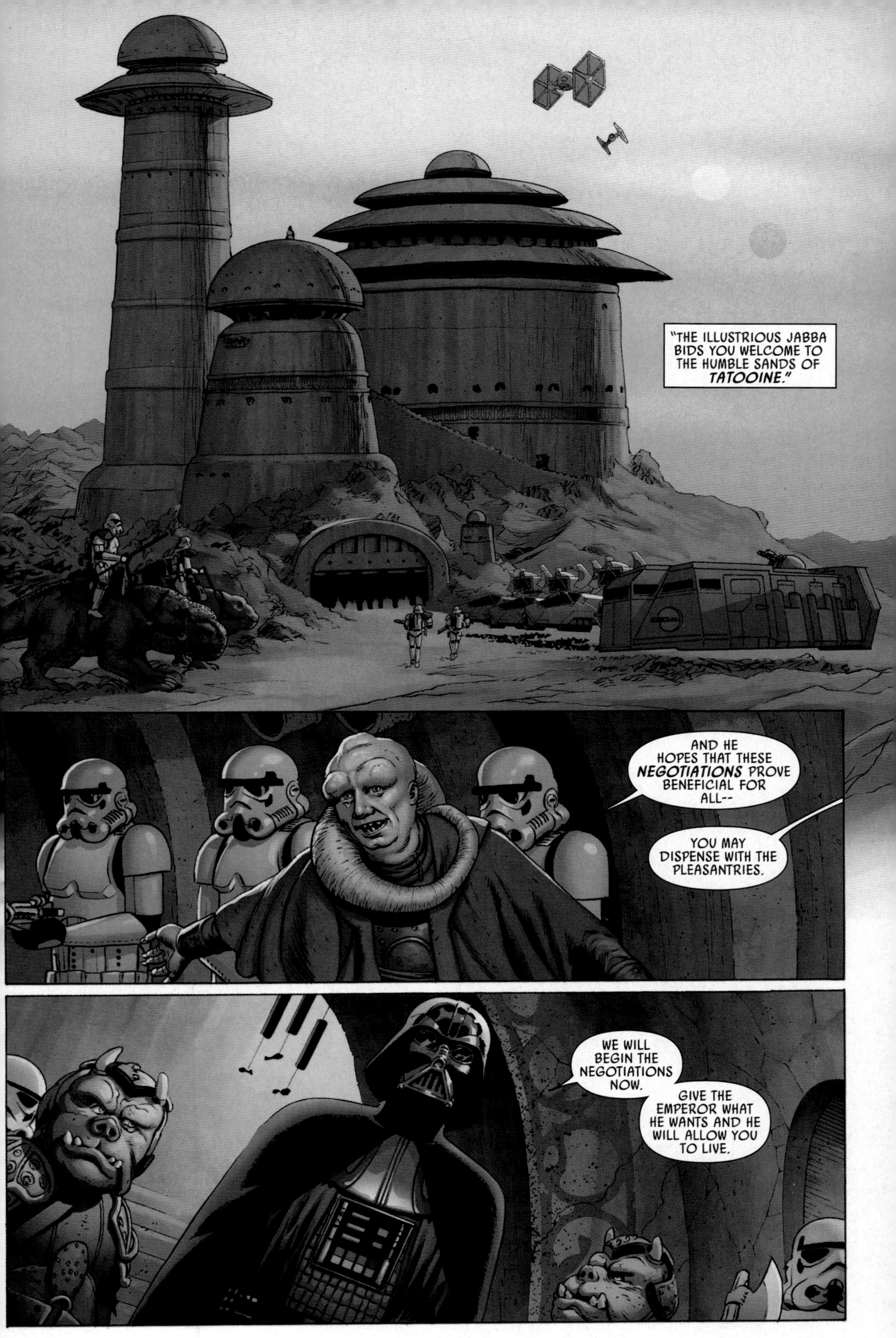
"THE ILLUSTRIOUS JABBA BIDS YOU WELCOME TO THE HUMBLE SANDS OF TATOOINE."
AND HE HOPES THAT THESE NEGOTIATIONS PROVE BENEFICIAL FOR ALL--
YOU MAY DISPENSE WITH THE PLEASANTRIES.
WE WILL BEGIN THE NEGOTIATIONS NOW.
GIVE THE EMPEROR WHAT HE WANTS AND HE WILL ALLOW YOU TO LIVE.

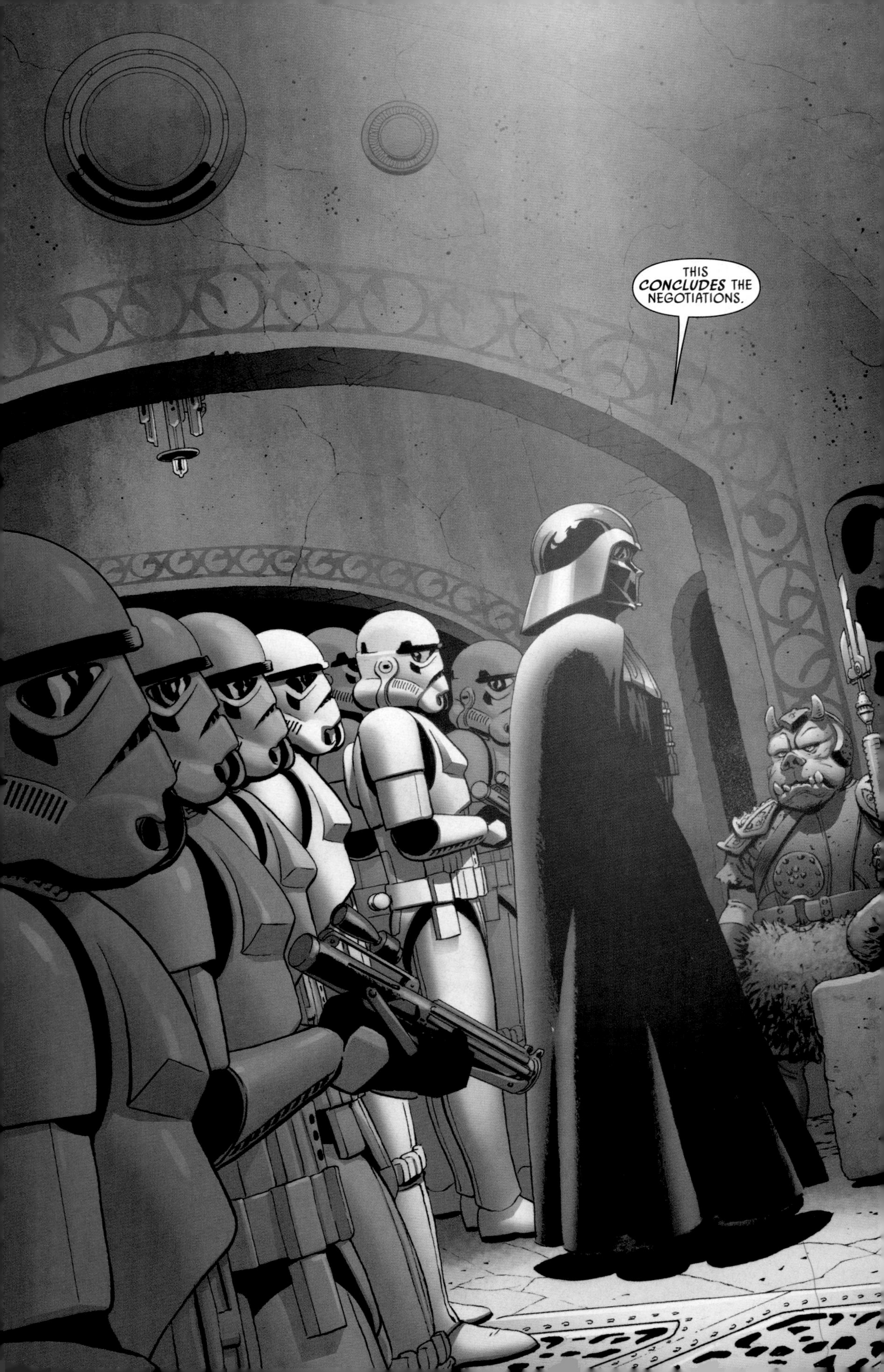
THIS CONCLUDES THE NEGOTIATIONS.

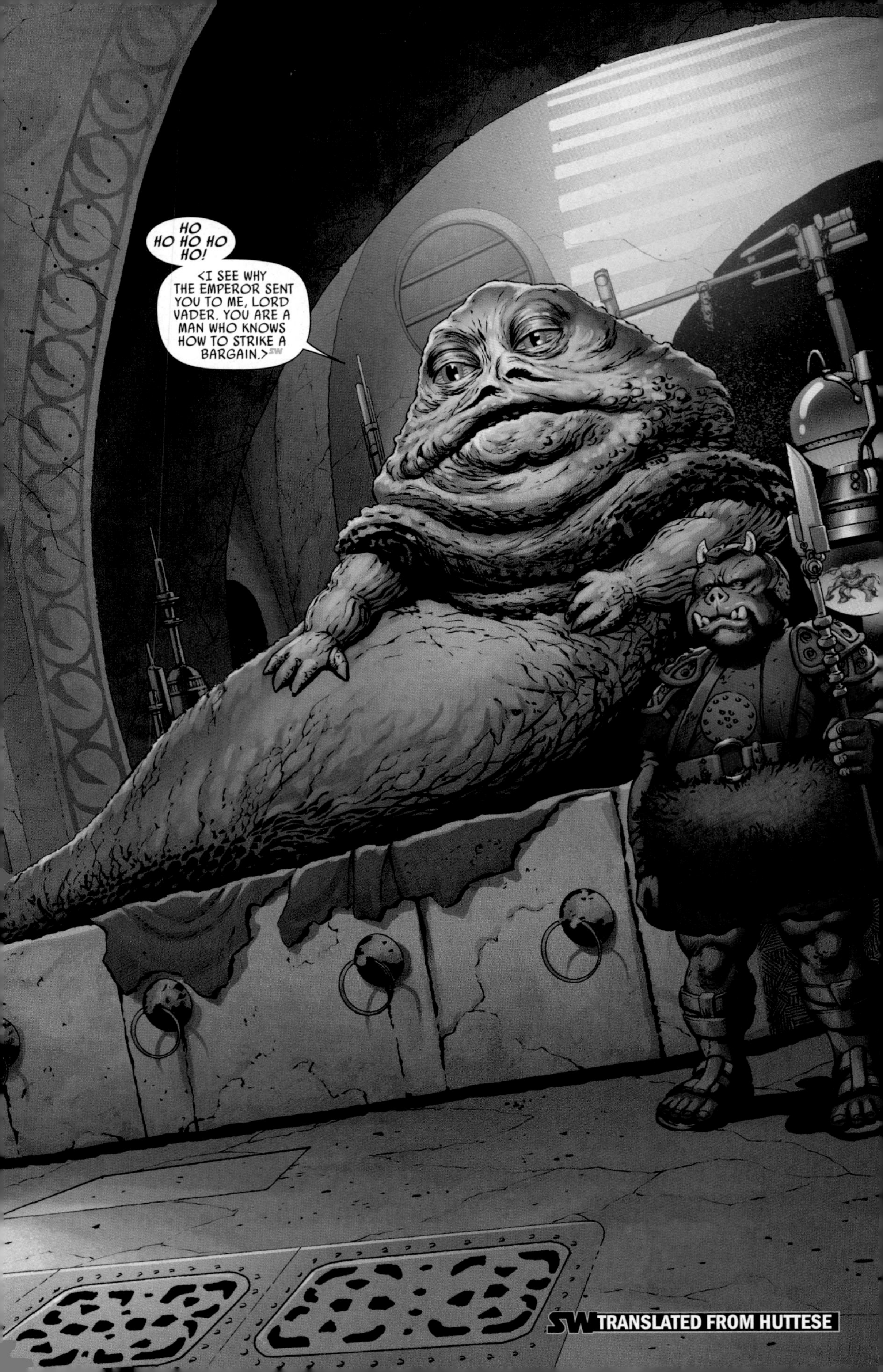
HO HO HO HO HO!
<I SEE WHY THE EMPEROR SENT YOU TO ME, LORD VADER. YOU ARE A MAN WHO KNOWS HOW TO STRIKE A BARGAIN.>
SW TRANSLATED FROM HUTTESE

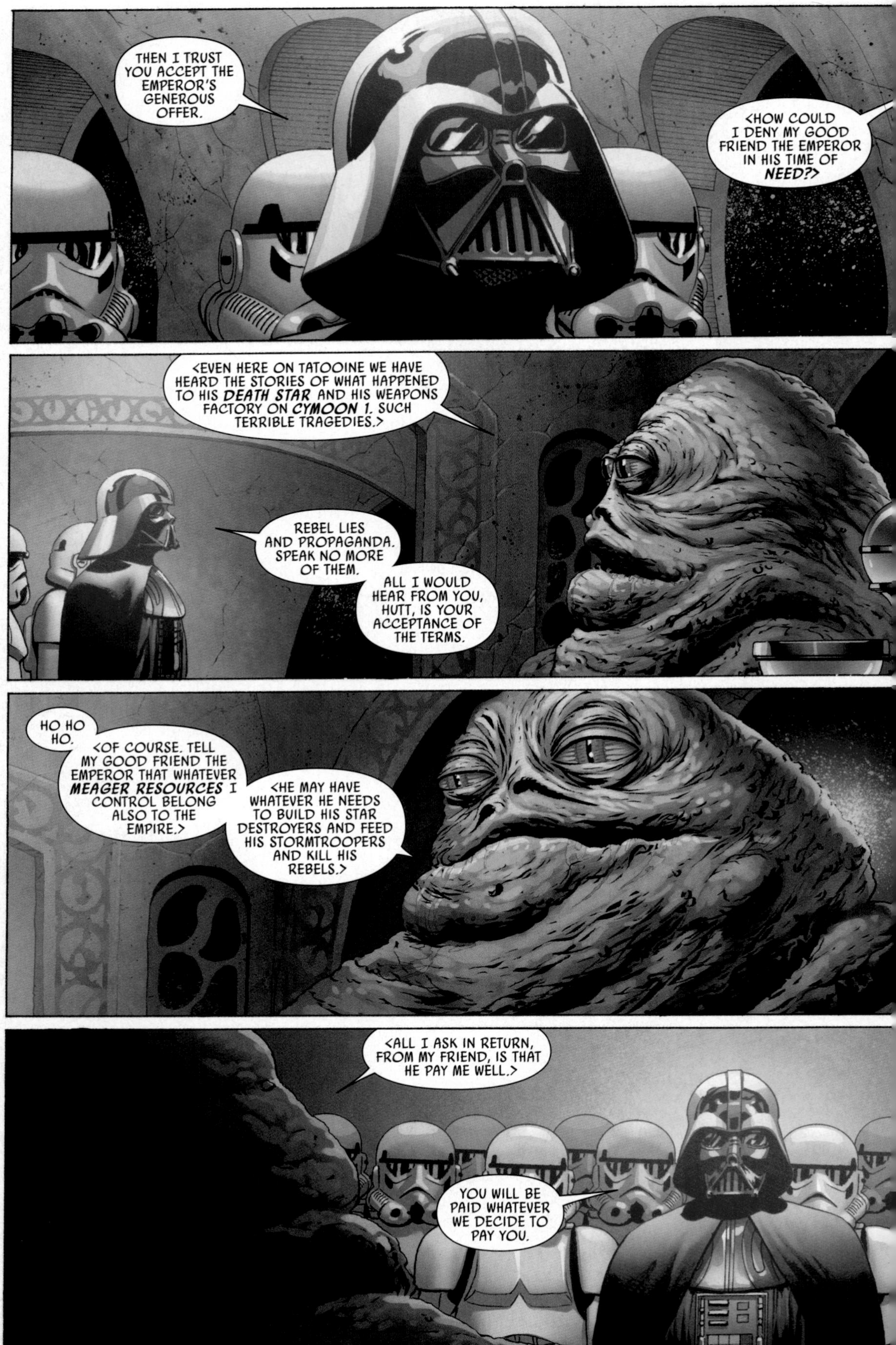
THEN I TRUST YOU ACCEPT THE EMPEROR'S GENEROUS OFFER.
<HOW COULD I DENY MY GOOD FRIEND THE EMPEROR IN HIS TIME OF NEED?>
<EVEN HERE ON TATOOINE WE HAVE HEARD THE STORIES OF WHAT HAPPENED TO HIS DEATH STAR AND HIS WEAPONS FACTORY ON CYMOON 1. SUCH TERRIBLE TRAGEDIES.>
REBEL LIES AND PROPAGANDA. SPEAK NO MORE OF THEM.
ALL I WOULD HEAR FROM YOU, HUTT, IS YOUR ACCEPTANCE OF THE TERMS.
HO HO HO.
<OF COURSE. TELL MY GOOD FRIEND THE EMPEROR THAT WHATEVER MEAGER RESOURCES I CONTROL BELONG ALSO TO THE EMPIRE.>
<HE MAY HAVE WHATEVER HE NEEDS TO BUILD HIS STAR DESTROYERS AND FEED HIS STORMTROOPERS AND KILL HIS REBELS.>
<ALL I ASK IN RETURN, FROM MY FRIEND, IS THAT HE PAY ME WELL.>
YOU WILL BE PAID WHATEVER WE DECIDE TO PAY YOU.

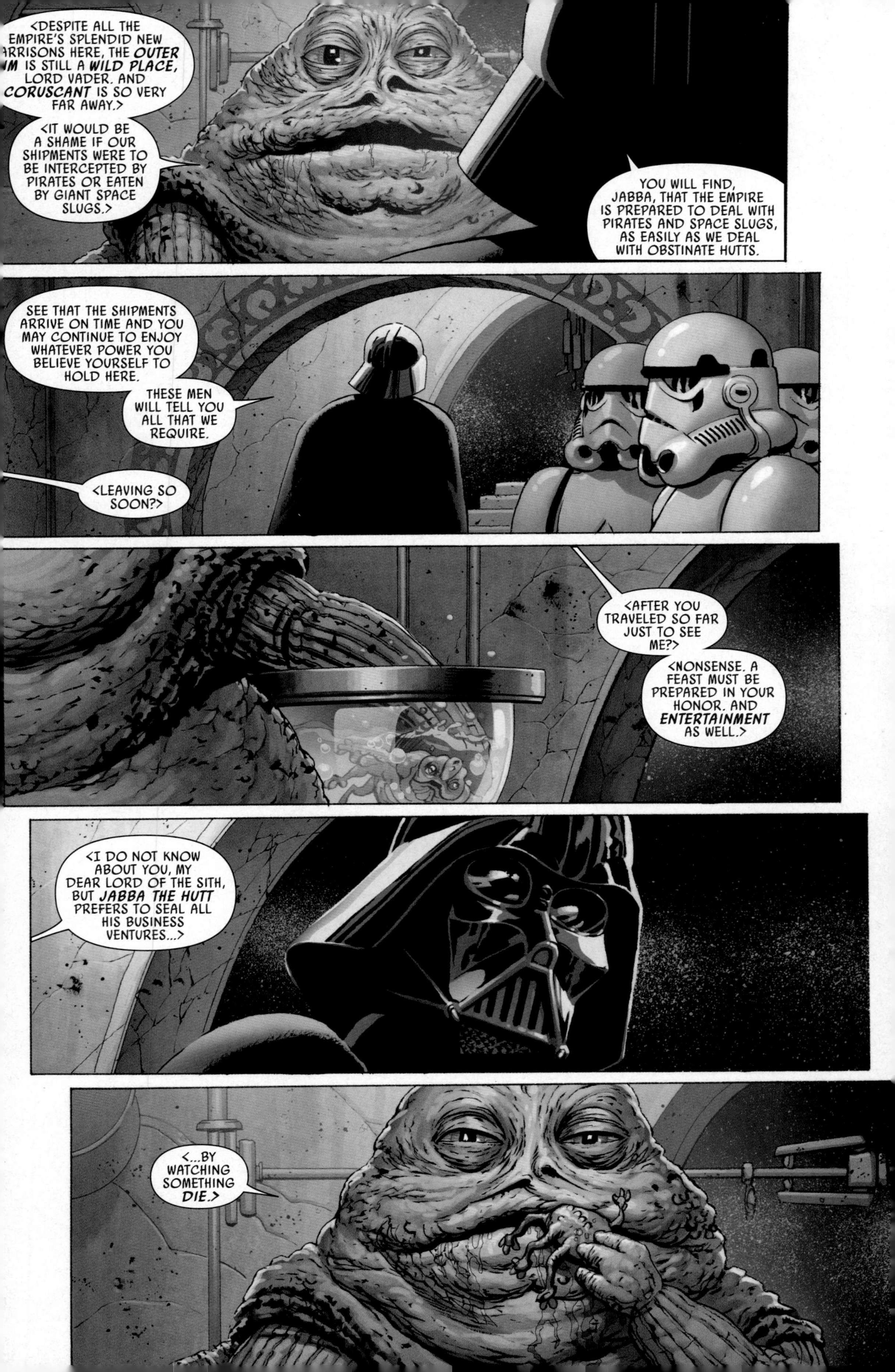
<DESPITE ALL THE EMPIRE'S SPLENDID NEW ARRISONS HERE, THE OUTER IM IS STILL A WILD PLACE, LORD VADER. AND CORUSCANT IS SO VERY FAR AWAY.>
<IT WOULD BE A SHAME IF OUR SHIPMENTS WERE TO BE INTERCEPTED BY PIRATES OR EATEN BY GIANT SPACE SLUGS.>
YOU WILL FIND, JABBA, THAT THE EMPIRE IS PREPARED TO DEAL WITH PIRATES AND SPACE SLUGS, AS EASILY AS WE DEAL WITH OBSTINATE HUTTS.
SEE THAT THE SHIPMENTS ARRIVE ON TIME AND YOU MAY CONTINUE TO ENJOY WHATEVER POWER YOU BELIEVE YOURSELF TO HOLD HERE.
THESE MEN WILL TELL YOU ALL THAT WE REQUIRE.
<LEAVING SO SOON?>
<AFTER YOU TRAVELED SO FAR JUST TO SEE ME?>
<NONSENSE. A FEAST MUST BE PREPARED IN YOUR HONOR. AND ENTERTAINMENT AS WELL.>
<I DO NOT KNOW ABOUT YOU, MY DEAR LORD OF THE SITH, BUT JABBA THE HUTT PREFERS TO SEAL ALL HIS BUSINESS VENTURES...>
<...BY WATCHING SOMETHING DIE.>

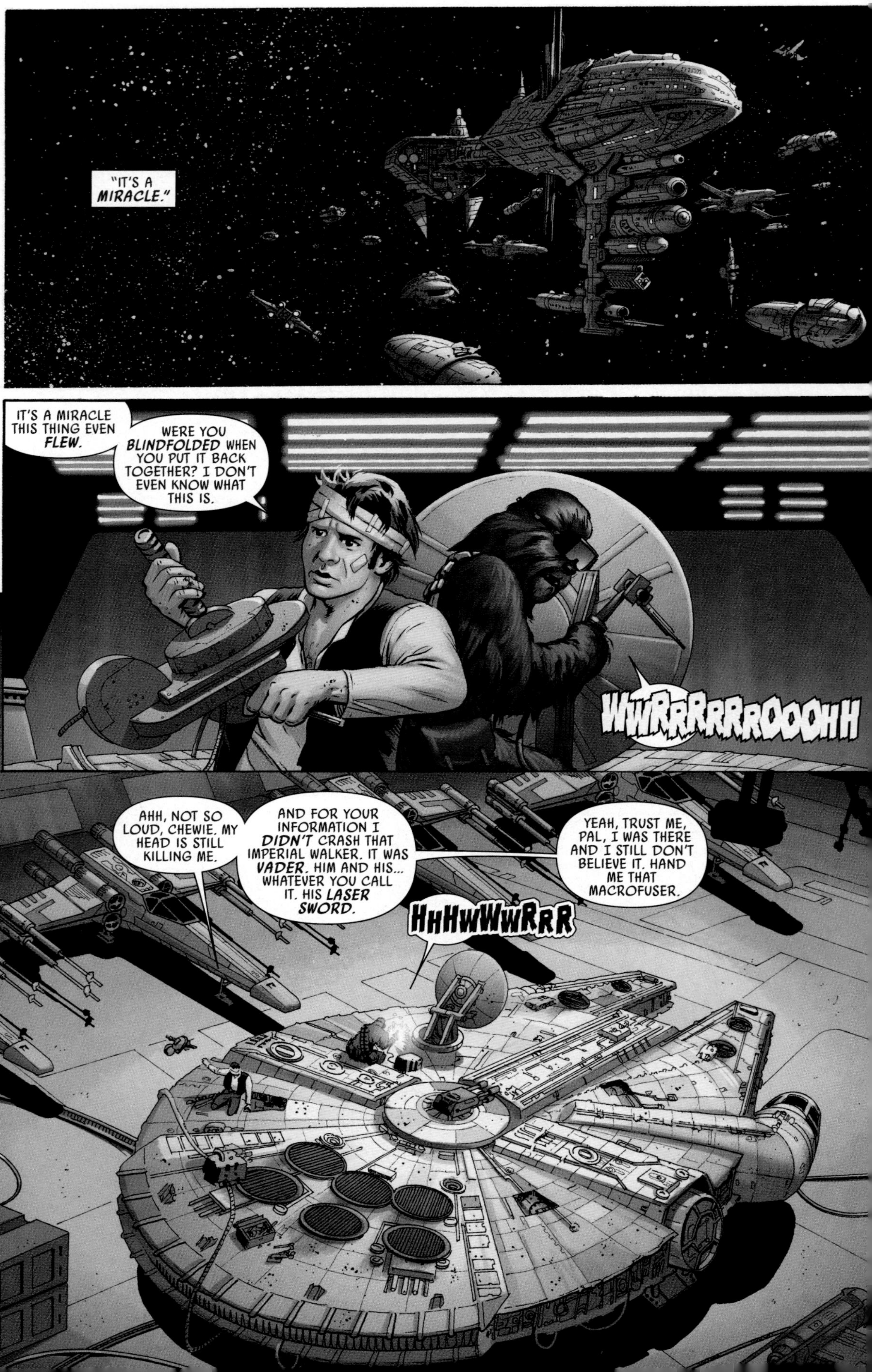
"IT'S A MIRACLE."
IT'S A MIRACLE THIS THING EVEN FLEW.
WERE YOU BLINDFOLDED WHEN YOU PUT IT BACK TOGETHER? I DON'T EVEN KNOW WHAT THIS IS.
WWRRRRRRROOOHH
AHH, NOT SO LOUD, CHEWIE. MY HEAD IS STILL KILLING ME.
AND FOR YOUR INFORMATION I DIDN'T CRASH THAT IMPERIAL WALKER. IT WAS VADER. HIM AND HIS... WHATEVER YOU CALL IT. HIS LASER SWORD.
HHHWWWRRR
YEAH, TRUST ME, PAL, I WAS THERE AND I STILL DON'T BELIEVE IT. HAND ME THAT MACROFUSER.

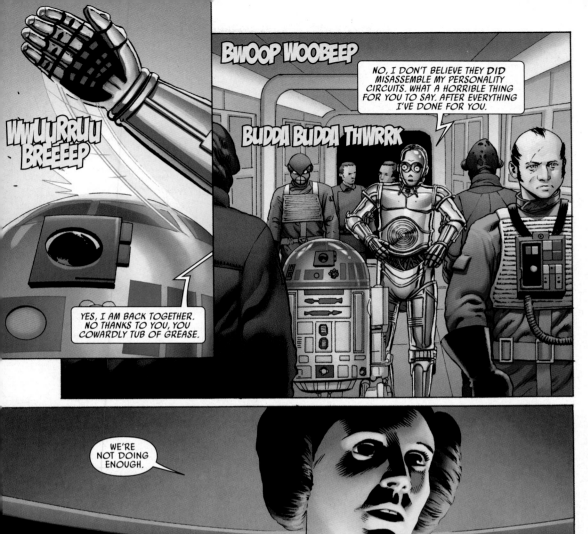

WWUURRUU BREEEEP

YES, I AM BACK TOGETHER. NO THANKS TO YOU, YOU COWARDLY TUB OF GREASE.

BWOOP WOOBEEP

BUDDA BUDDA THWRRK

NO, I DON'T BELIEVE THEY *DID* MISASSEMBLE MY PERSONALITY CIRCUITS. WHAT A HORRIBLE THING FOR YOU TO SAY. AFTER EVERYTHING I'VE DONE FOR YOU.

WE'RE NOT DOING ENOUGH.

SINCE THE BATTLE OF YAVIN AND THE DESTRUCTION OF THE DEATH STAR, THE REBEL ALLIANCE HAS STAGED MORE THAN A DOZEN DIFFERENT ATTACKS ON ALMOST AS MANY WORLDS.

WE'VE BOMBED THE SHIPYARDS AT KUAT AND THE SUPPLY BASE ON IMDAAR. YOU YOURSELF, PRINCESS, JUST DESTROYED ONE OF THE LARGEST WEAPONS FACTORIES IN THE GALAXY. I'M NOT SURE WHAT MORE WE COULD POSSIBLY BE DOING.

WE MAY HAVE *WOUNDED* THE EMPIRE, BUT THEY'RE FAR FROM CRIPPLED. WE HAVE TO PRESS OUR ADVANTAGE NOW, OR EVERYTHING WE'VE DONE WILL HAVE BEEN FOR NOTHING.

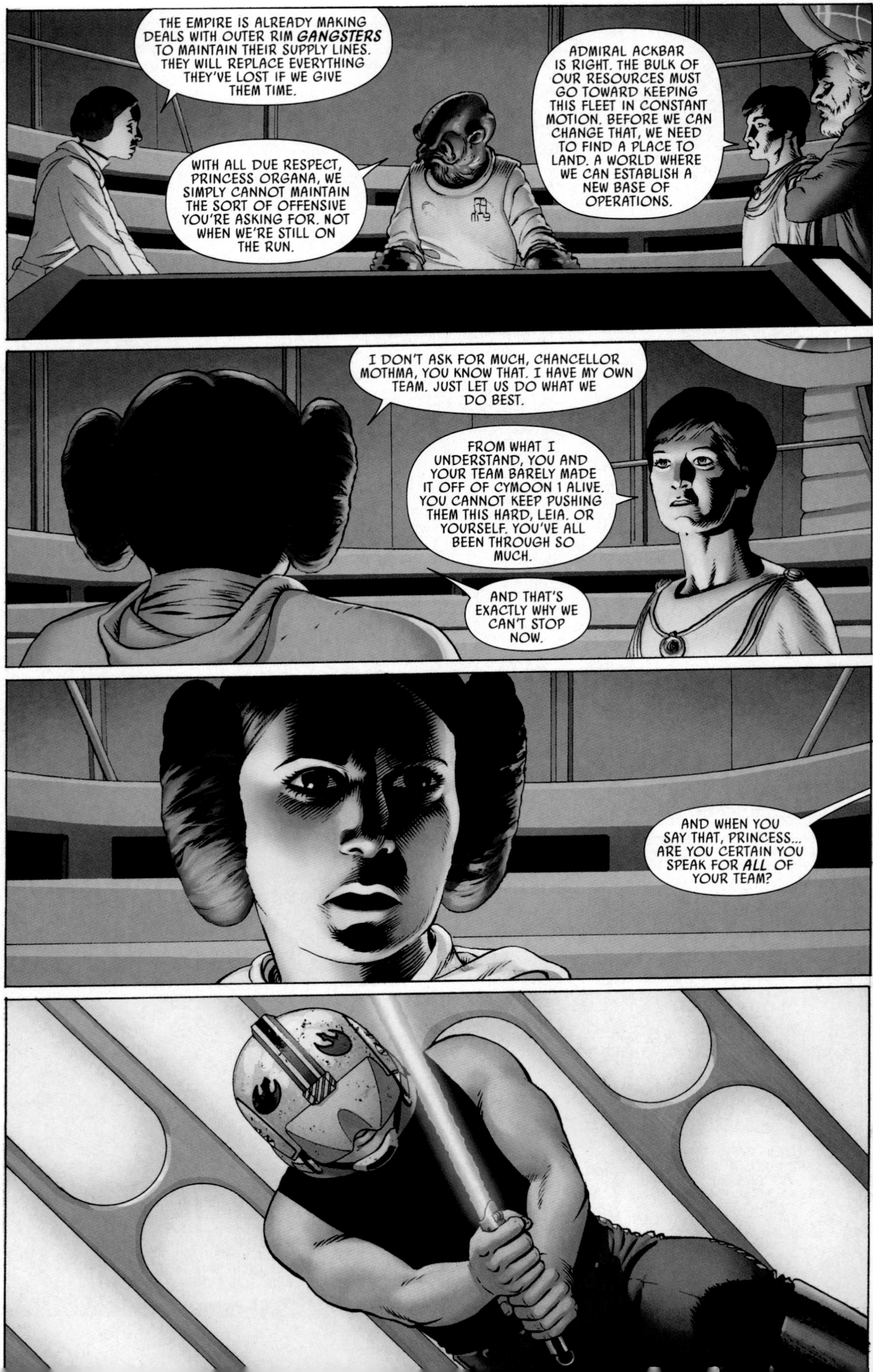
THE EMPIRE IS ALREADY MAKING DEALS WITH OUTER RIM GANGSTERS TO MAINTAIN THEIR SUPPLY LINES. THEY WILL REPLACE EVERYTHING THEY'VE LOST IF WE GIVE THEM TIME.
WITH ALL DUE RESPECT, PRINCESS ORGANA, WE SIMPLY CANNOT MAINTAIN THE SORT OF OFFENSIVE YOU'RE ASKING FOR. NOT WHEN WE'RE STILL ON THE RUN.
ADMIRAL ACKBAR IS RIGHT. THE BULK OF OUR RESOURCES MUST GO TOWARD KEEPING THIS FLEET IN CONSTANT MOTION. BEFORE WE CAN CHANGE THAT, WE NEED TO FIND A PLACE TO LAND. A WORLD WHERE WE CAN ESTABLISH A NEW BASE OF OPERATIONS.
I DON'T ASK FOR MUCH, CHANCELLOR MOTHMA, YOU KNOW THAT. I HAVE MY OWN TEAM. JUST LET US DO WHAT WE DO BEST.
FROM WHAT I UNDERSTAND, YOU AND YOUR TEAM BARELY MADE IT OFF OF CYMOON 1 ALIVE. YOU CANNOT KEEP PUSHING THEM THIS HARD, LEIA. OR YOURSELF. YOU'VE ALL BEEN THROUGH SO MUCH.
AND THAT'S EXACTLY WHY WE CAN'T STOP NOW.
AND WHEN YOU SAY THAT, PRINCESS... ARE YOU CERTAIN YOU SPEAK FOR ALL OF YOUR TEAM?

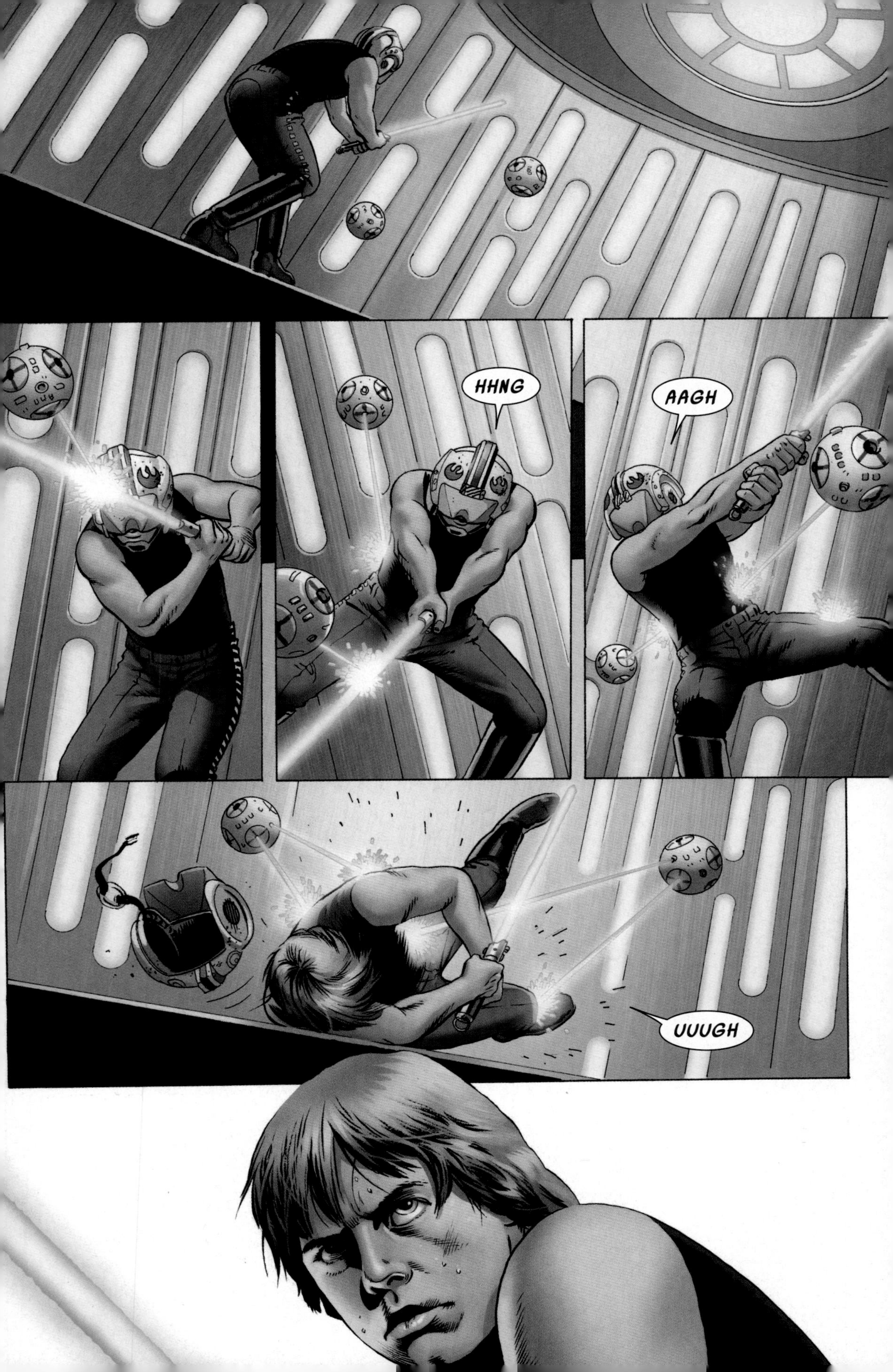
HHNG
AAGH
UUUGH

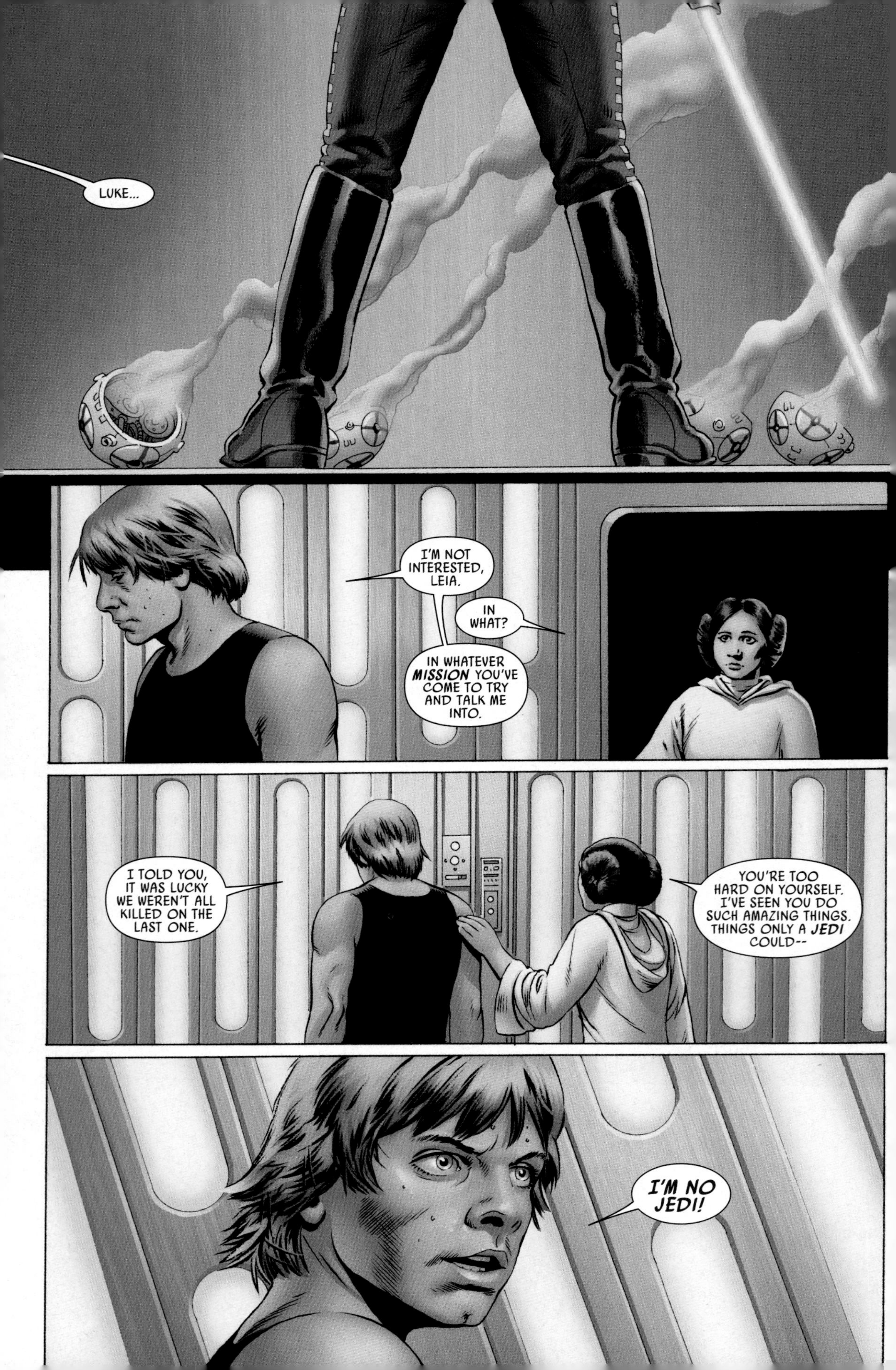
LUKE...
I'M NOT INTERESTED, LEIA.
IN WHAT?
IN WHATEVER MISSION YOU'VE COME TO TRY AND TALK ME INTO.
I TOLD YOU, IT WAS LUCKY WE WEREN'T ALL KILLED ON THE LAST ONE.
YOU'RE TOO HARD ON YOURSELF. I'VE SEEN YOU DO SUCH AMAZING THINGS. THINGS ONLY A JEDI COULD--
I'M NO JEDI!

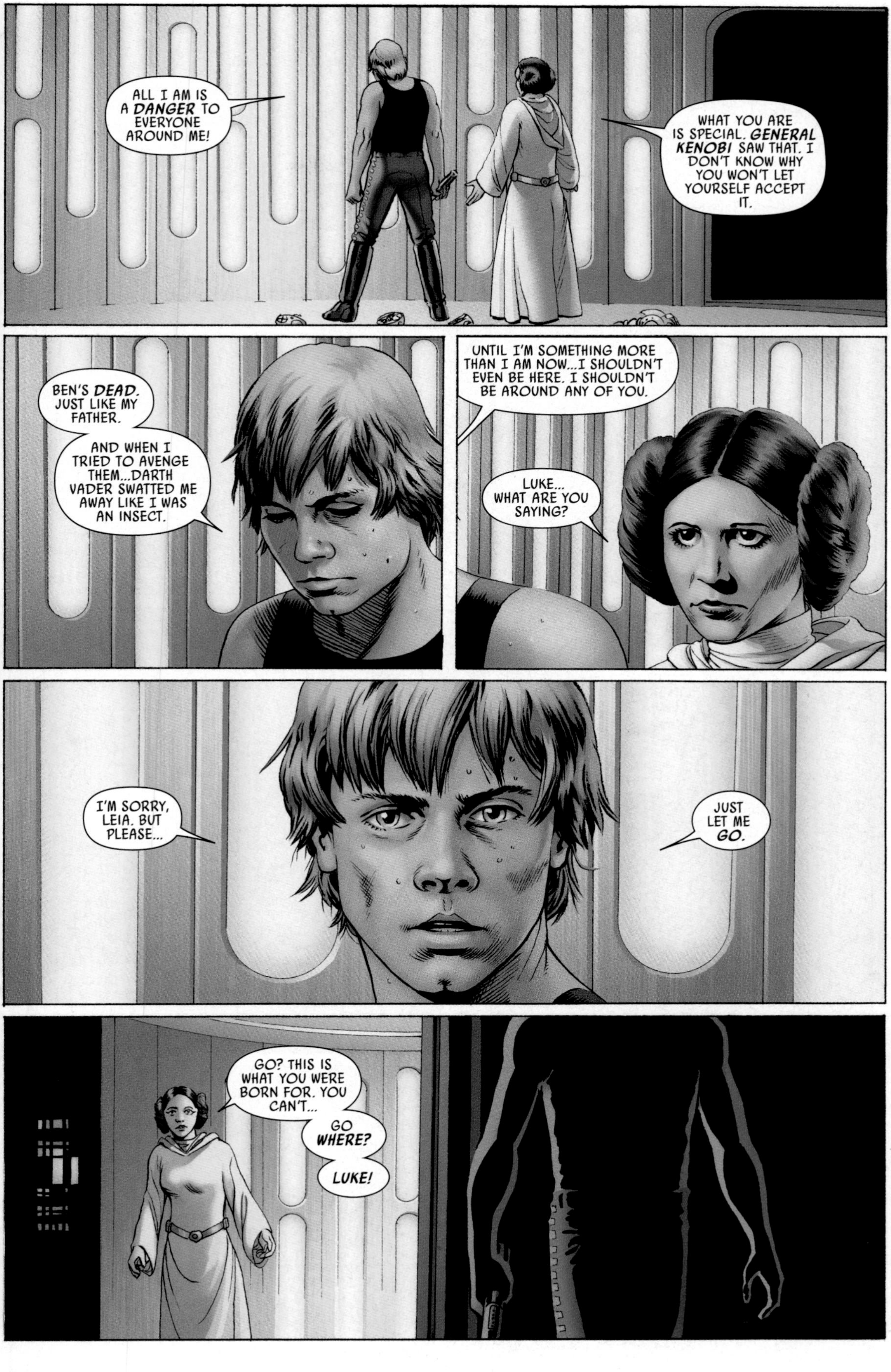
ALL I AM IS A DANGER TO EVERYONE AROUND ME!
WHAT YOU ARE IS SPECIAL. GENERAL KENOBI SAW THAT. I DON'T KNOW WHY YOU WON'T LET YOURSELF ACCEPT IT.
BEN'S DEAD. JUST LIKE MY FATHER.
AND WHEN I TRIED TO AVENGE THEM...DARTH VADER SWATTED ME AWAY LIKE I WAS AN INSECT.
UNTIL I'M SOMETHING MORE THAN I AM NOW...I SHOULDN'T EVEN BE HERE. I SHOULDN'T BE AROUND ANY OF YOU.
LUKE... WHAT ARE YOU SAYING?
I'M SORRY, LEIA. BUT PLEASE...
JUST LET ME GO.
GO? THIS IS WHAT YOU WERE BORN FOR. YOU CAN'T...
GO WHERE?
LUKE!

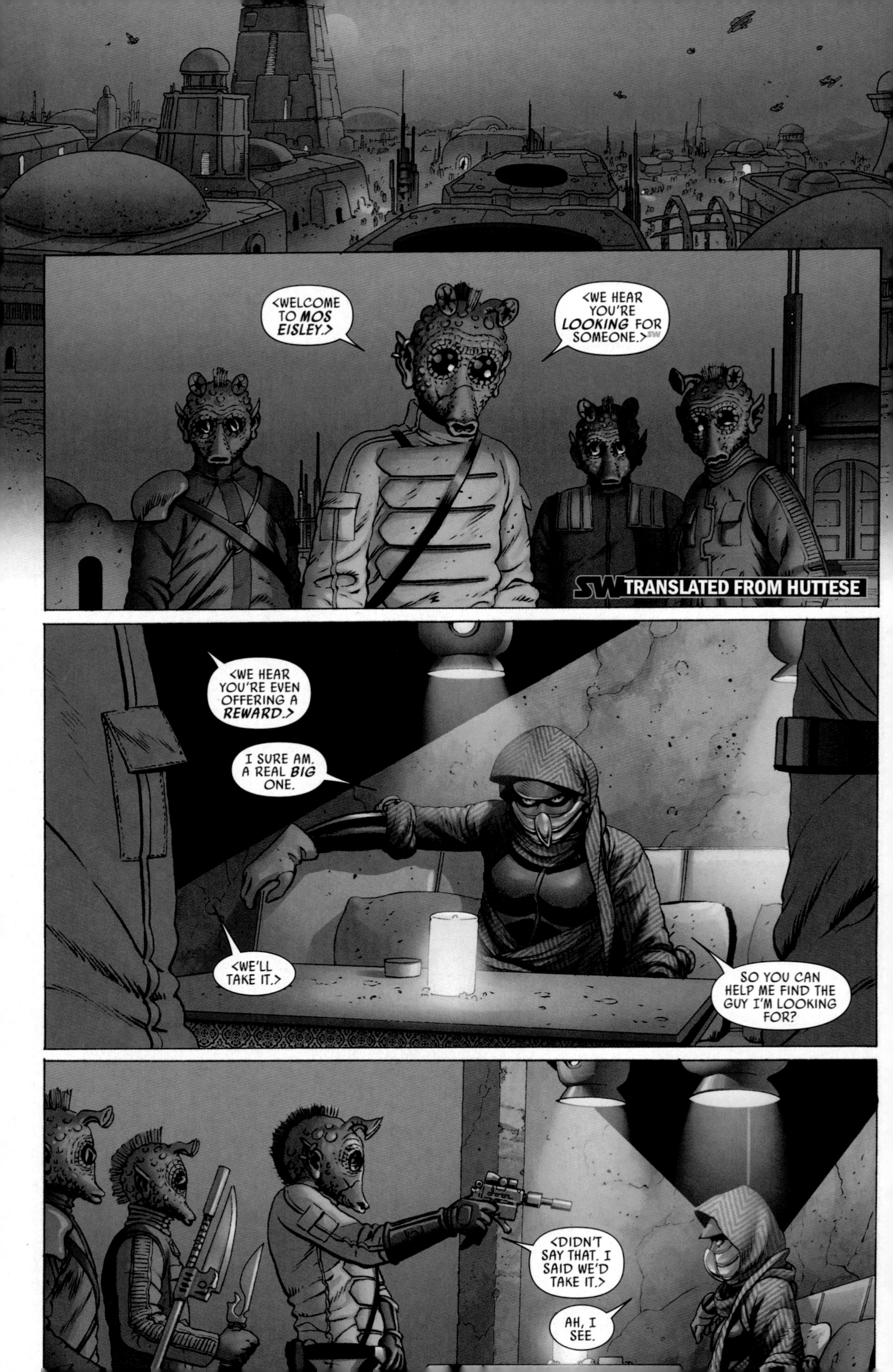
<WELCOME TO MOS EISLEY.>
<WE HEAR YOU'RE LOOKING FOR SOMEONE.>
TRANSLATED FROM HUTTESE
<WE HEAR YOU'RE EVEN OFFERING A REWARD.>
I SURE AM. A REAL BIG ONE.
<WE'LL TAKE IT.>
SO YOU CAN HELP ME FIND THE GUY I'M LOOKING FOR?
<DIDN'T SAY THAT. I SAID WE'D TAKE IT.>
AH, I SEE.

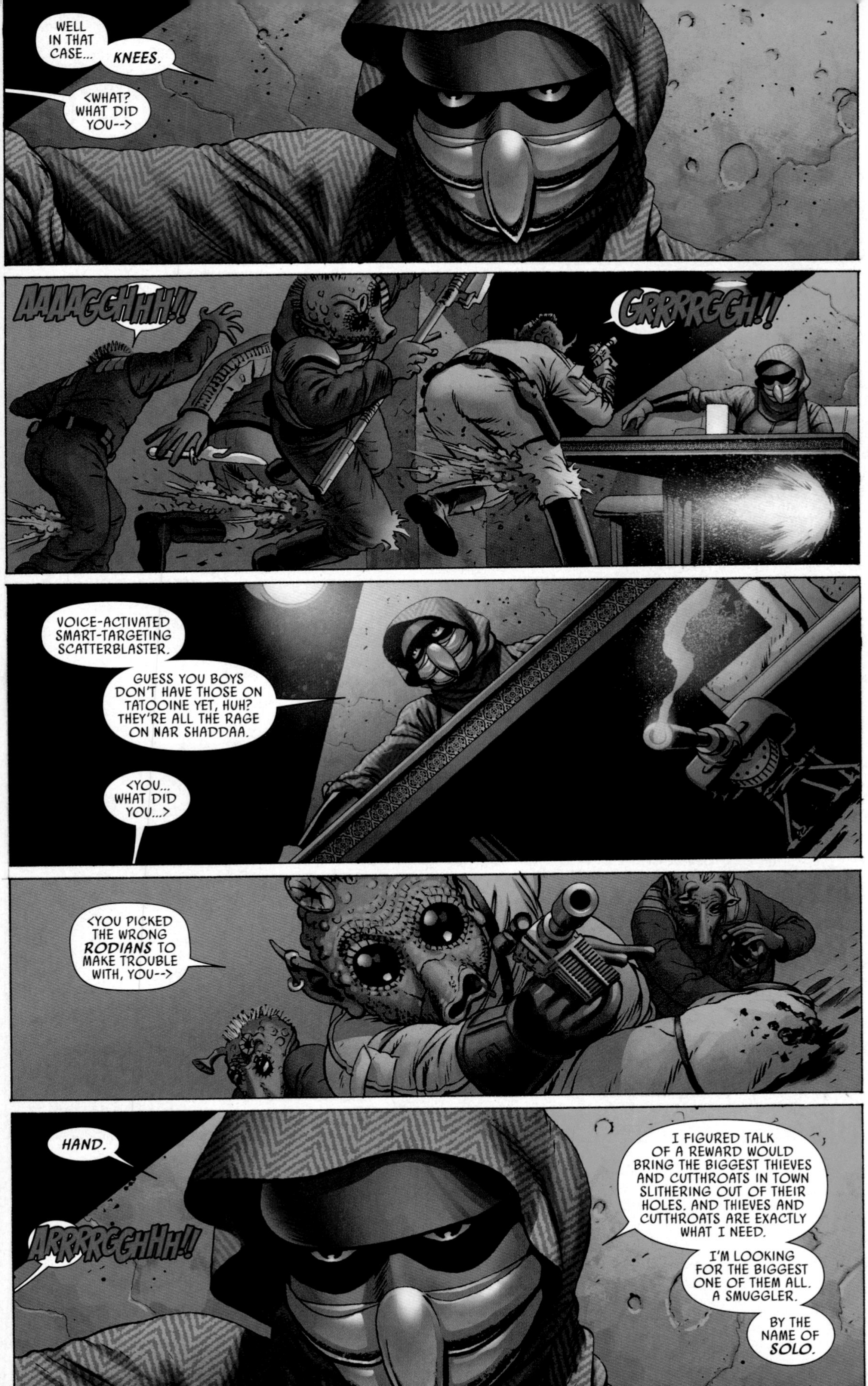
WELL IN THAT CASE... KNEES.
<WHAT? WHAT DID YOU-->
AAAAGGHHH!!
GRRRRGGH!!
VOICE-ACTIVATED SMART-TARGETING SCATTERBLASTER.
GUESS YOU BOYS DON'T HAVE THOSE ON TATOOINE YET, HUH? THEY'RE ALL THE RAGE ON NAR SHADDAA.
<YOU... WHAT DID YOU...>
<YOU PICKED THE WRONG RODIANS TO MAKE TROUBLE WITH, YOU-->
HAND.
ARRRRGGHHH!!
I FIGURED TALK OF A REWARD WOULD BRING THE BIGGEST THIEVES AND CUTTHROATS IN TOWN SLITHERING OUT OF THEIR HOLES. AND THIEVES AND CUTTHROATS ARE EXACTLY WHAT I NEED.
I'M LOOKING FOR THE BIGGEST ONE OF THEM ALL. A SMUGGLER.
BY THE NAME OF SOLO.

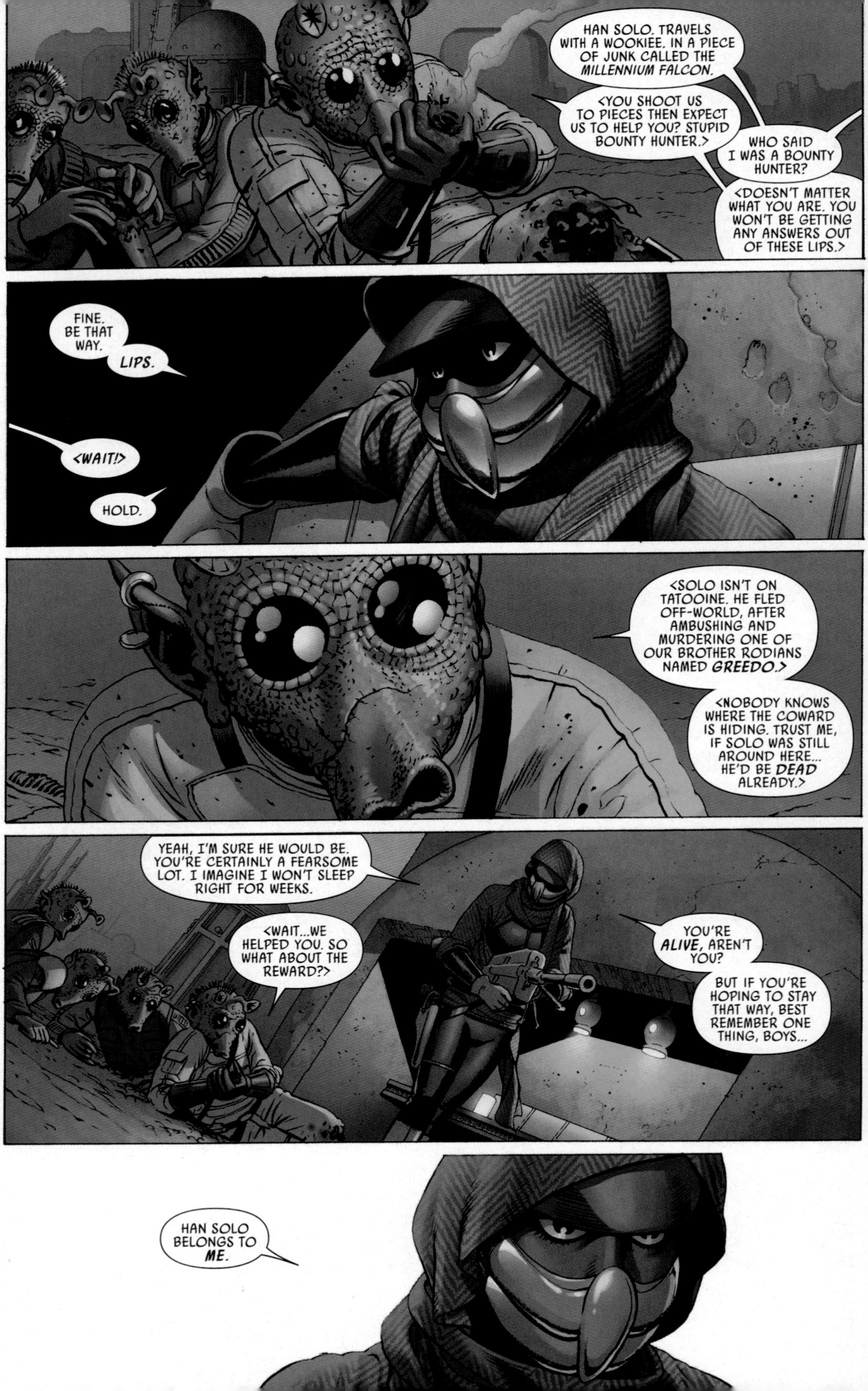
HAN SOLO. TRAVELS WITH A WOOKIEE. IN A PIECE OF JUNK CALLED THE *MILLENNIUM FALCON.*
<YOU SHOOT US TO PIECES THEN EXPECT US TO HELP YOU? STUPID BOUNTY HUNTER.>
WHO SAID I WAS A BOUNTY HUNTER?
<DOESN'T MATTER WHAT YOU ARE. YOU WON'T BE GETTING ANY ANSWERS OUT OF THESE LIPS.>
FINE. BE THAT WAY.
LIPS.
<WAIT!>
HOLD.
<SOLO ISN'T ON TATOOINE. HE FLED OFF-WORLD, AFTER AMBUSHING AND MURDERING ONE OF OUR BROTHER RODIANS NAMED ***GREEDO.***>
<NOBODY KNOWS WHERE THE COWARD IS HIDING. TRUST ME, IF SOLO WAS STILL AROUND HERE... HE'D BE ***DEAD*** ALREADY.>
YEAH, I'M SURE HE WOULD BE. YOU'RE CERTAINLY A FEARSOME LOT. I IMAGINE I WON'T SLEEP RIGHT FOR WEEKS.
<WAIT...WE HELPED YOU. SO WHAT ABOUT THE REWARD?>
YOU'RE ***ALIVE,*** AREN'T YOU?
BUT IF YOU'RE HOPING TO STAY THAT WAY, BEST REMEMBER ONE THING, BOYS...
HAN SOLO BELONGS TO ***ME.***

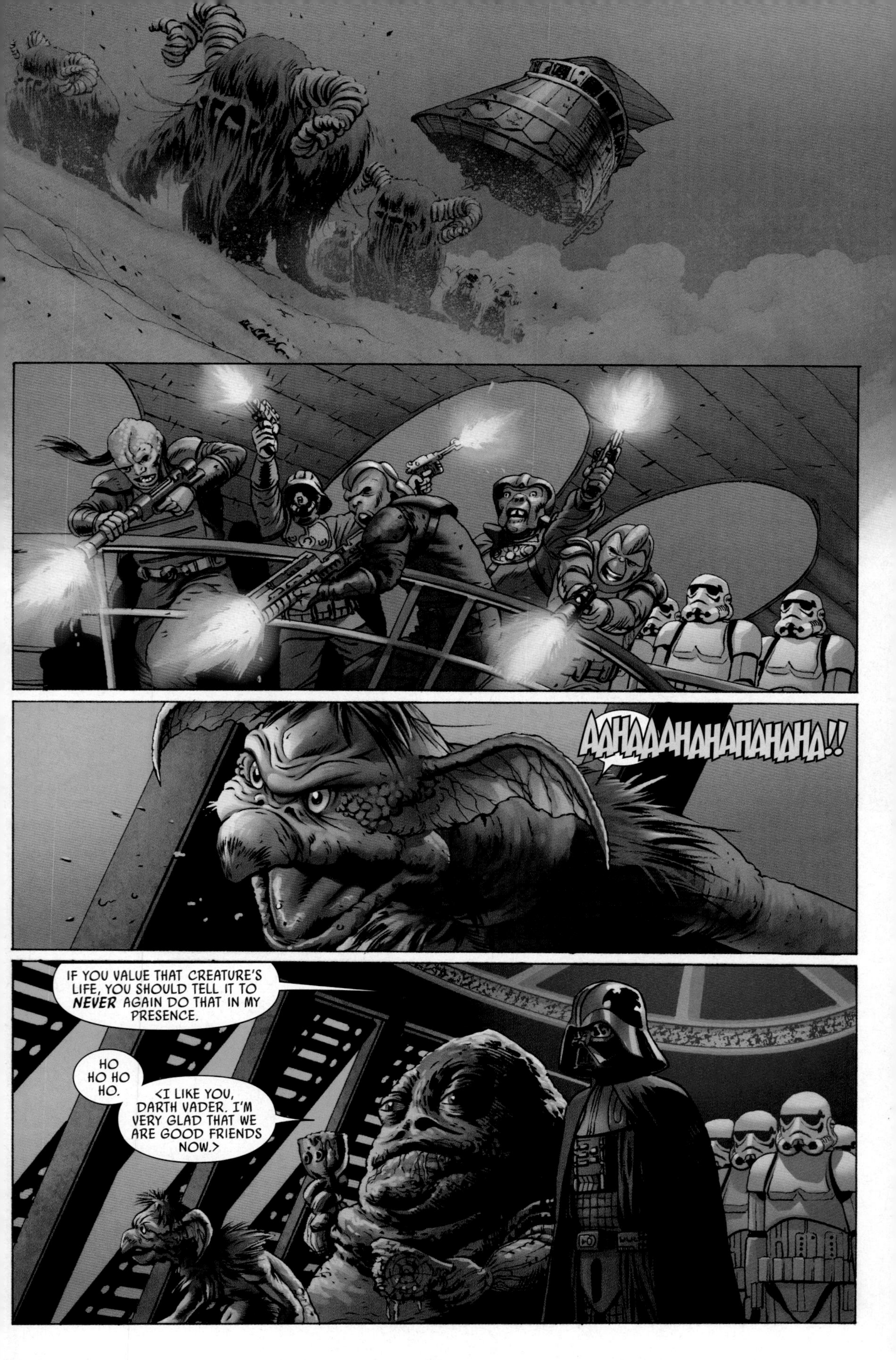
AAHAAAHAHAHAHAHA!!
IF YOU VALUE THAT CREATURE'S LIFE, YOU SHOULD TELL IT TO NEVER AGAIN DO THAT IN MY PRESENCE.
HO HO HO HO.
<I LIKE YOU, DARTH VADER. I'M VERY GLAD THAT WE ARE GOOD FRIENDS NOW.>

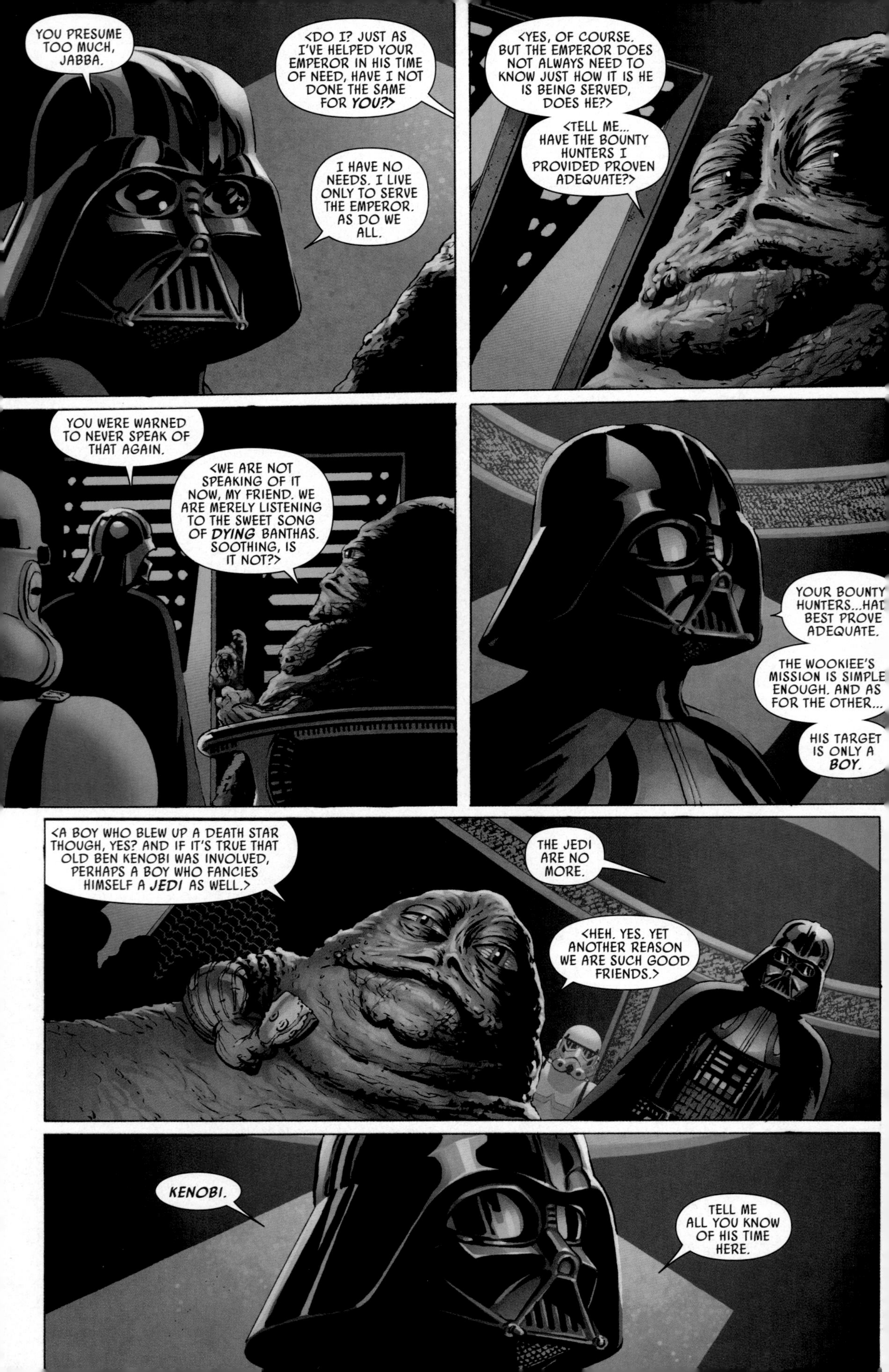
YOU PRESUME TOO MUCH, JABBA.
<DO I? JUST AS I'VE HELPED YOUR EMPEROR IN HIS TIME OF NEED, HAVE I NOT DONE THE SAME FOR *YOU?*>
I HAVE NO NEEDS. I LIVE ONLY TO SERVE THE EMPEROR. AS DO WE ALL.
<YES, OF COURSE. BUT THE EMPEROR DOES NOT ALWAYS NEED TO KNOW JUST HOW IT IS HE IS BEING SERVED, DOES HE?>
<TELL ME... HAVE THE BOUNTY HUNTERS I PROVIDED PROVEN ADEQUATE?>
YOU WERE WARNED TO NEVER SPEAK OF THAT AGAIN.
<WE ARE NOT SPEAKING OF IT NOW, MY FRIEND. WE ARE MERELY LISTENING TO THE SWEET SONG OF *DYING* BANTHAS. SOOTHING, IS IT NOT?>
YOUR BOUNTY HUNTERS...HAD BEST PROVE ADEQUATE.
THE WOOKIEE'S MISSION IS SIMPLE ENOUGH. AND AS FOR THE OTHER...
HIS TARGET IS ONLY A *BOY.*
<A BOY WHO BLEW UP A DEATH STAR THOUGH, YES? AND IF IT'S TRUE THAT OLD BEN KENOBI WAS INVOLVED, PERHAPS A BOY WHO FANCIES HIMSELF A *JEDI* AS WELL.>
THE JEDI ARE NO MORE.
<HEH. YES. YET ANOTHER REASON WE ARE SUCH GOOD FRIENDS.>
KENOBI.
TELL ME ALL YOU KNOW OF HIS TIME HERE.

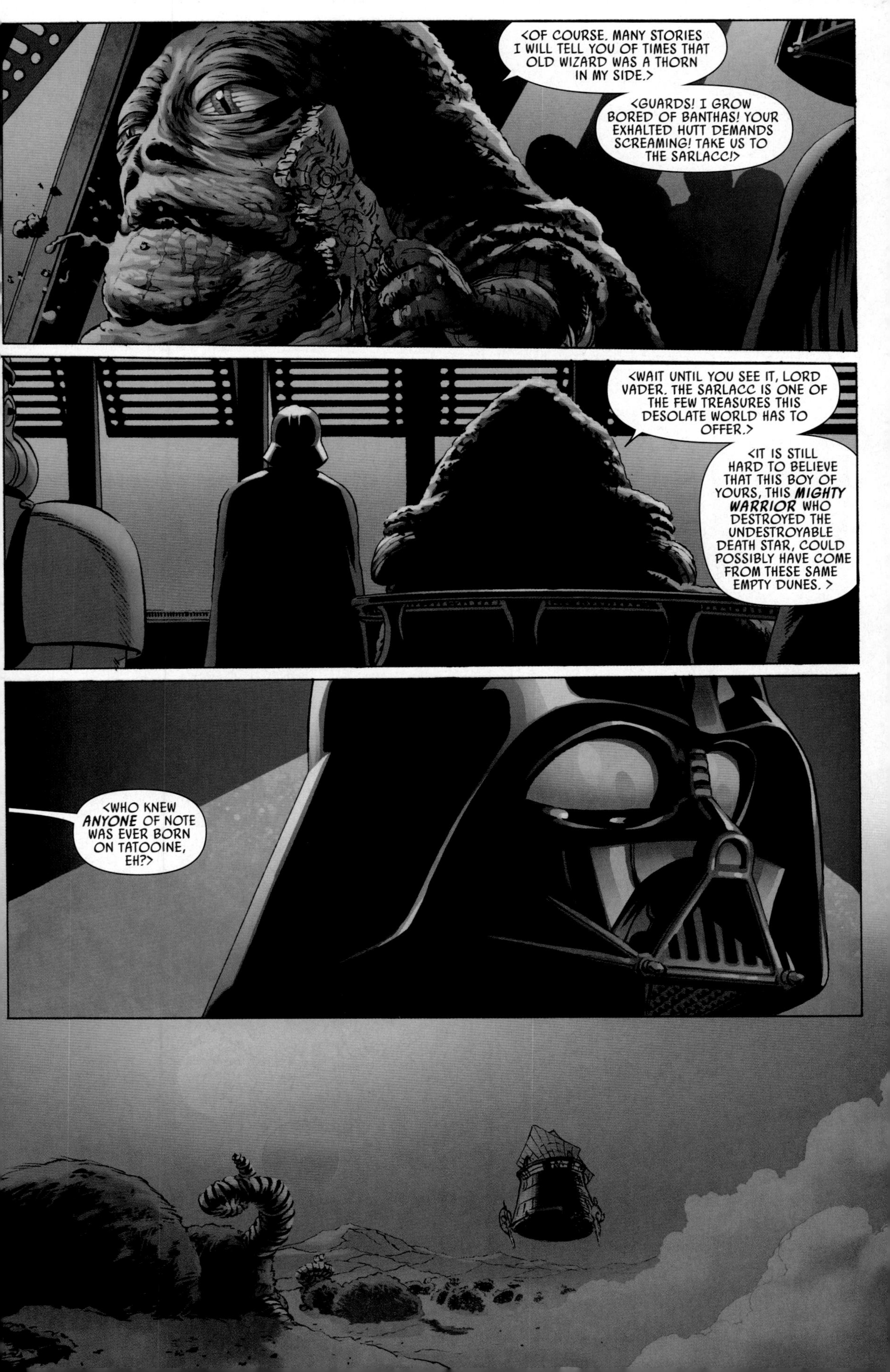
<OF COURSE. MANY STORIES I WILL TELL YOU OF TIMES THAT OLD WIZARD WAS A THORN IN MY SIDE.>
<GUARDS! I GROW BORED OF BANTHAS! YOUR EXHALTED HUTT DEMANDS SCREAMING! TAKE US TO THE SARLACC!>
<WAIT UNTIL YOU SEE IT, LORD VADER. THE SARLACC IS ONE OF THE FEW TREASURES THIS DESOLATE WORLD HAS TO OFFER.>
<IT IS STILL HARD TO BELIEVE THAT THIS BOY OF YOURS, THIS MIGHTY WARRIOR WHO DESTROYED THE UNDESTROYABLE DEATH STAR, COULD POSSIBLY HAVE COME FROM THESE SAME EMPTY DUNES. >
<WHO KNEW ANYONE OF NOTE WAS EVER BORN ON TATOOINE, EH?>

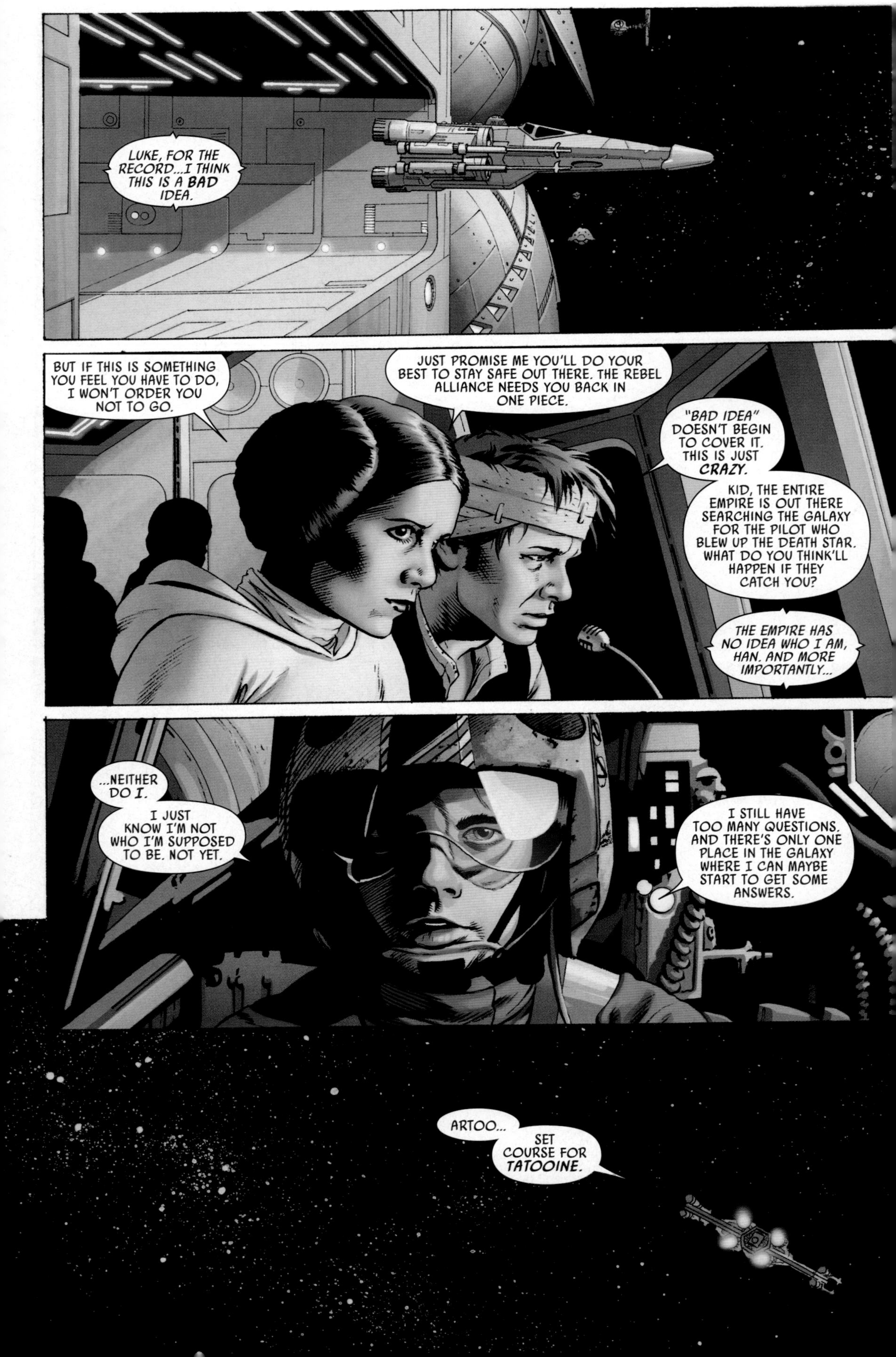
LUKE, FOR THE RECORD...I THINK THIS IS A BAD IDEA.
BUT IF THIS IS SOMETHING YOU FEEL YOU HAVE TO DO, I WON'T ORDER YOU NOT TO GO.
JUST PROMISE ME YOU'LL DO YOUR BEST TO STAY SAFE OUT THERE. THE REBEL ALLIANCE NEEDS YOU BACK IN ONE PIECE.
"BAD IDEA" DOESN'T BEGIN TO COVER IT. THIS IS JUST CRAZY.
KID, THE ENTIRE EMPIRE IS OUT THERE SEARCHING THE GALAXY FOR THE PILOT WHO BLEW UP THE DEATH STAR. WHAT DO YOU THINK'LL HAPPEN IF THEY CATCH YOU?
THE EMPIRE HAS NO IDEA WHO I AM, HAN. AND MORE IMPORTANTLY...
...NEITHER DO I.
I JUST KNOW I'M NOT WHO I'M SUPPOSED TO BE. NOT YET.
I STILL HAVE TOO MANY QUESTIONS. AND THERE'S ONLY ONE PLACE IN THE GALAXY WHERE I CAN MAYBE START TO GET SOME ANSWERS.
ARTOO...
SET COURSE FOR TATOOINE.

"I'M *LOOKING* FOR SOMEONE."

<NOT YOU *TOO*.>

<LIKE WE TOLD THE *OTHER* BOUNTY HUNTER, WE DON'T KNOW WHERE SOLO'S RUN OFF TO.>

SOLO CAN WAIT.

TELL ME ALL YOU KNOW ABOUT A MAN NAMED *KENOBI*.

<KENOBI? THERE'S A KENOBI WHO LIVES WAY OUTSIDE OF TOWN, OUT IN THE DUNE SEA. SOME CRAZY OLD WIZARD.>

<WHY ARE YOU LOOKING FOR HIM?>

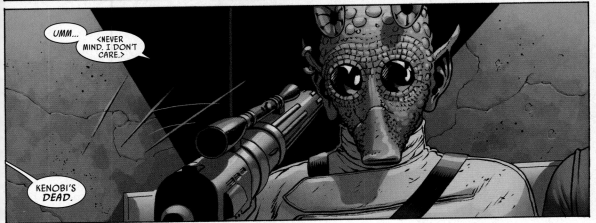

UMM...

<NEVER MIND. I DON'T CARE.>

KENOBI'S *DEAD*.

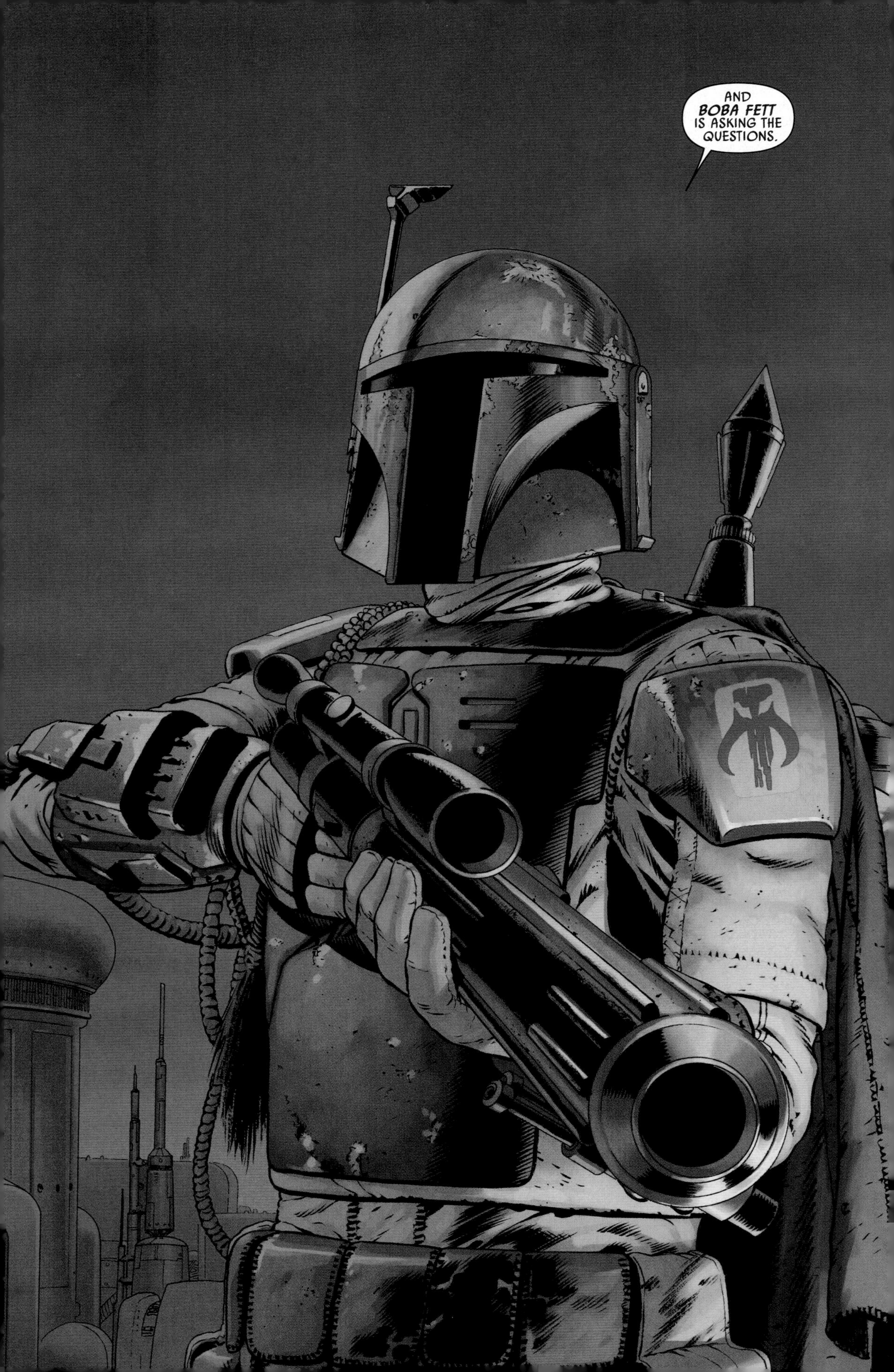
AND BOBA FETT IS ASKING THE QUESTIONS.

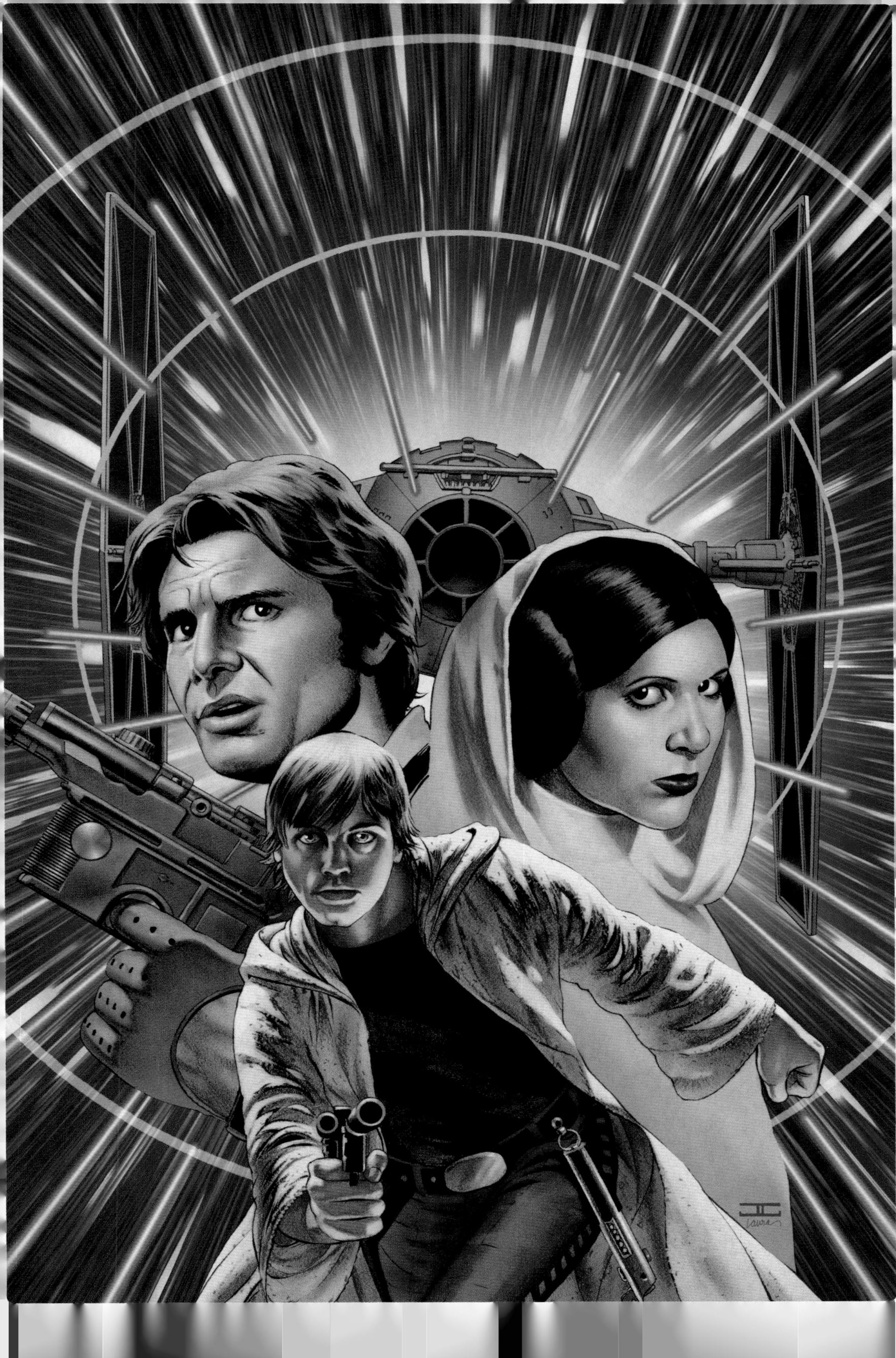

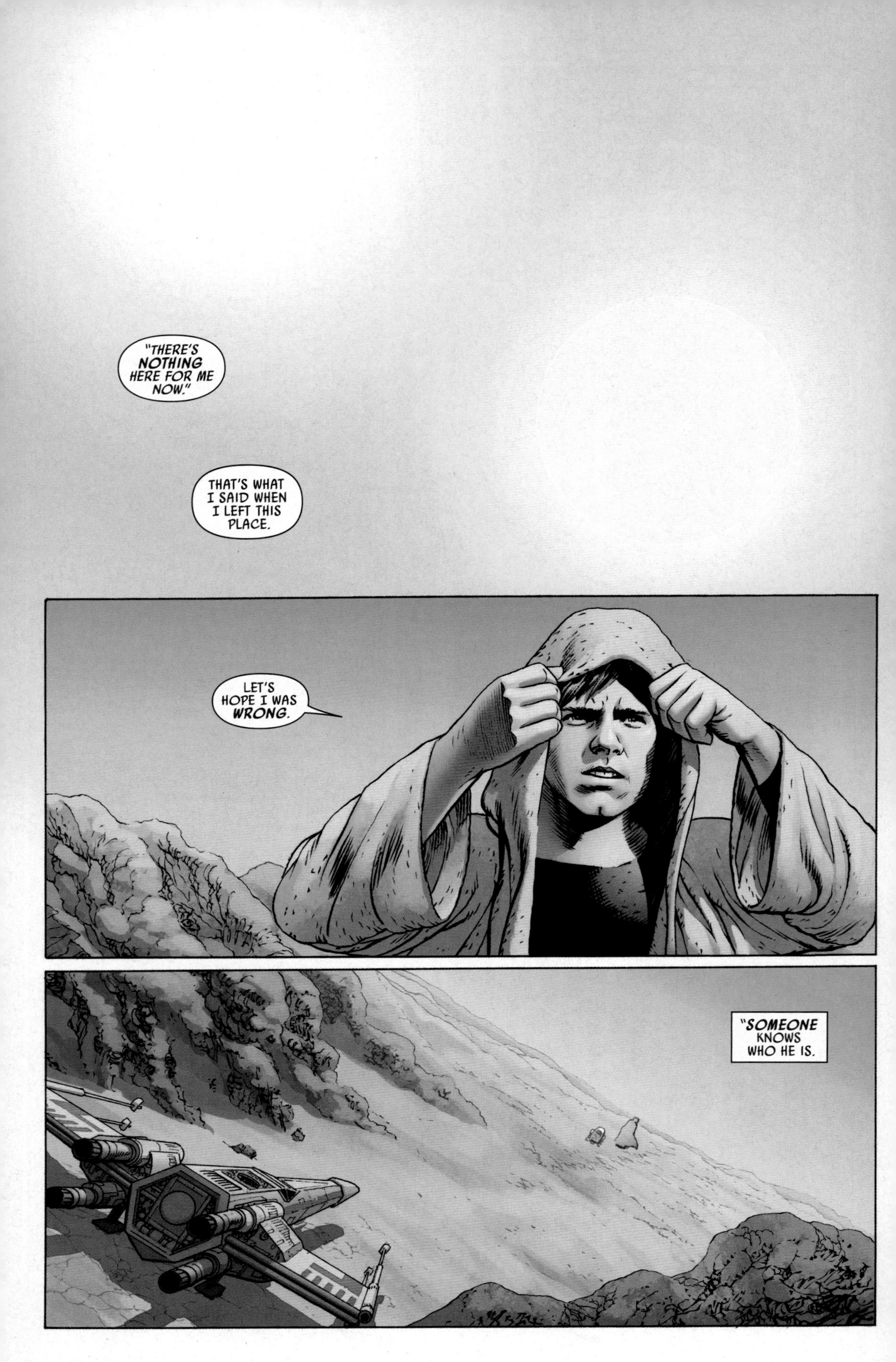

"THERE'S NOTHING HERE FOR ME NOW."
THAT'S WHAT I SAID WHEN I LEFT THIS PLACE.
LET'S HOPE I WAS WRONG.
"SOMEONE KNOWS WHO HE IS.

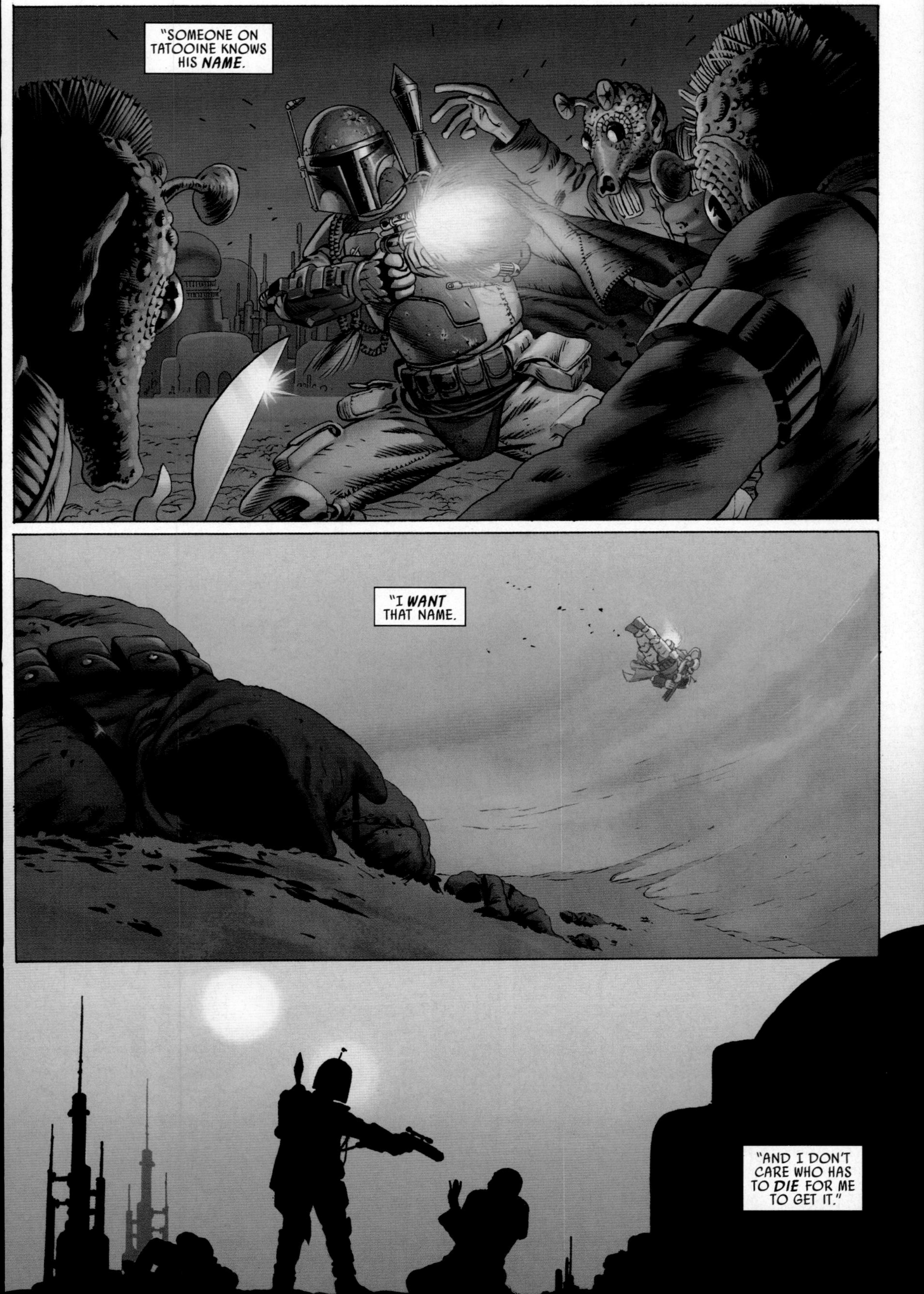
"SOMEONE ON TATOOINE KNOWS HIS NAME.
"I WANT THAT NAME.
"AND I DON'T CARE WHO HAS TO DIE FOR ME TO GET IT."

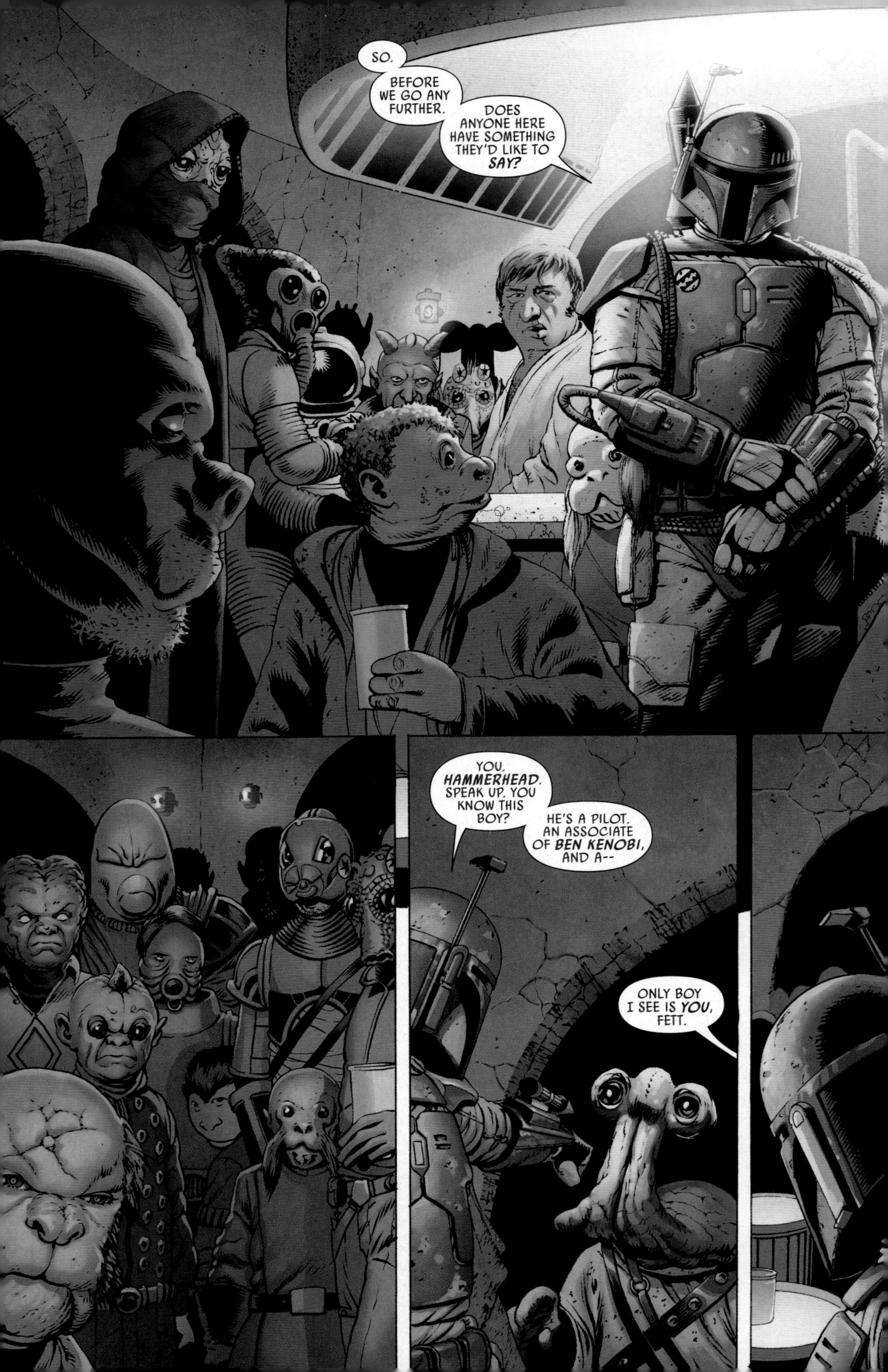
SO.
BEFORE WE GO ANY FURTHER.
DOES ANYONE HERE HAVE SOMETHING THEY'D LIKE TO SAY?
YOU. HAMMERHEAD. SPEAK UP. YOU KNOW THIS BOY?
HE'S A PILOT. AN ASSOCIATE OF BEN KENOBI, AND A--
ONLY BOY I SEE IS YOU, FETT.

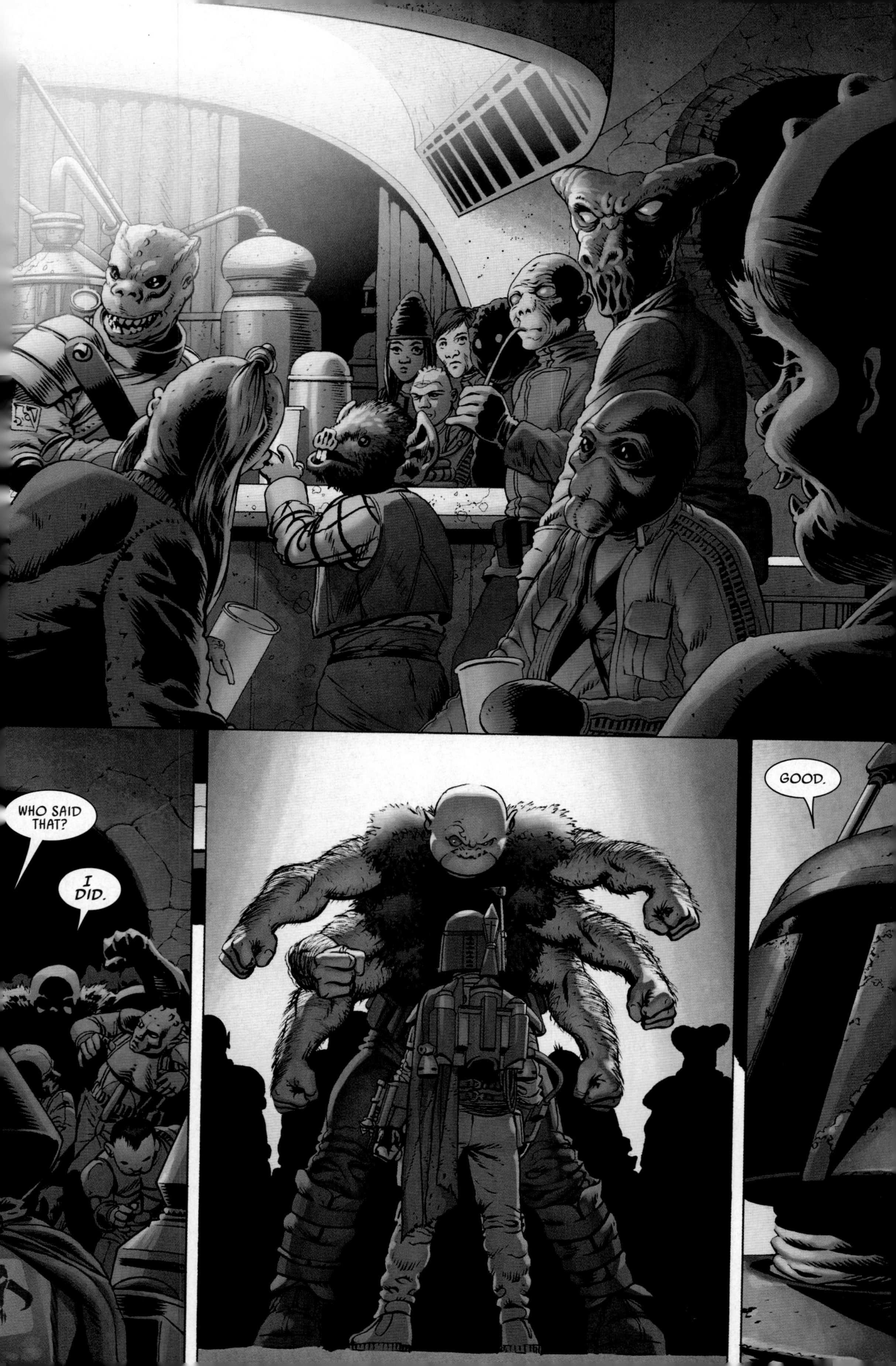
WHO SAID THAT?
I DID.
GOOD.

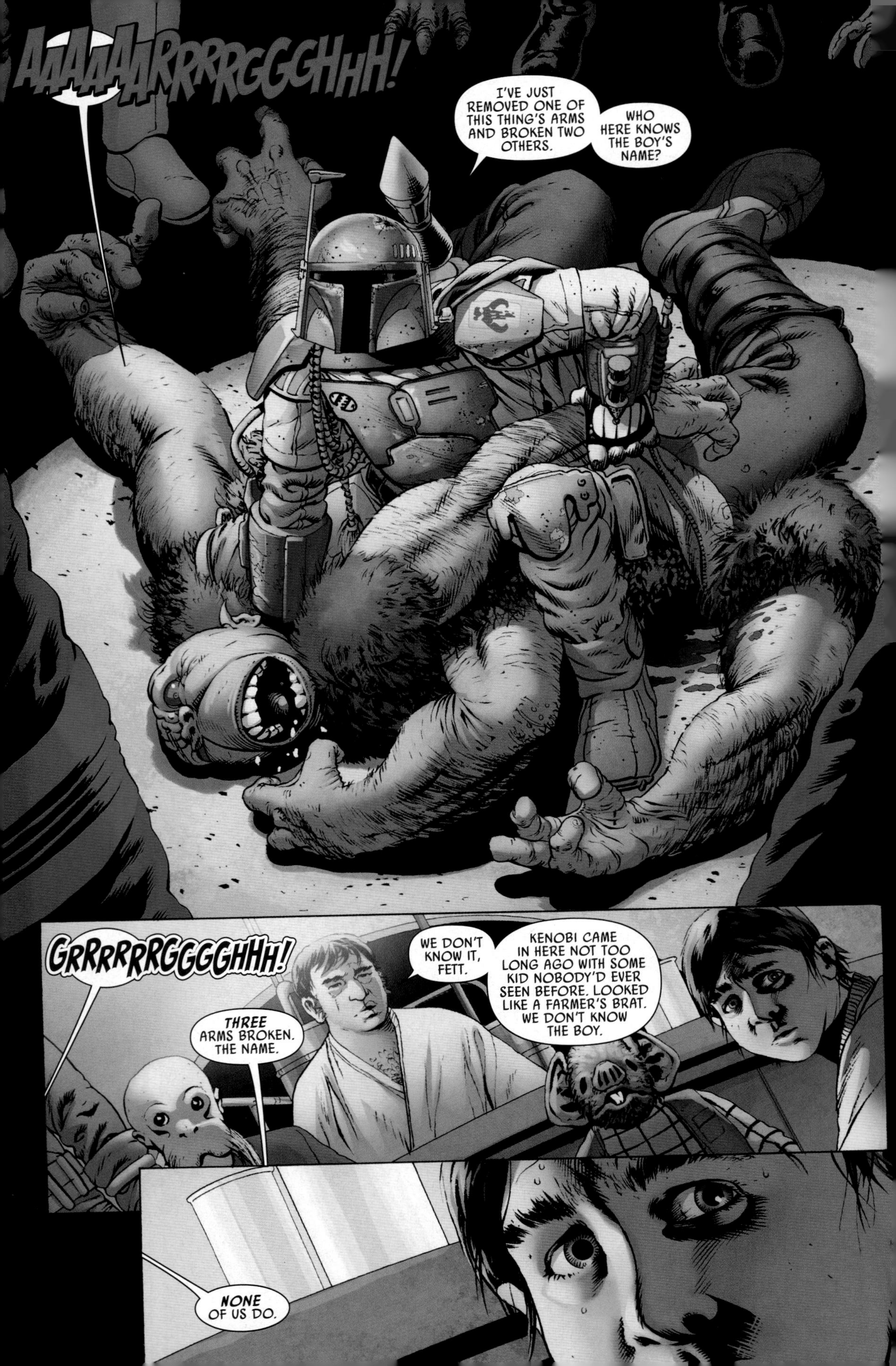
AAAAAARRRRRGGGHHH!
I'VE JUST REMOVED ONE OF THIS THING'S ARMS AND BROKEN TWO OTHERS.
WHO HERE KNOWS THE BOY'S NAME?
GRRRRRRGGGGHHH!
THREE ARMS BROKEN. THE NAME.
WE DON'T KNOW IT, FETT.
KENOBI CAME IN HERE NOT TOO LONG AGO WITH SOME KID NOBODY'D EVER SEEN BEFORE. LOOKED LIKE A FARMER'S BRAT. WE DON'T KNOW THE BOY.
NONE OF US DO.

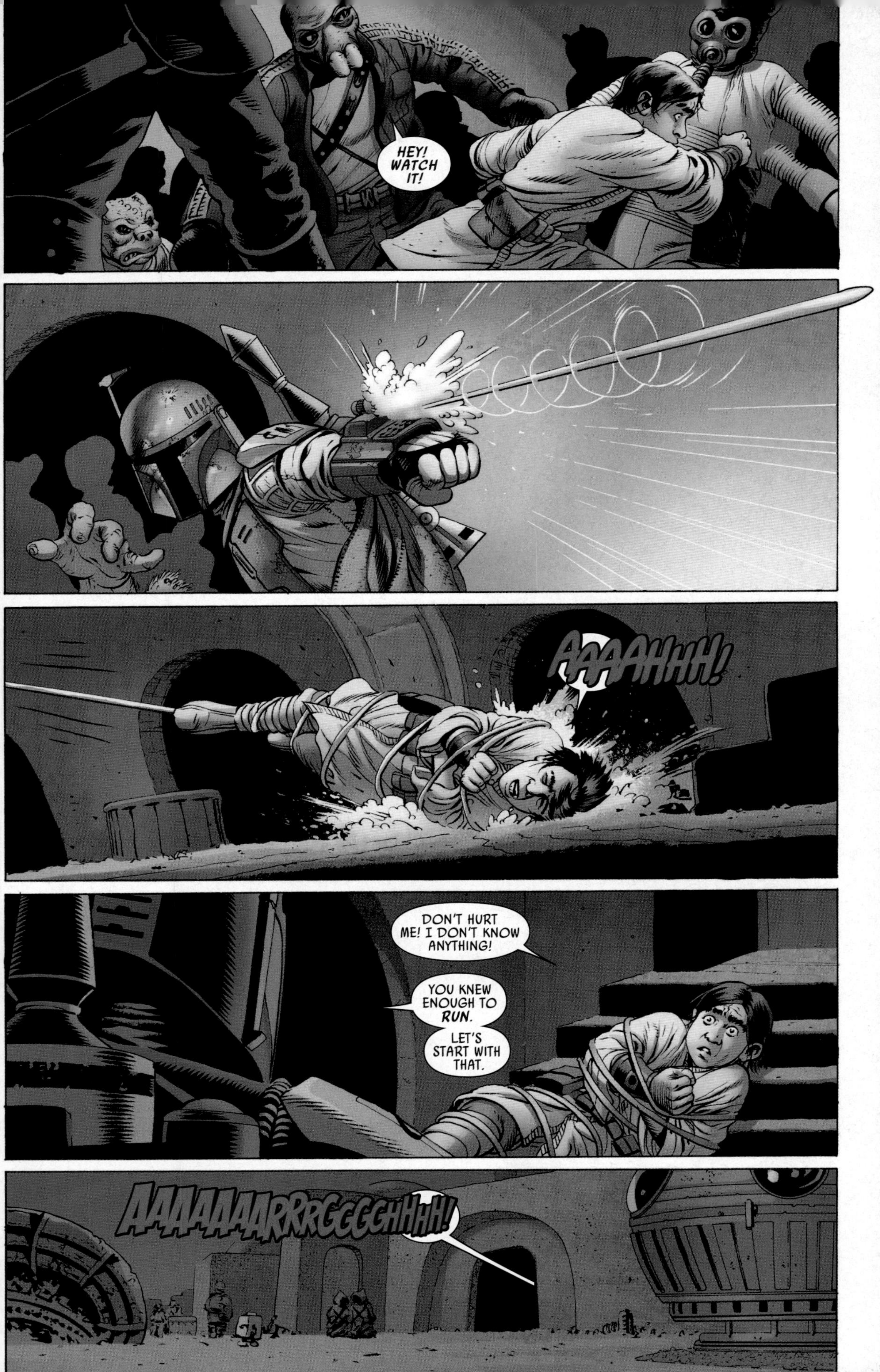
HEY! WATCH IT!
AAAAHHH!
DON'T HURT ME! I DON'T KNOW ANYTHING!
YOU KNEW ENOUGH TO RUN.
LET'S START WITH THAT.
AAAAAAARRRGGGGHHHH!

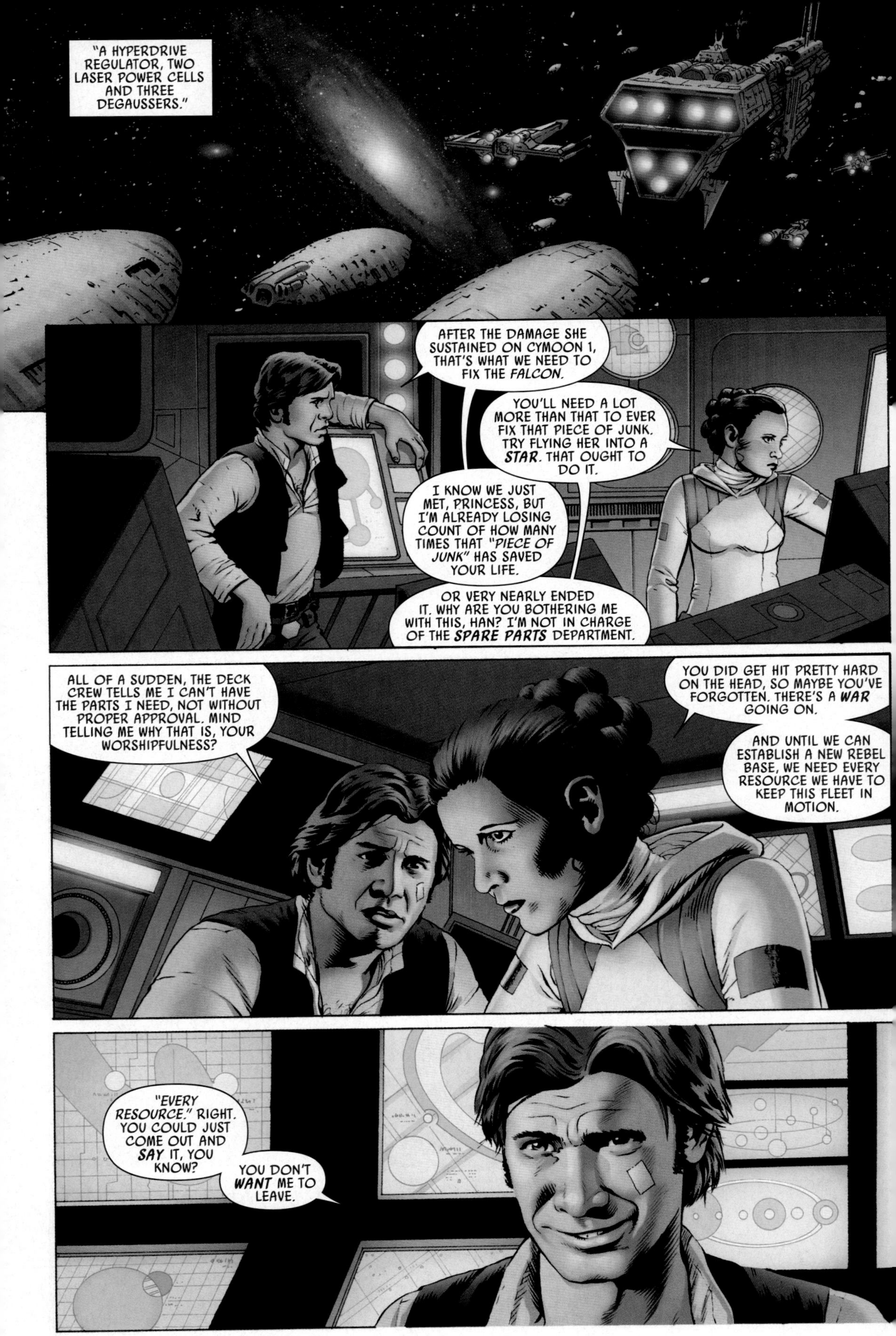

"A HYPERDRIVE REGULATOR, TWO LASER POWER CELLS AND THREE DEGAUSSERS."
AFTER THE DAMAGE SHE SUSTAINED ON CYMOON 1, THAT'S WHAT WE NEED TO FIX THE FALCON.
YOU'LL NEED A LOT MORE THAN THAT TO EVER FIX THAT PIECE OF JUNK. TRY FLYING HER INTO A STAR. THAT OUGHT TO DO IT.
I KNOW WE JUST MET, PRINCESS, BUT I'M ALREADY LOSING COUNT OF HOW MANY TIMES THAT "PIECE OF JUNK" HAS SAVED YOUR LIFE.
OR VERY NEARLY ENDED IT. WHY ARE YOU BOTHERING ME WITH THIS, HAN? I'M NOT IN CHARGE OF THE SPARE PARTS DEPARTMENT.
ALL OF A SUDDEN, THE DECK CREW TELLS ME I CAN'T HAVE THE PARTS I NEED, NOT WITHOUT PROPER APPROVAL. MIND TELLING ME WHY THAT IS, YOUR WORSHIPFULNESS?
YOU DID GET HIT PRETTY HARD ON THE HEAD, SO MAYBE YOU'VE FORGOTTEN. THERE'S A WAR GOING ON.
AND UNTIL WE CAN ESTABLISH A NEW REBEL BASE, WE NEED EVERY RESOURCE WE HAVE TO KEEP THIS FLEET IN MOTION.
"EVERY RESOURCE." RIGHT. YOU COULD JUST COME OUT AND SAY IT, YOU KNOW?
YOU DON'T WANT ME TO LEAVE.

OH, YOU ARE *SO* WRONG ABOUT THAT. SUDDENLY I *VERY MUCH* WANT YOU TO LEAVE.

THEN GIVE ME THE PARTS I NEED AND LET ME BE ON MY WAY.

WE'RE NOT RUNNING A CHARITY HERE. EVERYONE ON BOARD THIS FLEET *WORKS* FOR WHAT THEY GET.

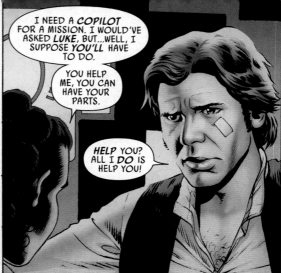

I NEED A *COPILOT* FOR A MISSION. I WOULD'VE ASKED *LUKE*, BUT...WELL, I SUPPOSE *YOU'LL* HAVE TO DO.

YOU HELP ME, YOU CAN HAVE YOUR PARTS.

HELP YOU? ALL I *DO* IS HELP YOU!

I JUST HELPED YOU *BLOW UP* THE BIGGEST WEAPONS FACTORY IN THE GALAXY. I PUT MY *NAME* ON THE EMPIRE'S MOST WANTED LIST FOR YOU.

THAT WAS *DAYS* AGO. YOU NEED TO STOP LIVING IN THE *PAST*, CAPTAIN SOLO.

I HELP YOU *ONE* LAST TIME, I GET WHATEVER I NEED TO FIX MY SHIP. IS THAT THE DEAL?

IF THAT'S WHAT YOU--

I'LL DO IT.

AND... *AFTER* YOU FIX YOUR SHIP?

YOU NEED TO STOP LIVING IN THE *FUTURE*, PRINCESS.

LET'S GET THIS OVER WITH.

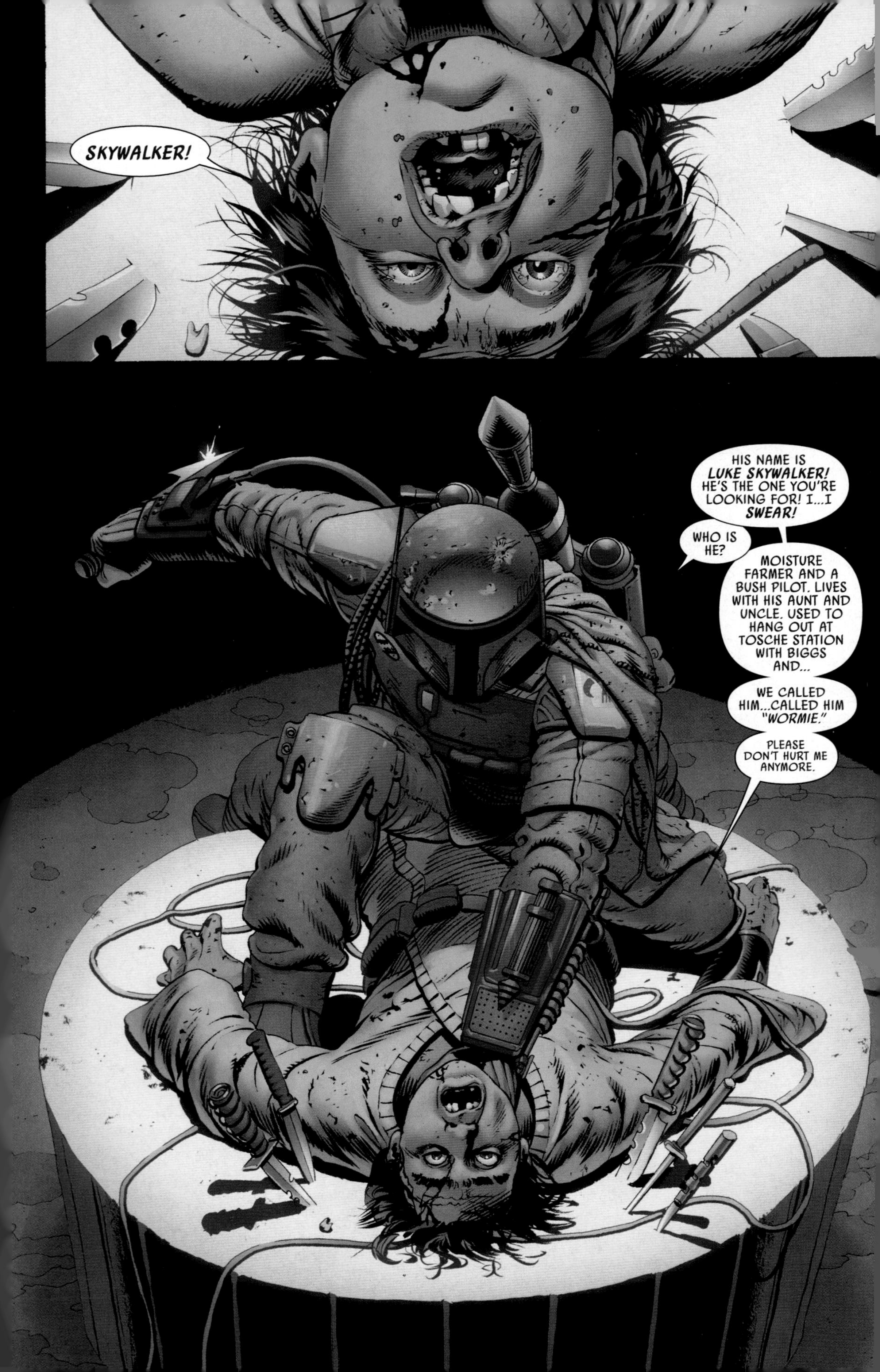
SKYWALKER!
HIS NAME IS LUKE SKYWALKER! HE'S THE ONE YOU'RE LOOKING FOR! I...I SWEAR!
WHO IS HE?
MOISTURE FARMER AND A BUSH PILOT. LIVES WITH HIS AUNT AND UNCLE. USED TO HANG OUT AT TOSCHE STATION WITH BIGGS AND...
WE CALLED HIM...CALLED HIM "WORMIE."
PLEASE DON'T HURT ME ANYMORE.

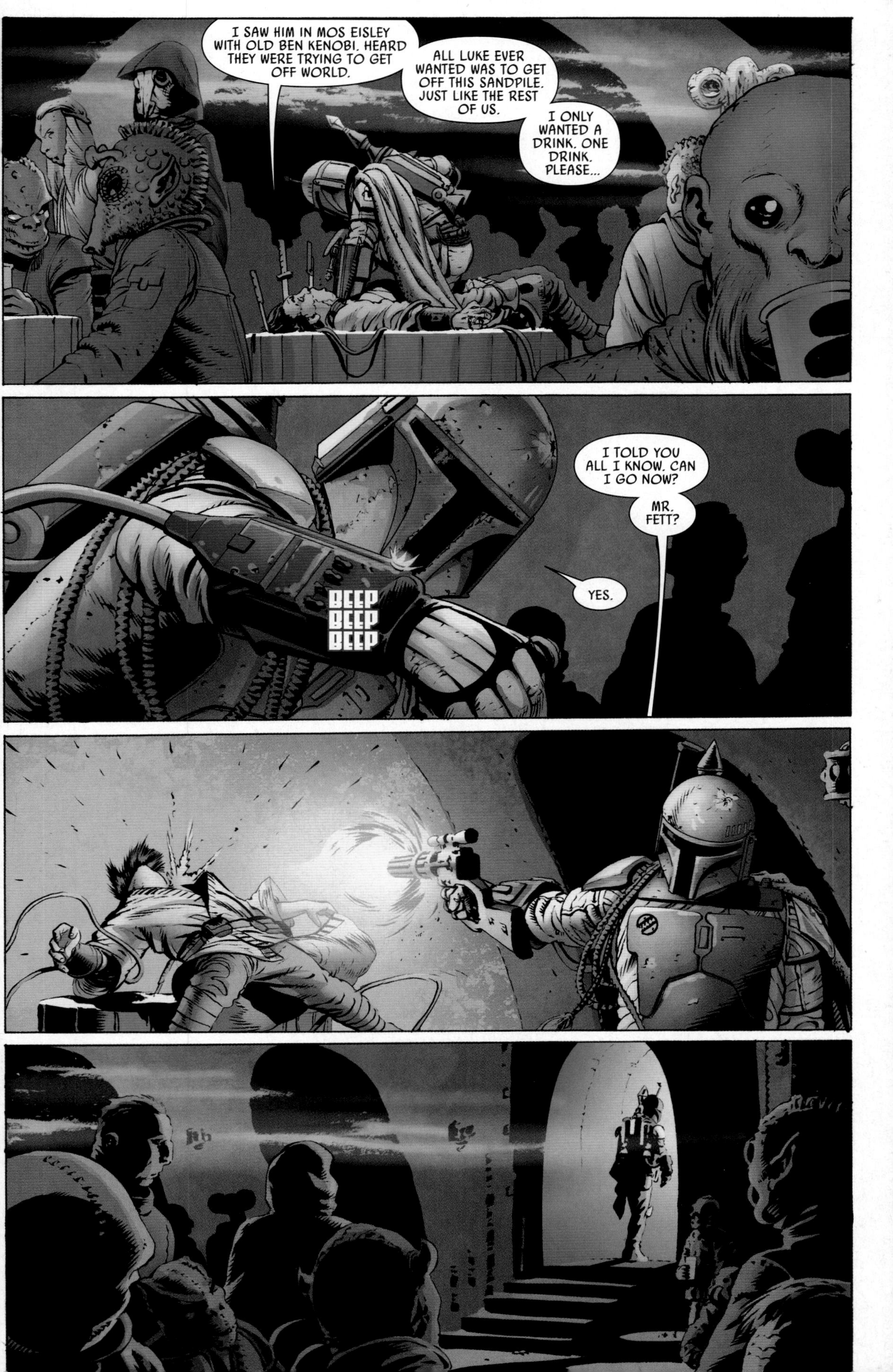
I SAW HIM IN MOS EISLEY WITH OLD BEN KENOBI. HEARD THEY WERE TRYING TO GET OFF WORLD.
ALL LUKE EVER WANTED WAS TO GET OFF THIS SANDPILE. JUST LIKE THE REST OF US.
I ONLY WANTED A DRINK. ONE DRINK. PLEASE...
I TOLD YOU ALL I KNOW. CAN I GO NOW?
MR. FETT?
BEEP BEEP BEEP
YES.

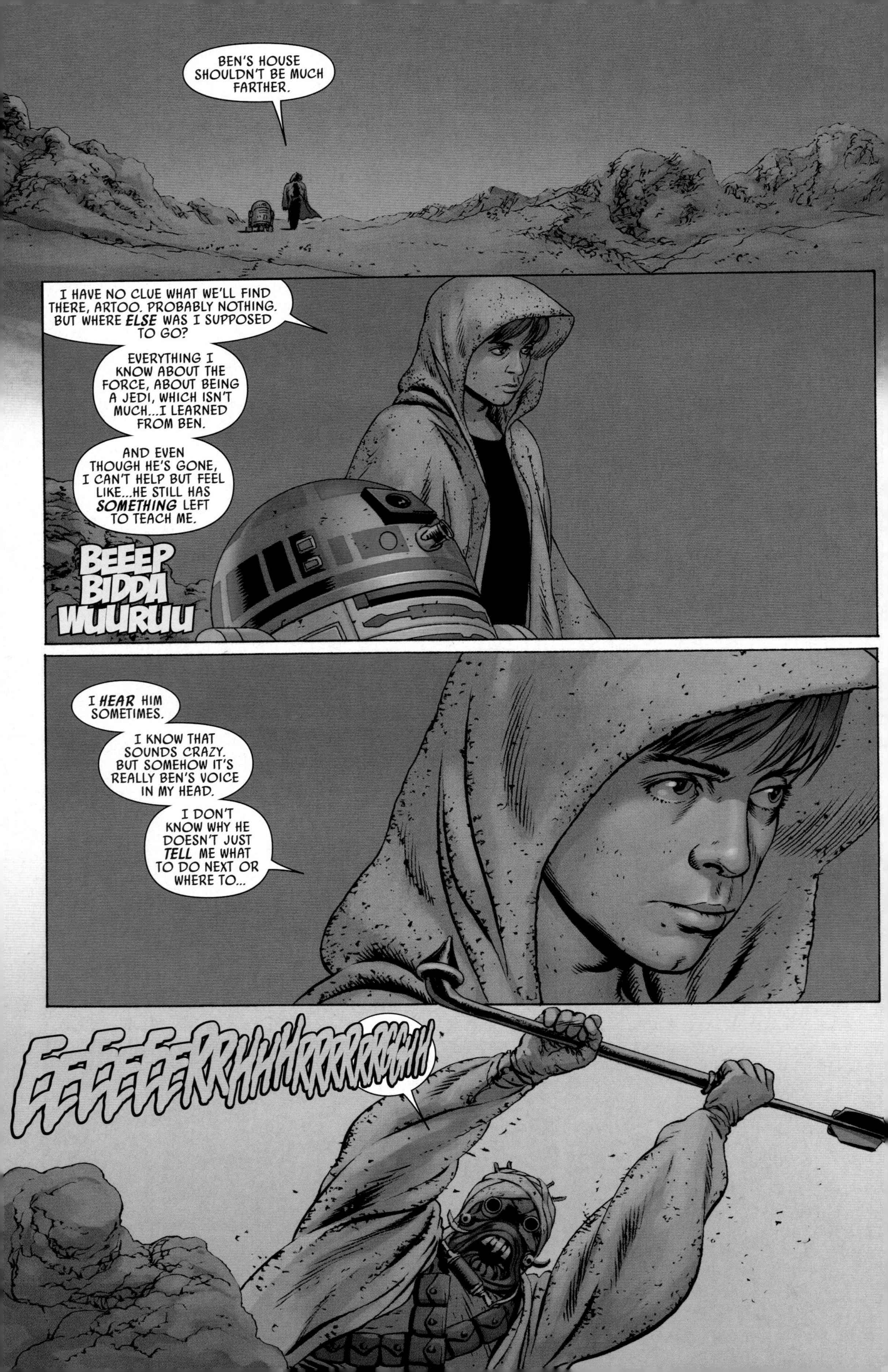
BEN'S HOUSE SHOULDN'T BE MUCH FARTHER.
I HAVE NO CLUE WHAT WE'LL FIND THERE, ARTOO. PROBABLY NOTHING. BUT WHERE ELSE WAS I SUPPOSED TO GO?
EVERYTHING I KNOW ABOUT THE FORCE, ABOUT BEING A JEDI, WHICH ISN'T MUCH...I LEARNED FROM BEN.
AND EVEN THOUGH HE'S GONE, I CAN'T HELP BUT FEEL LIKE...HE STILL HAS SOMETHING LEFT TO TEACH ME.
BEEEP BIDDA WUURUU
I HEAR HIM SOMETIMES.
I KNOW THAT SOUNDS CRAZY. BUT SOMEHOW IT'S REALLY BEN'S VOICE IN MY HEAD.
I DON'T KNOW WHY HE DOESN'T JUST TELL ME WHAT TO DO NEXT OR WHERE TO...
EEEEEERRHHHRRRRRRGHH

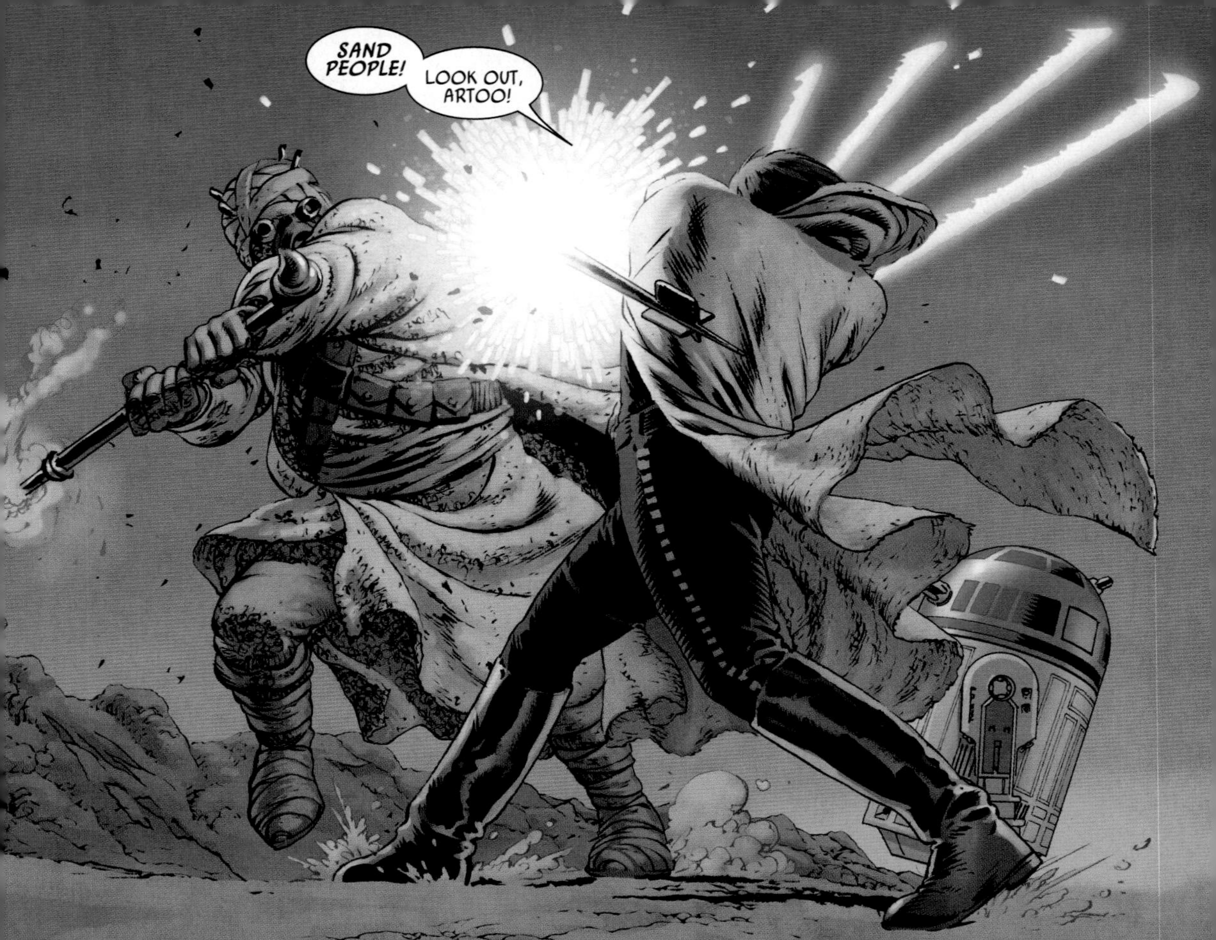
SAND PEOPLE!
LOOK OUT, ARTOO!

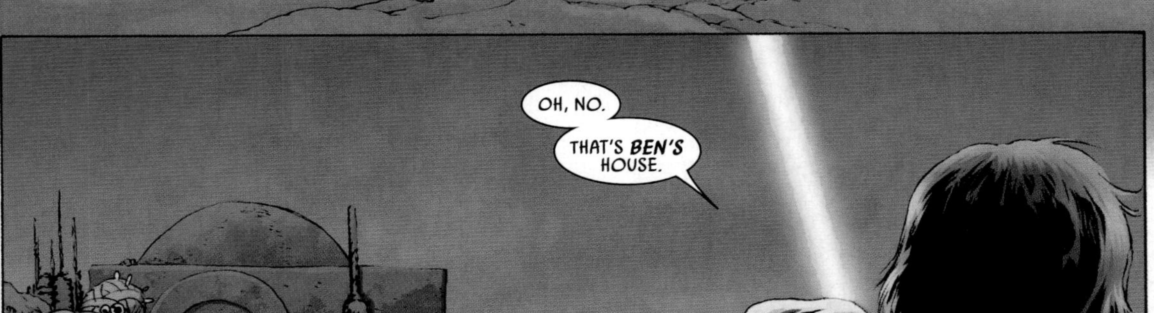
OH, NO.
THAT'S **BEN'S** HOUSE.

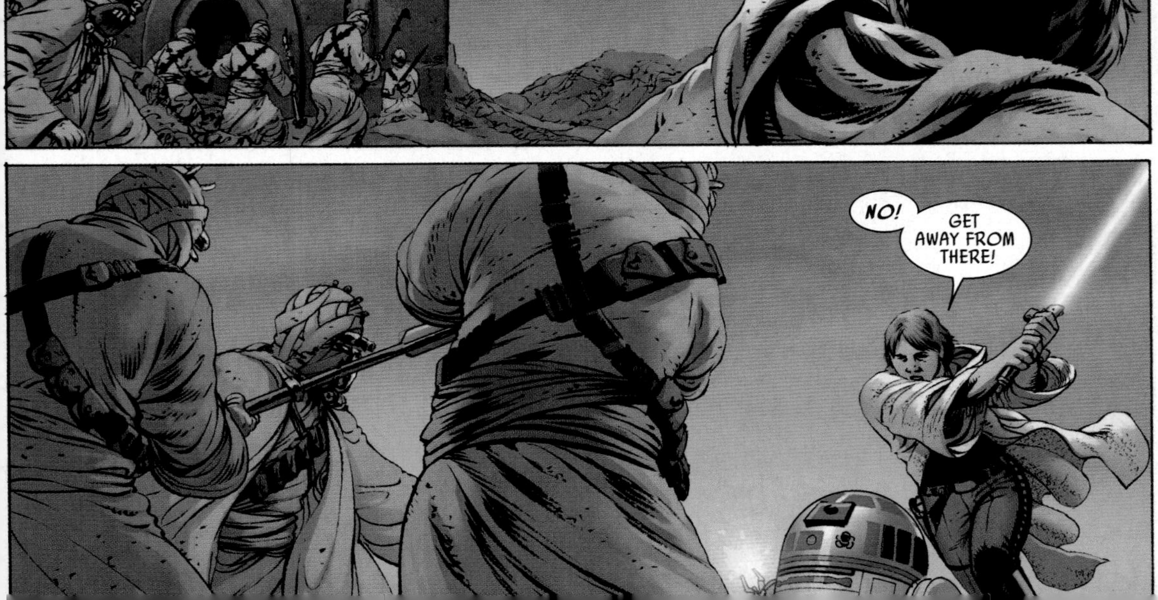
NO!
GET AWAY FROM THERE!

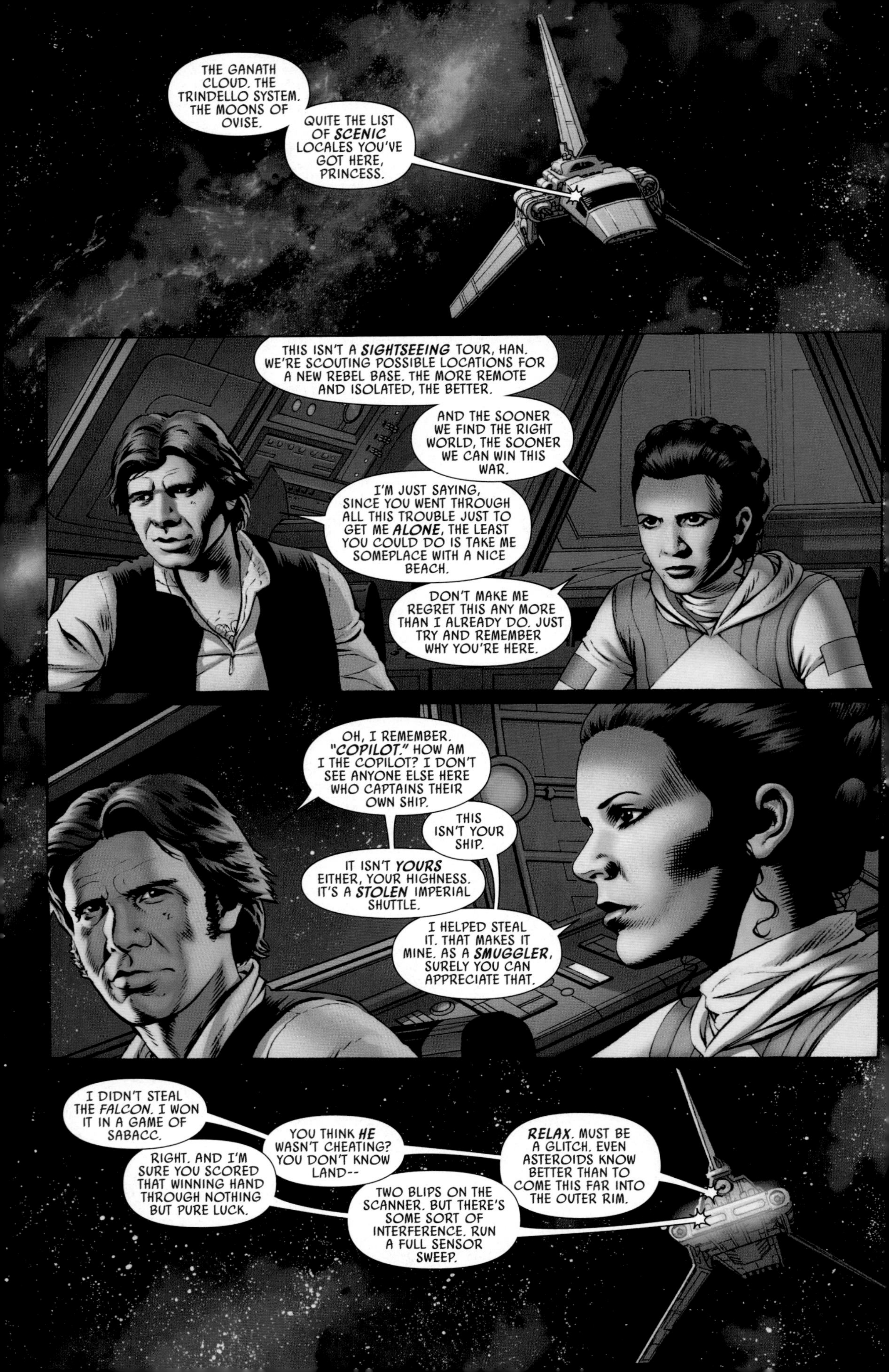
THE GANATH CLOUD. THE TRINDELLO SYSTEM. THE MOONS OF OVISE.
QUITE THE LIST OF SCENIC LOCALES YOU'VE GOT HERE, PRINCESS.
THIS ISN'T A SIGHTSEEING TOUR, HAN. WE'RE SCOUTING POSSIBLE LOCATIONS FOR A NEW REBEL BASE. THE MORE REMOTE AND ISOLATED, THE BETTER.
AND THE SOONER WE FIND THE RIGHT WORLD, THE SOONER WE CAN WIN THIS WAR.
I'M JUST SAYING, SINCE YOU WENT THROUGH ALL THIS TROUBLE JUST TO GET ME ALONE, THE LEAST YOU COULD DO IS TAKE ME SOMEPLACE WITH A NICE BEACH.
DON'T MAKE ME REGRET THIS ANY MORE THAN I ALREADY DO. JUST TRY AND REMEMBER WHY YOU'RE HERE.
OH, I REMEMBER. "COPILOT." HOW AM I THE COPILOT? I DON'T SEE ANYONE ELSE HERE WHO CAPTAINS THEIR OWN SHIP.
THIS ISN'T YOUR SHIP.
IT ISN'T YOURS EITHER, YOUR HIGHNESS. IT'S A STOLEN IMPERIAL SHUTTLE.
I HELPED STEAL IT. THAT MAKES IT MINE. AS A SMUGGLER, SURELY YOU CAN APPRECIATE THAT.
I DIDN'T STEAL THE FALCON. I WON IT IN A GAME OF SABACC.
RIGHT. AND I'M SURE YOU SCORED THAT WINNING HAND THROUGH NOTHING BUT PURE LUCK.
YOU THINK HE WASN'T CHEATING? YOU DON'T KNOW LAND--
TWO BLIPS ON THE SCANNER. BUT THERE'S SOME SORT OF INTERFERENCE. RUN A FULL SENSOR SWEEP.
RELAX. MUST BE A GLITCH. EVEN ASTEROIDS KNOW BETTER THAN TO COME THIS FAR INTO THE OUTER RIM.

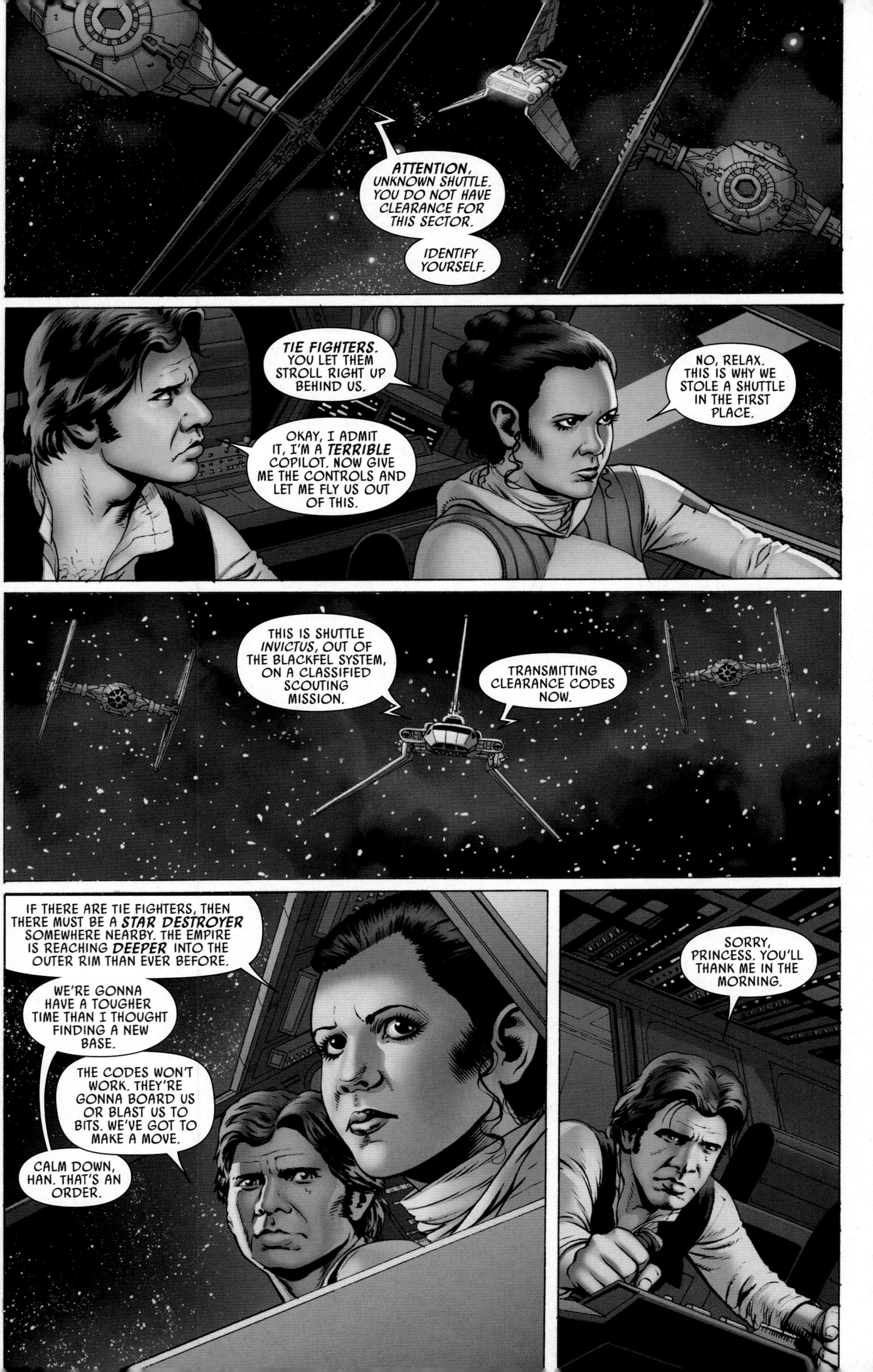
ATTENTION, UNKNOWN SHUTTLE. YOU DO NOT HAVE CLEARANCE FOR THIS SECTOR.
IDENTIFY YOURSELF.
TIE FIGHTERS. YOU LET THEM STROLL RIGHT UP BEHIND US.
OKAY, I ADMIT IT, I'M A TERRIBLE COPILOT. NOW GIVE ME THE CONTROLS AND LET ME FLY US OUT OF THIS.
NO, RELAX. THIS IS WHY WE STOLE A SHUTTLE IN THE FIRST PLACE.
THIS IS SHUTTLE INVICTUS, OUT OF THE BLACKFEL SYSTEM, ON A CLASSIFIED SCOUTING MISSION.
TRANSMITTING CLEARANCE CODES NOW.
IF THERE ARE TIE FIGHTERS, THEN THERE MUST BE A STAR DESTROYER SOMEWHERE NEARBY. THE EMPIRE IS REACHING DEEPER INTO THE OUTER RIM THAN EVER BEFORE.
WE'RE GONNA HAVE A TOUGHER TIME THAN I THOUGHT FINDING A NEW BASE.
THE CODES WON'T WORK. THEY'RE GONNA BOARD US OR BLAST US TO BITS. WE'VE GOT TO MAKE A MOVE.
CALM DOWN, HAN. THAT'S AN ORDER.
SORRY, PRINCESS. YOU'LL THANK ME IN THE MORNING.

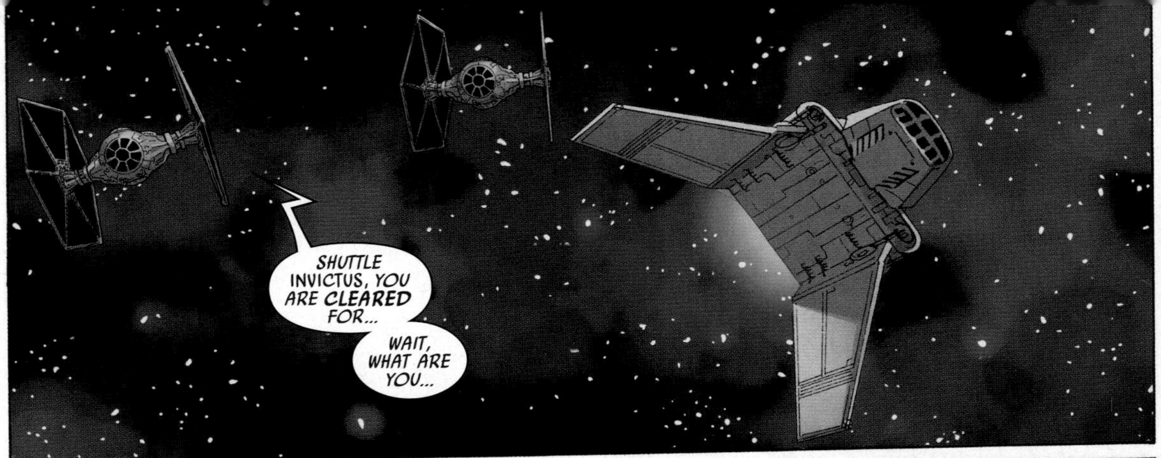
SHUTTLE INVICTUS, YOU ARE CLEARED FOR...
WAIT, WHAT ARE YOU...
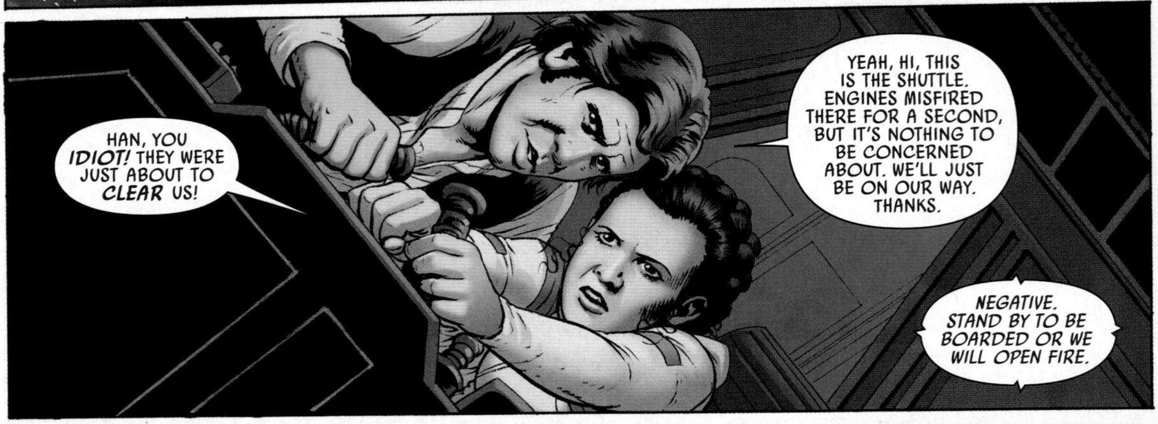
YEAH, HI, THIS IS THE SHUTTLE. ENGINES MISFIRED THERE FOR A SECOND, BUT IT'S NOTHING TO BE CONCERNED ABOUT. WE'LL JUST BE ON OUR WAY. THANKS.
HAN, YOU IDIOT! THEY WERE JUST ABOUT TO CLEAR US!
NEGATIVE. STAND BY TO BE BOARDED OR WE WILL OPEN FIRE.
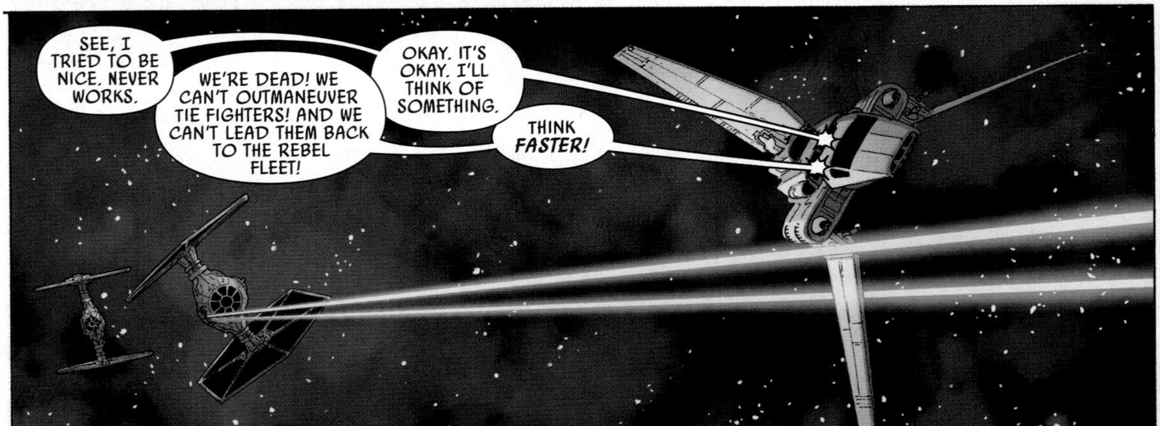
SEE, I TRIED TO BE NICE. NEVER WORKS.
WE'RE DEAD! WE CAN'T OUTMANEUVER TIE FIGHTERS! AND WE CAN'T LEAD THEM BACK TO THE REBEL FLEET!
OKAY. IT'S OKAY. I'LL THINK OF SOMETHING.
THINK FASTER!
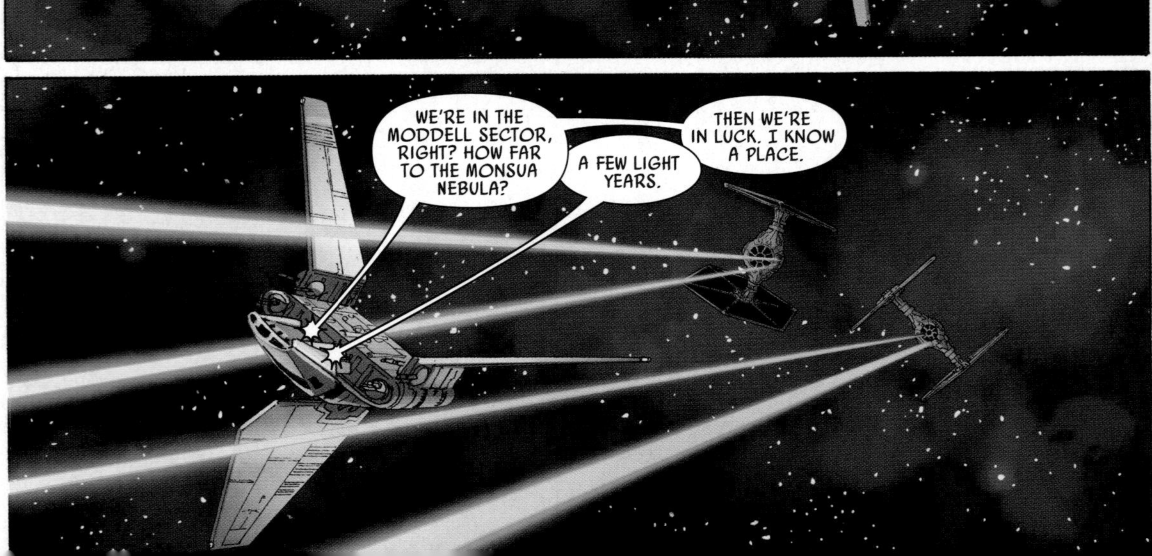
WE'RE IN THE MODDELL SECTOR, RIGHT? HOW FAR TO THE MONSUA NEBULA?
A FEW LIGHT YEARS.
THEN WE'RE IN LUCK. I KNOW A PLACE.

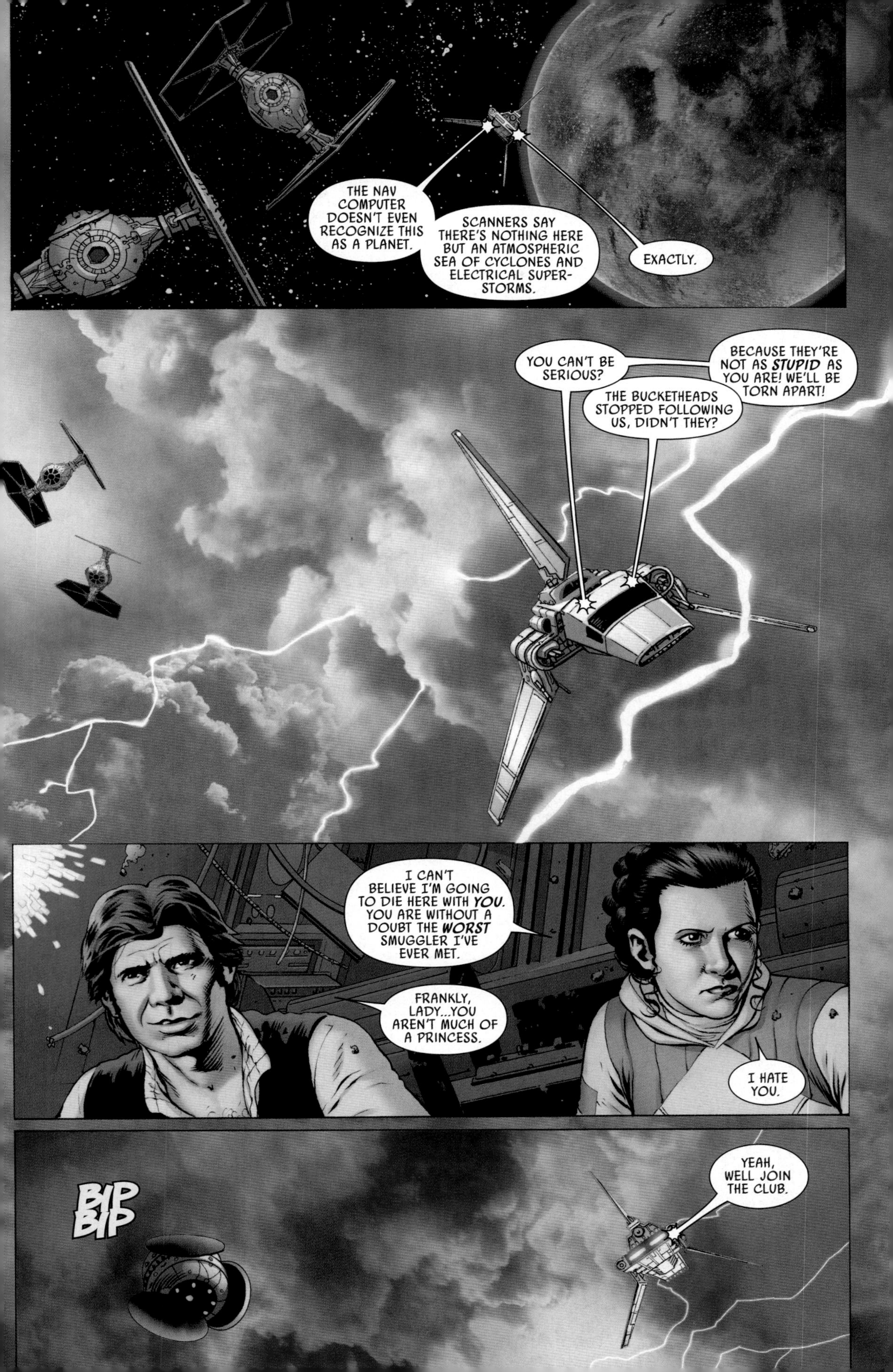
THE NAV COMPUTER DOESN'T EVEN RECOGNIZE THIS AS A PLANET.
SCANNERS SAY THERE'S NOTHING HERE BUT AN ATMOSPHERIC SEA OF CYCLONES AND ELECTRICAL SUPER-STORMS.
EXACTLY.
YOU CAN'T BE SERIOUS?
THE BUCKETHEADS STOPPED FOLLOWING US, DIDN'T THEY?
BECAUSE THEY'RE NOT AS STUPID AS YOU ARE! WE'LL BE TORN APART!
I CAN'T BELIEVE I'M GOING TO DIE HERE WITH YOU. YOU ARE WITHOUT A DOUBT THE WORST SMUGGLER I'VE EVER MET.
FRANKLY, LADY...YOU AREN'T MUCH OF A PRINCESS.
I HATE YOU.
BIP BIP
YEAH, WELL JOIN THE CLUB.

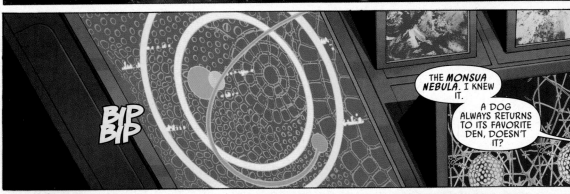

THE *MONSUA NEBULA*. I KNEW IT.

A DOG ALWAYS RETURNS TO ITS FAVORITE DEN, DOESN'T IT?

BIP BIP

I'VE GOT YOU NOW, YOU SORRY SON OF A BANTHA.

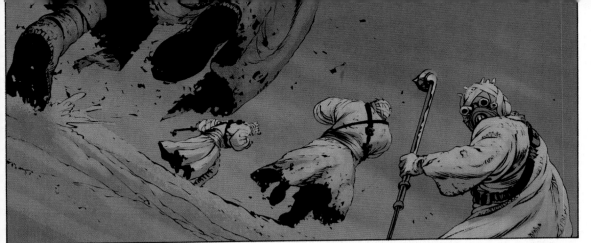

IF THEY HADN'T *RUN*...I MIGHT'VE...

I'M JUST *GLAD* THEY RAN.

ALL I FEEL IS ANGER. AND FRUSTRATION. SOMETHING TELLS ME THAT'S NOT THE PATH TO BECOMING A JEDI.

I NEED *ANSWERS*, ARTOO. LET'S HOPE BEN LEFT US A FEW.

SUDDENLY I'M NOT SO HOPEFUL. *LOOK* AT THIS MESS.

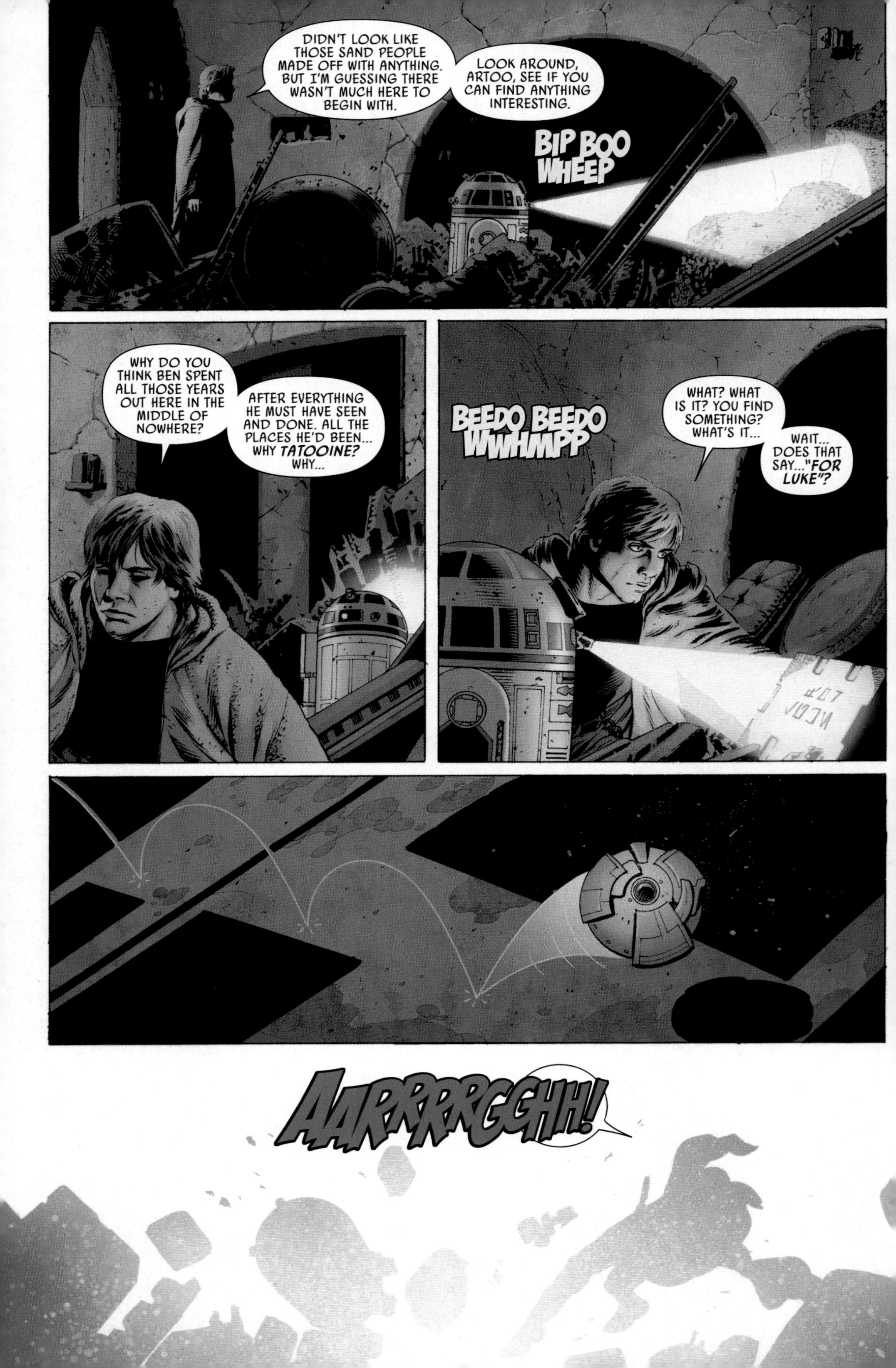
DIDN'T LOOK LIKE THOSE SAND PEOPLE MADE OFF WITH ANYTHING. BUT I'M GUESSING THERE WASN'T MUCH HERE TO BEGIN WITH.
LOOK AROUND, ARTOO, SEE IF YOU CAN FIND ANYTHING INTERESTING.
BIP BOO WHEEP
WHY DO YOU THINK BEN SPENT ALL THOSE YEARS OUT HERE IN THE MIDDLE OF NOWHERE?
AFTER EVERYTHING HE MUST HAVE SEEN AND DONE, ALL THE PLACES HE'D BEEN... WHY *TATOOINE?* WHY...
BEEDO BEEDO WWHMPP
WHAT? WHAT IS IT? YOU FIND SOMETHING? WHAT'S IT...
WAIT... DOES THAT SAY..."*FOR LUKE*"?
AARRRRRGGHH!

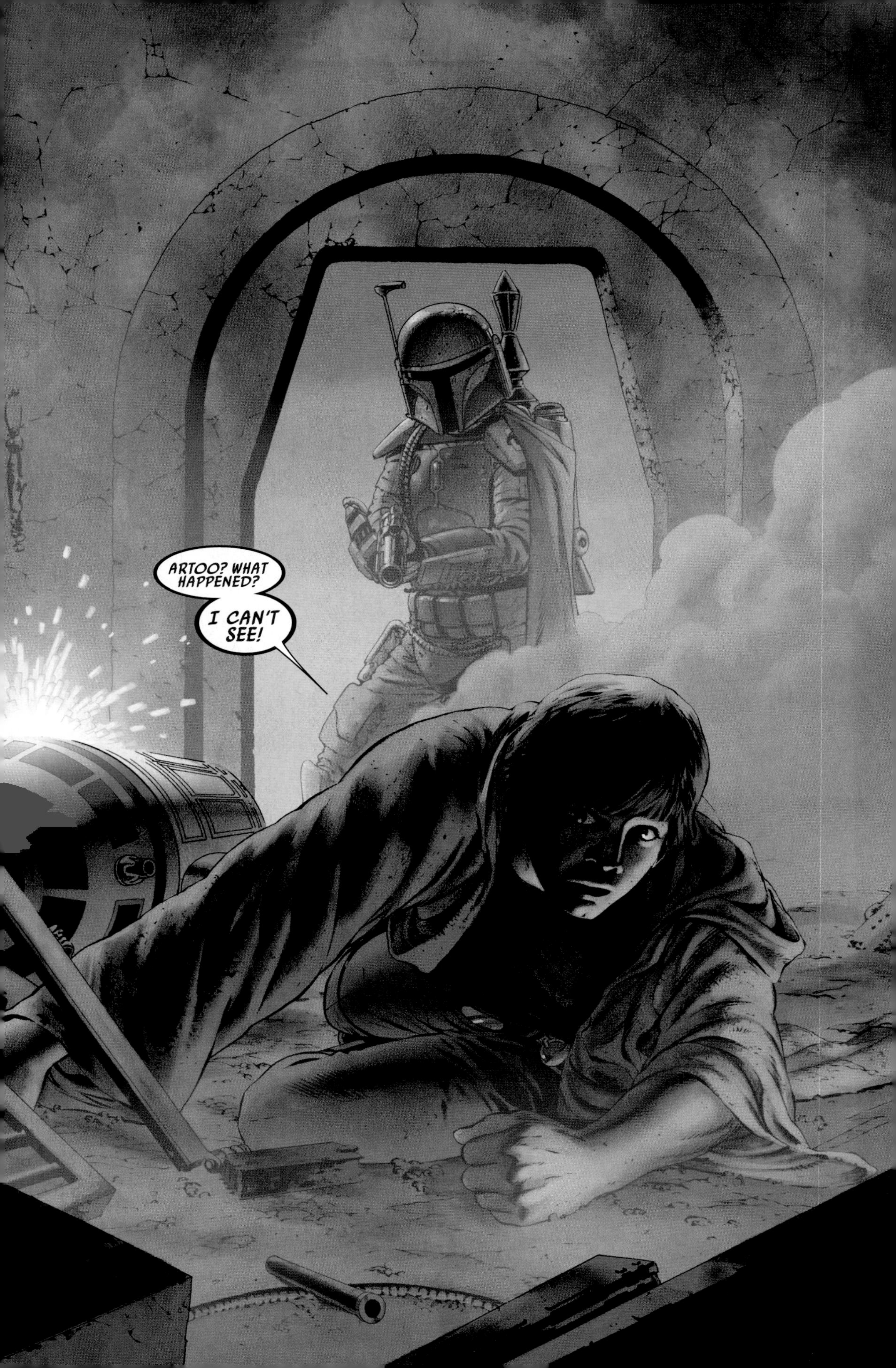
ARTOO? WHAT HAPPENED?
I CAN'T SEE!

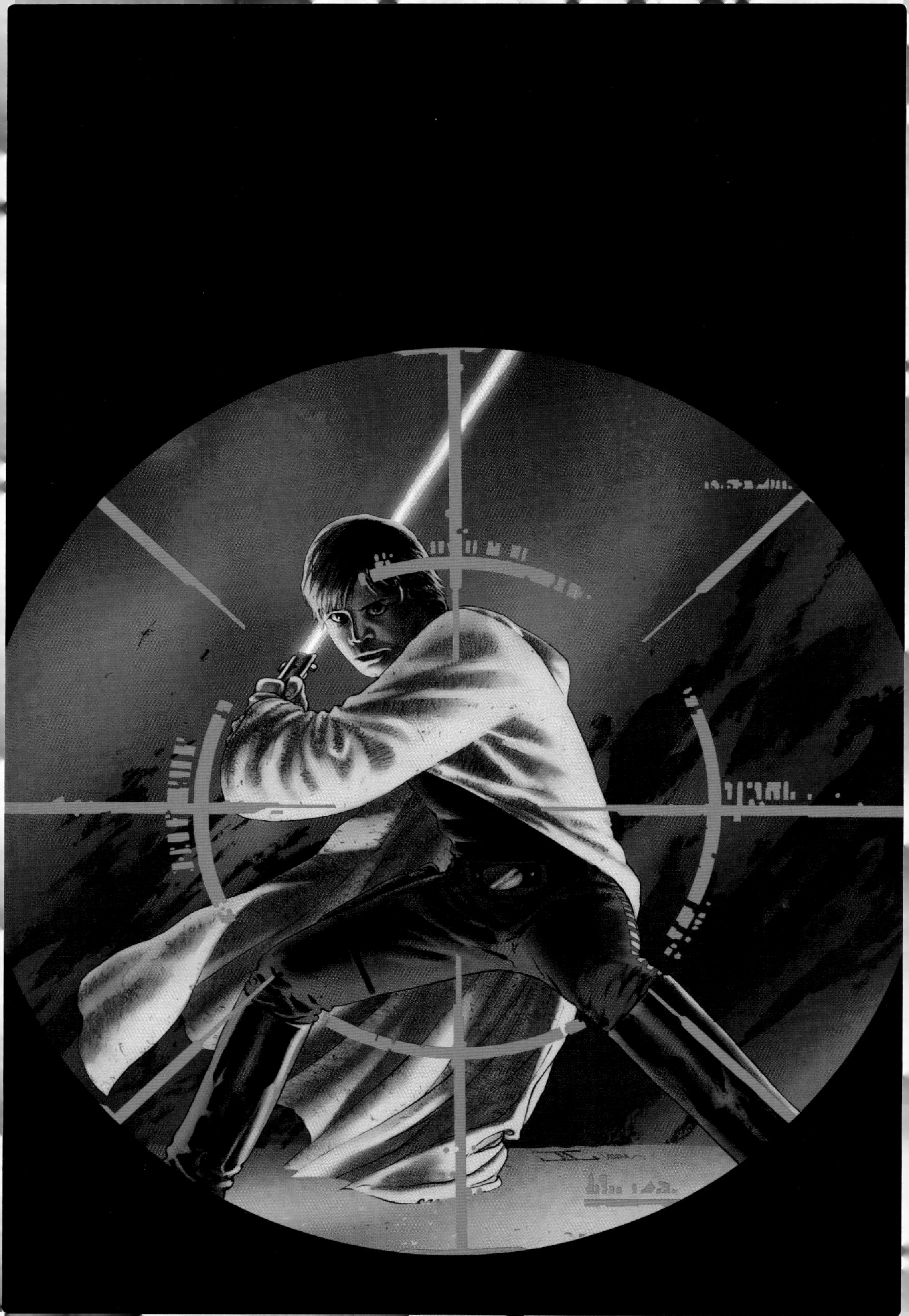

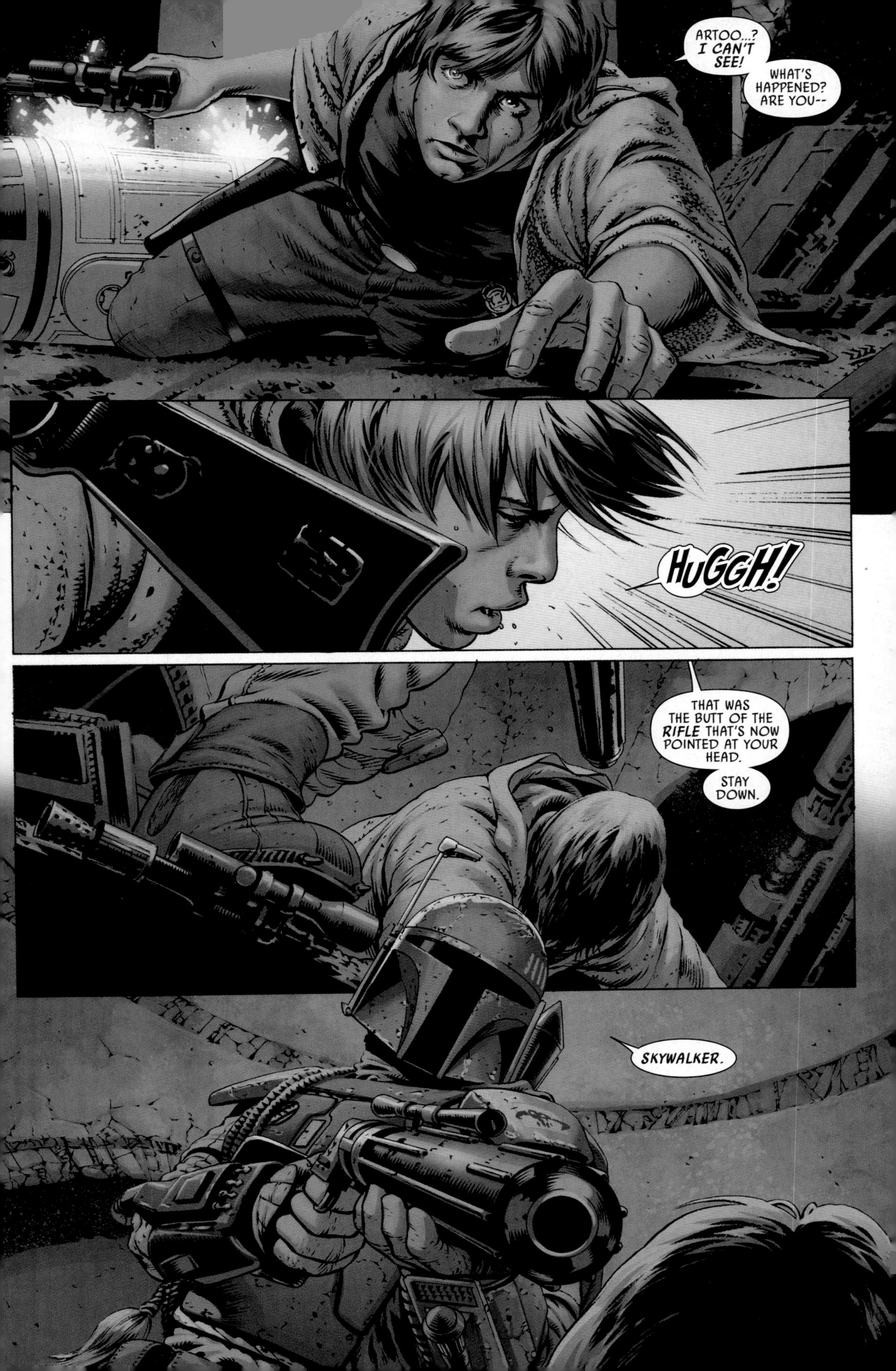

ARTOO...? I CAN'T SEE!
WHAT'S HAPPENED? ARE YOU--
HUGGH!
THAT WAS THE BUTT OF THE RIFLE THAT'S NOW POINTED AT YOUR HEAD.
STAY DOWN.
SKYWALKER.

SKY WHO?

ARRGHH!

DON'T WASTE MY TIME.

ARMOR. WHAT ARE STORMTROOPERS DOING IN THE DUNE SEA?

YOU'D HAVE TO ASK THE STORMTROOPERS. DON'T MOVE.

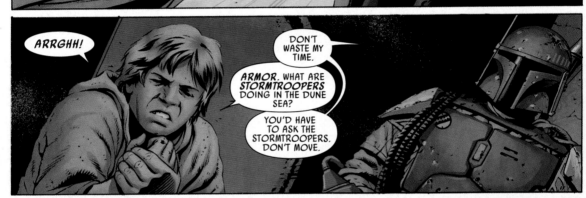

WHY CAN'T I SEE? WHAT WAS THAT, A FLASH GRENADE?

I SAID DON'T MOVE.

IF YOU WERE GONNA KILL ME, YOU'D HAVE DONE IT ALREADY. WHO HIRED YOU? WHERE ARE YOU PLANNING ON TAKING--

GGUGH!

YOU COULD'VE WALKED.

BUT I CAN JUST AS EASILY CARRY YOU TO MY SHIP.

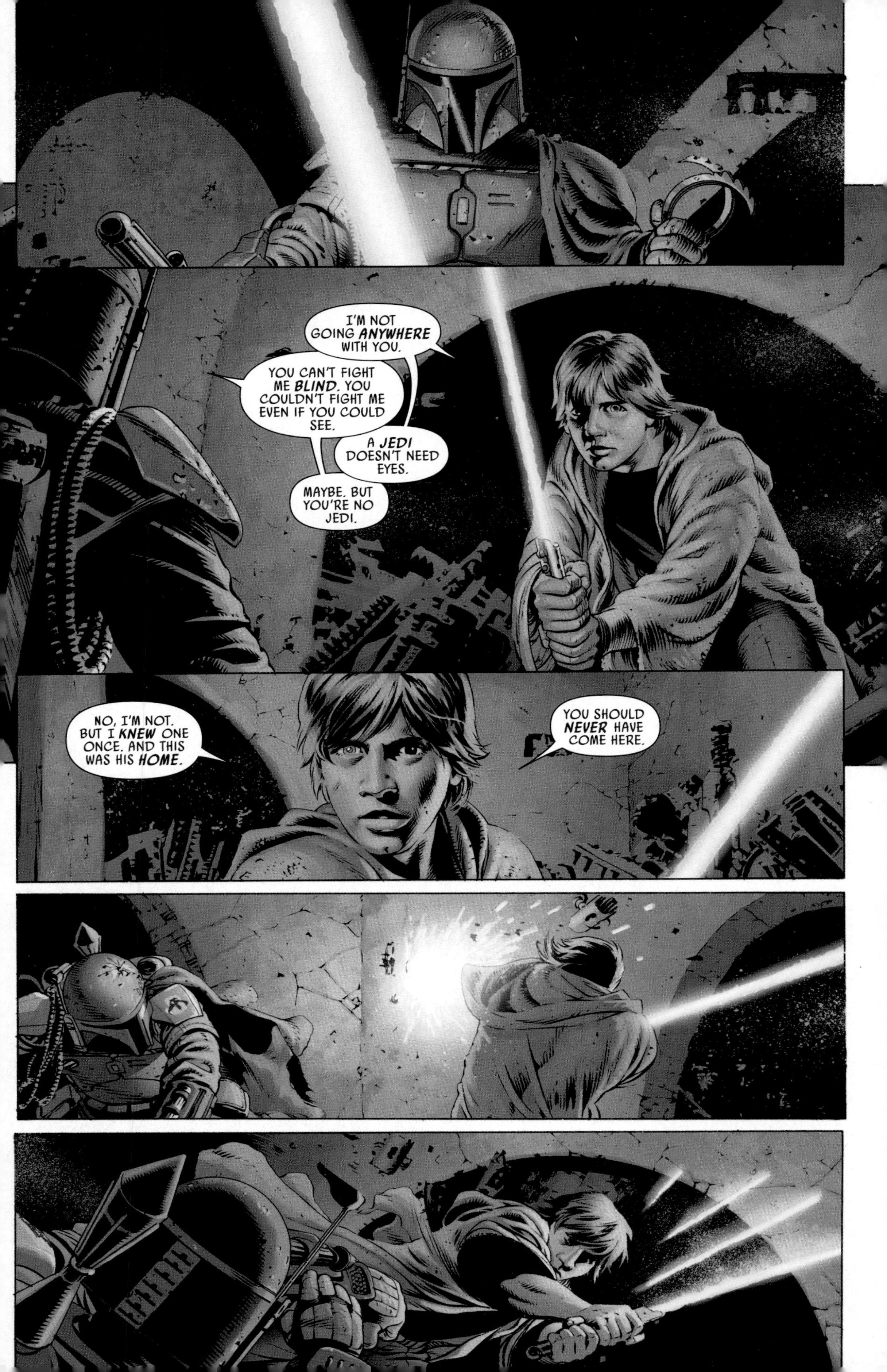
I'M NOT GOING ANYWHERE WITH YOU.
YOU CAN'T FIGHT ME BLIND. YOU COULDN'T FIGHT ME EVEN IF YOU COULD SEE.
A JEDI DOESN'T NEED EYES.
MAYBE. BUT YOU'RE NO JEDI.
NO, I'M NOT. BUT I KNEW ONE ONCE. AND THIS WAS HIS HOME.
YOU SHOULD NEVER HAVE COME HERE.

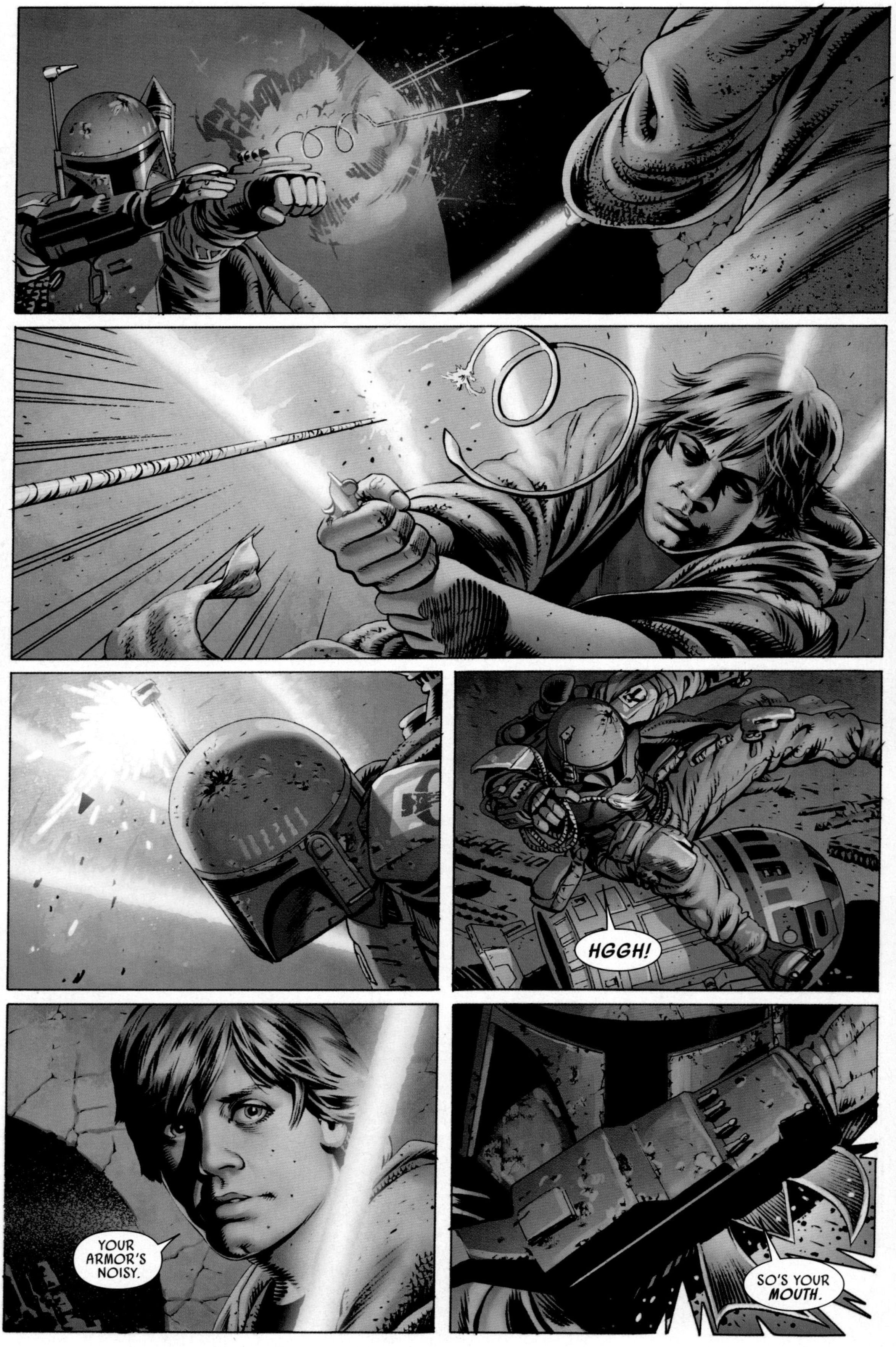
HGGH!
YOUR ARMOR'S NOISY.
SO'S YOUR MOUTH.

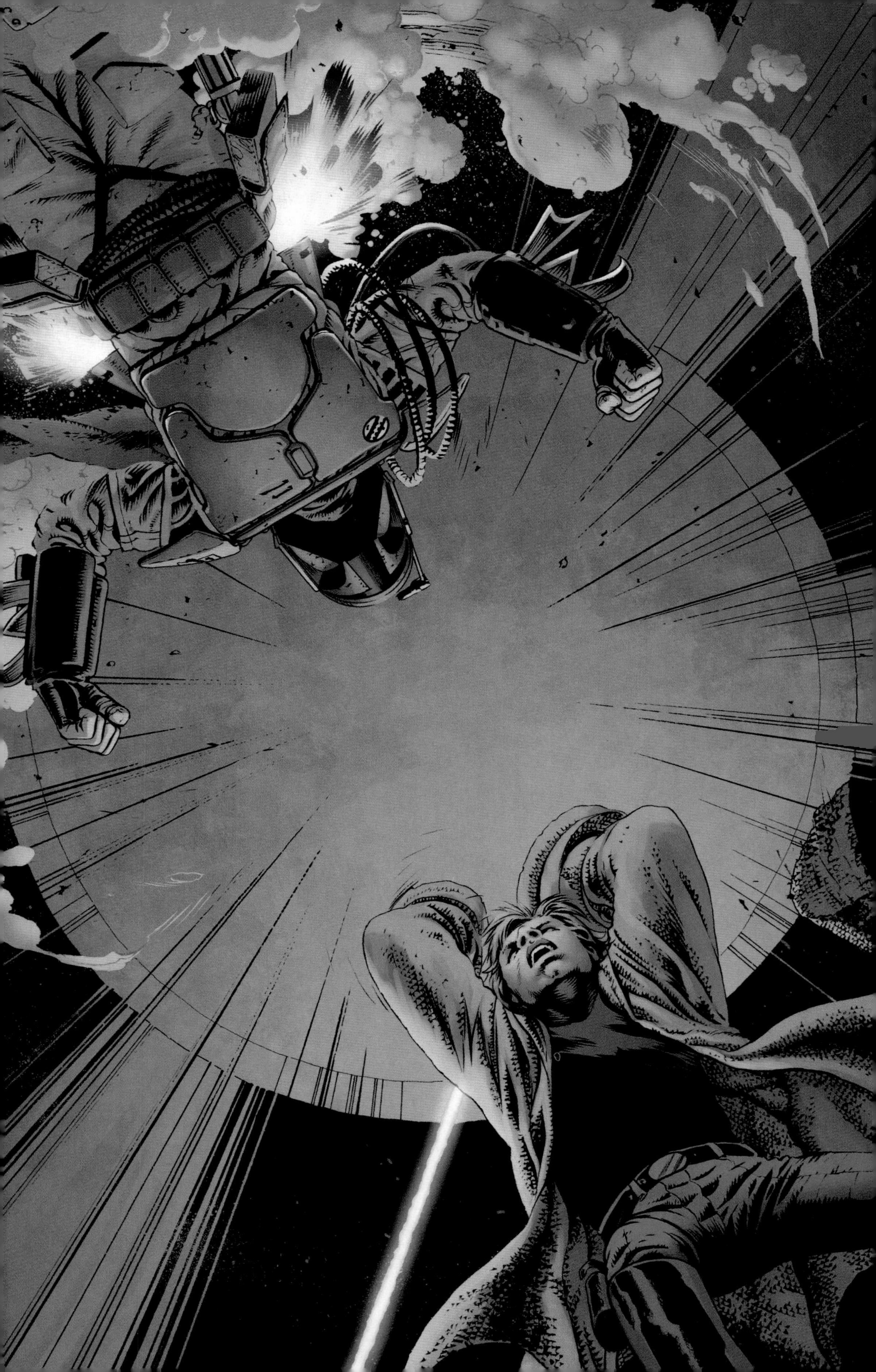

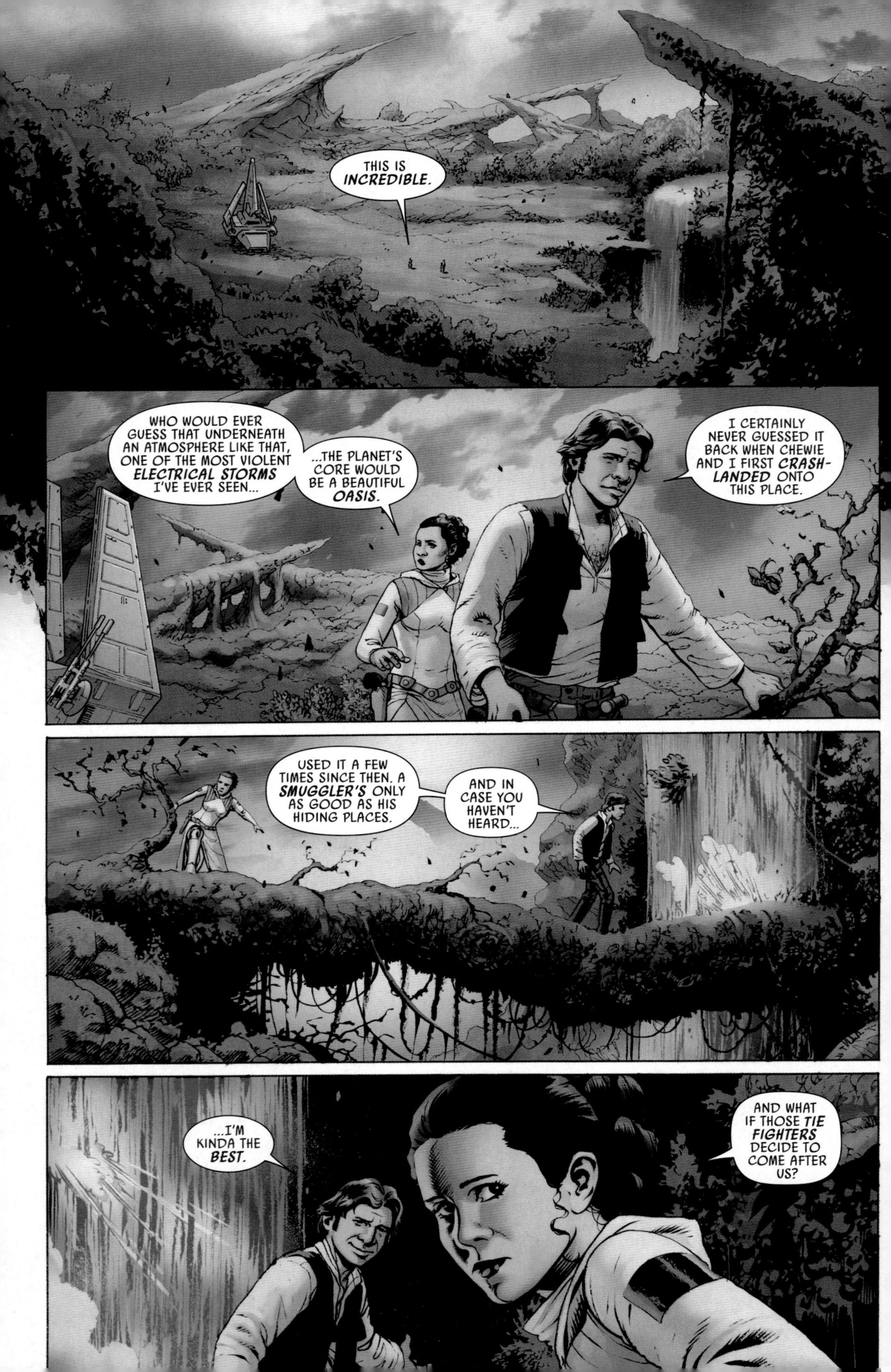
THIS IS INCREDIBLE.
WHO WOULD EVER GUESS THAT UNDERNEATH AN ATMOSPHERE LIKE THAT, ONE OF THE MOST VIOLENT ELECTRICAL STORMS I'VE EVER SEEN...
...THE PLANET'S CORE WOULD BE A BEAUTIFUL OASIS.
I CERTAINLY NEVER GUESSED IT BACK WHEN CHEWIE AND I FIRST CRASH-LANDED ONTO THIS PLACE.
USED IT A FEW TIMES SINCE THEN. A SMUGGLER'S ONLY AS GOOD AS HIS HIDING PLACES.
AND IN CASE YOU HAVEN'T HEARD...
...I'M KINDA THE BEST.
AND WHAT IF THOSE TIE FIGHTERS DECIDE TO COME AFTER US?

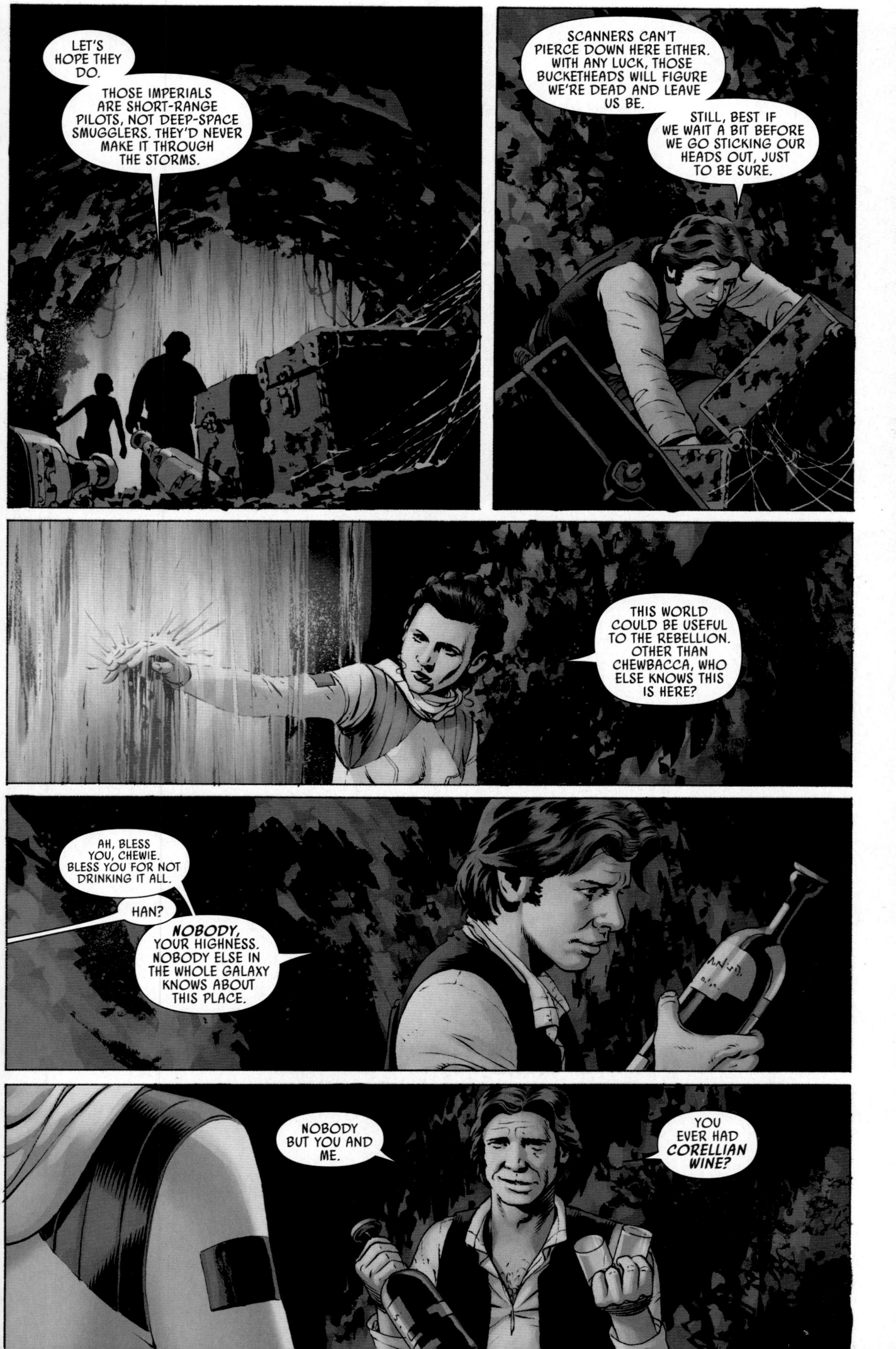
LET'S HOPE THEY DO.
THOSE IMPERIALS ARE SHORT-RANGE PILOTS, NOT DEEP-SPACE SMUGGLERS. THEY'D NEVER MAKE IT THROUGH THE STORMS.
SCANNERS CAN'T PIERCE DOWN HERE EITHER. WITH ANY LUCK, THOSE BUCKETHEADS WILL FIGURE WE'RE DEAD AND LEAVE US BE.
STILL, BEST IF WE WAIT A BIT BEFORE WE GO STICKING OUR HEADS OUT, JUST TO BE SURE.
THIS WORLD COULD BE USEFUL TO THE REBELLION. OTHER THAN CHEWBACCA, WHO ELSE KNOWS THIS IS HERE?
AH, BLESS YOU, CHEWIE. BLESS YOU FOR NOT DRINKING IT ALL.
HAN?
NOBODY, YOUR HIGHNESS. NOBODY ELSE IN THE WHOLE GALAXY KNOWS ABOUT THIS PLACE.
NOBODY BUT YOU AND ME.
YOU EVER HAD CORELLIAN WINE?

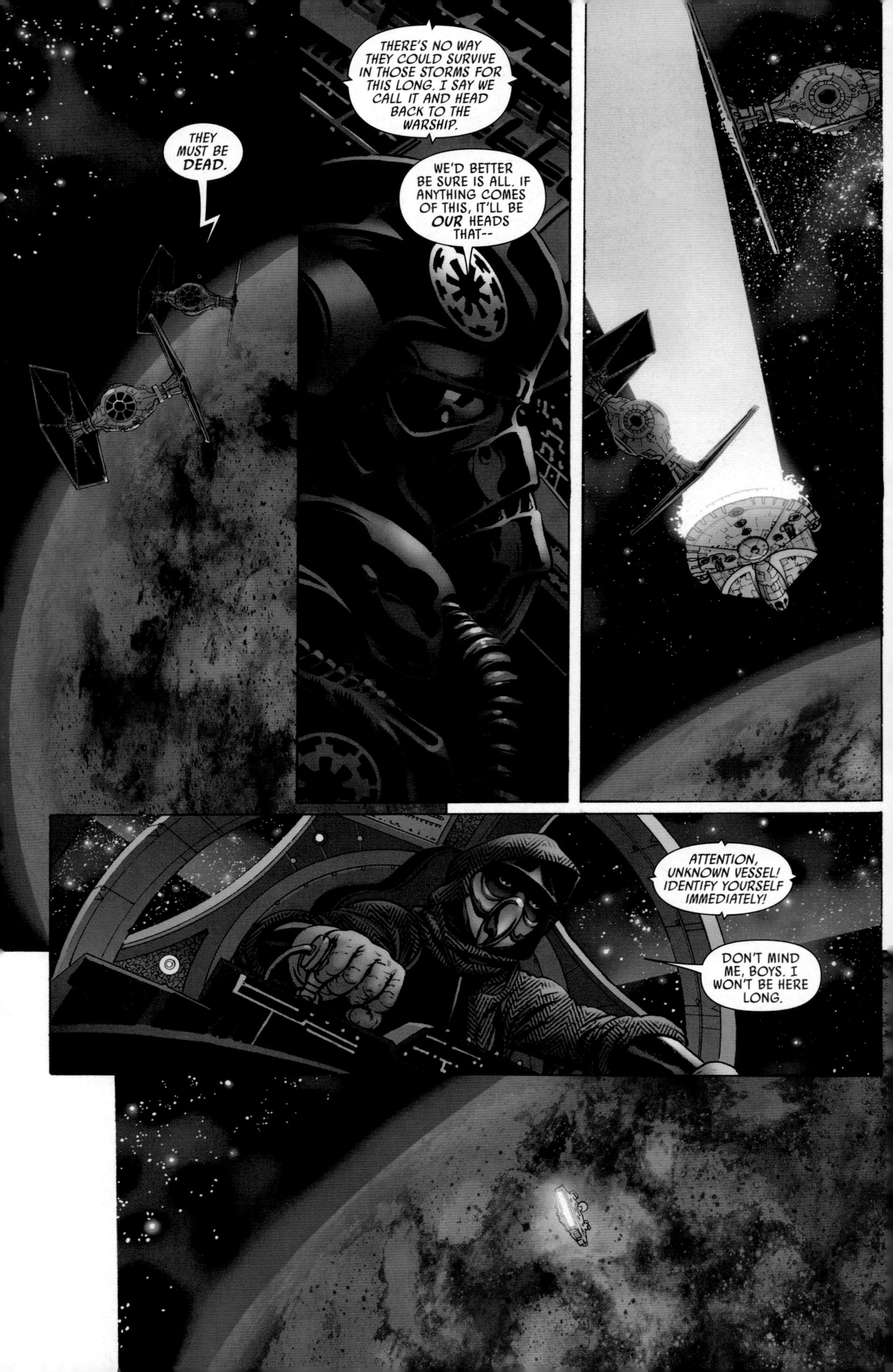
THEY MUST BE DEAD.
THERE'S NO WAY THEY COULD SURVIVE IN THOSE STORMS FOR THIS LONG. I SAY WE CALL IT AND HEAD BACK TO THE WARSHIP.
WE'D BETTER BE SURE IS ALL. IF ANYTHING COMES OF THIS, IT'LL BE OUR HEADS THAT--
ATTENTION, UNKNOWN VESSEL! IDENTIFY YOURSELF IMMEDIATELY!
DON'T MIND ME, BOYS. I WON'T BE HERE LONG.

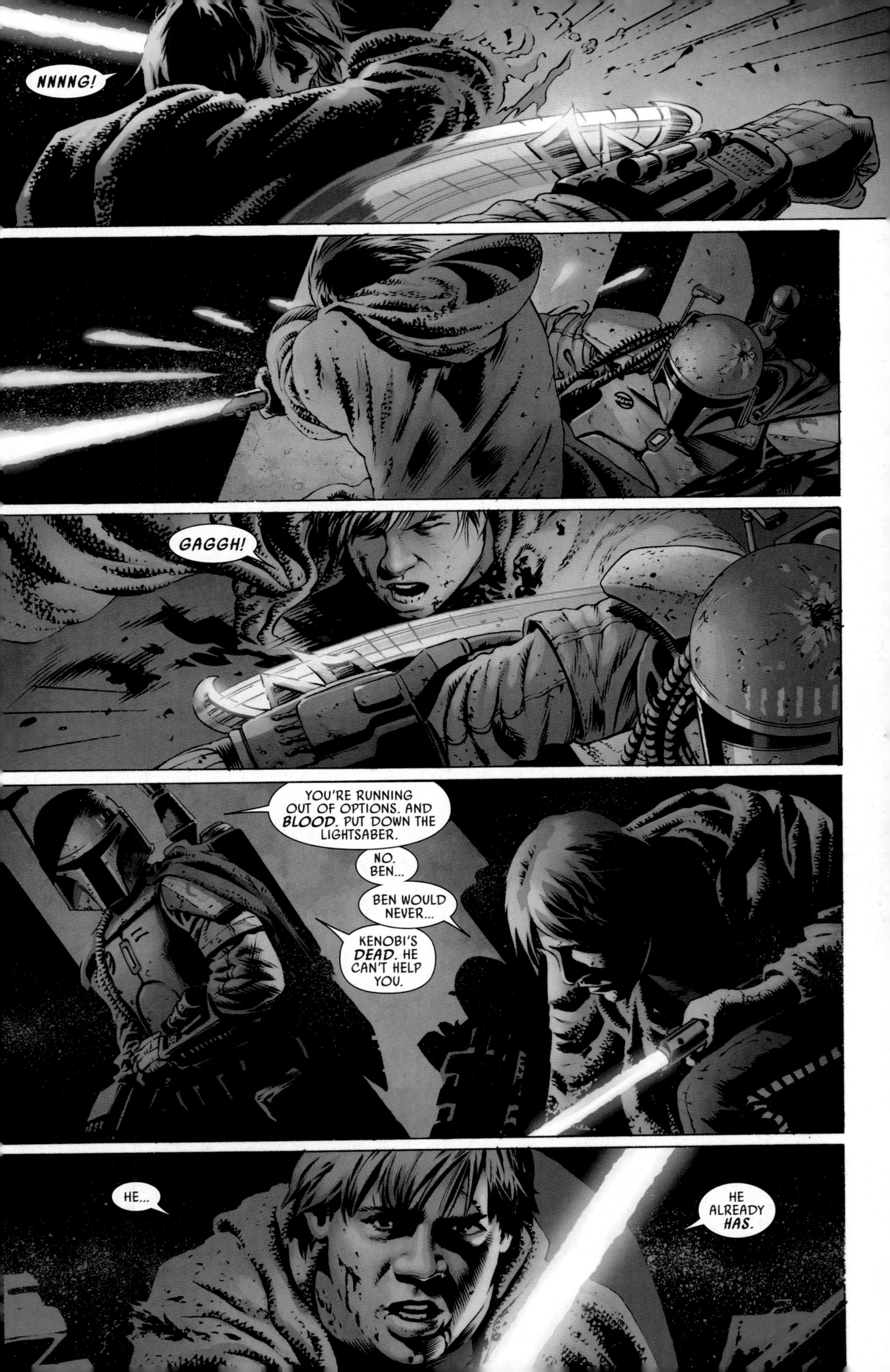
NNNNG!
GAGGH!
YOU'RE RUNNING OUT OF OPTIONS. AND BLOOD. PUT DOWN THE LIGHTSABER.
NO. BEN...
BEN WOULD NEVER...
KENOBI'S DEAD. HE CAN'T HELP YOU.
HE...
HE ALREADY HAS.

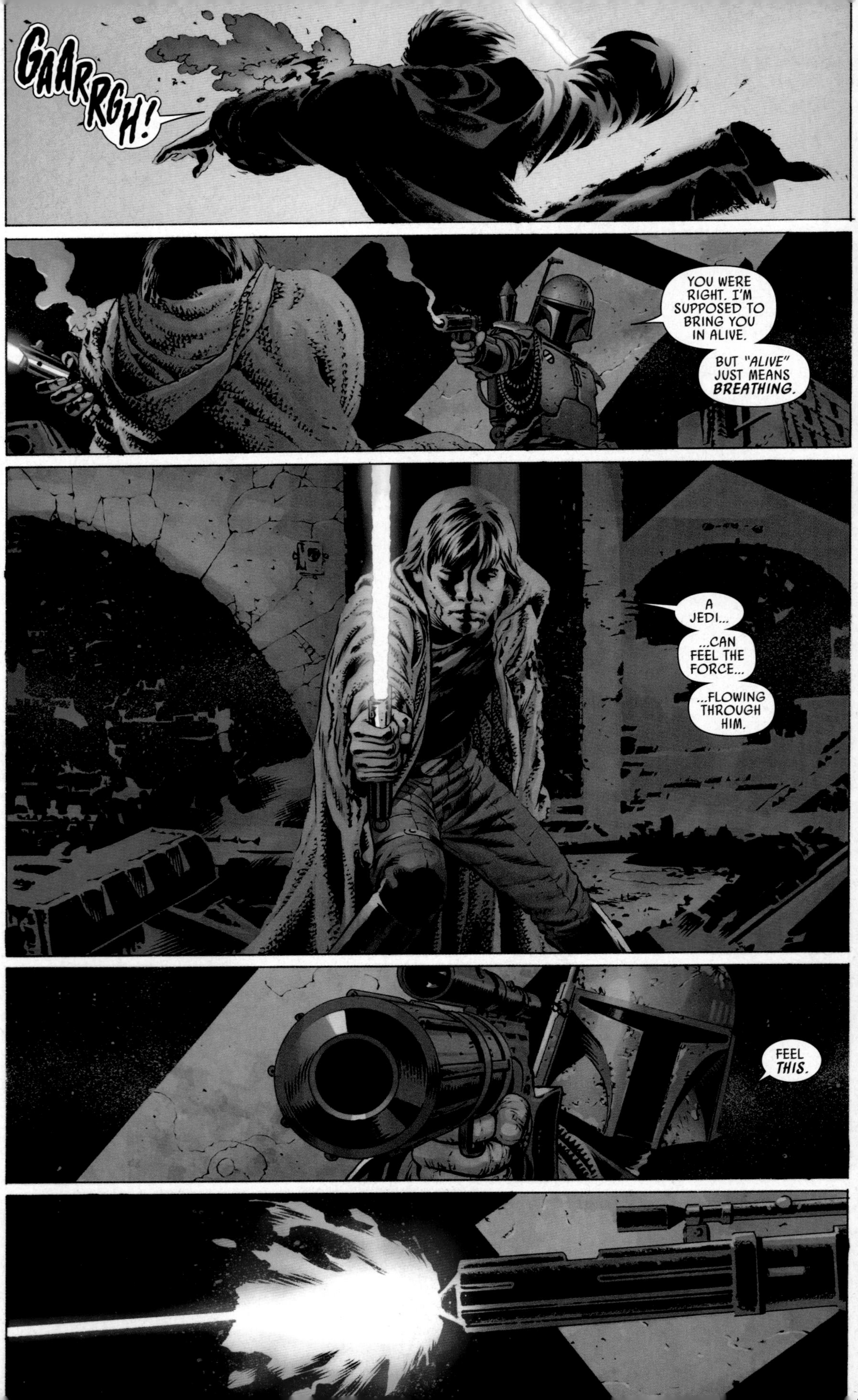
GAARRGH!
YOU WERE RIGHT. I'M SUPPOSED TO BRING YOU IN ALIVE.
BUT "ALIVE" JUST MEANS BREATHING.
A JEDI...
...CAN FEEL THE FORCE...
...FLOWING THROUGH HIM.
FEEL THIS.

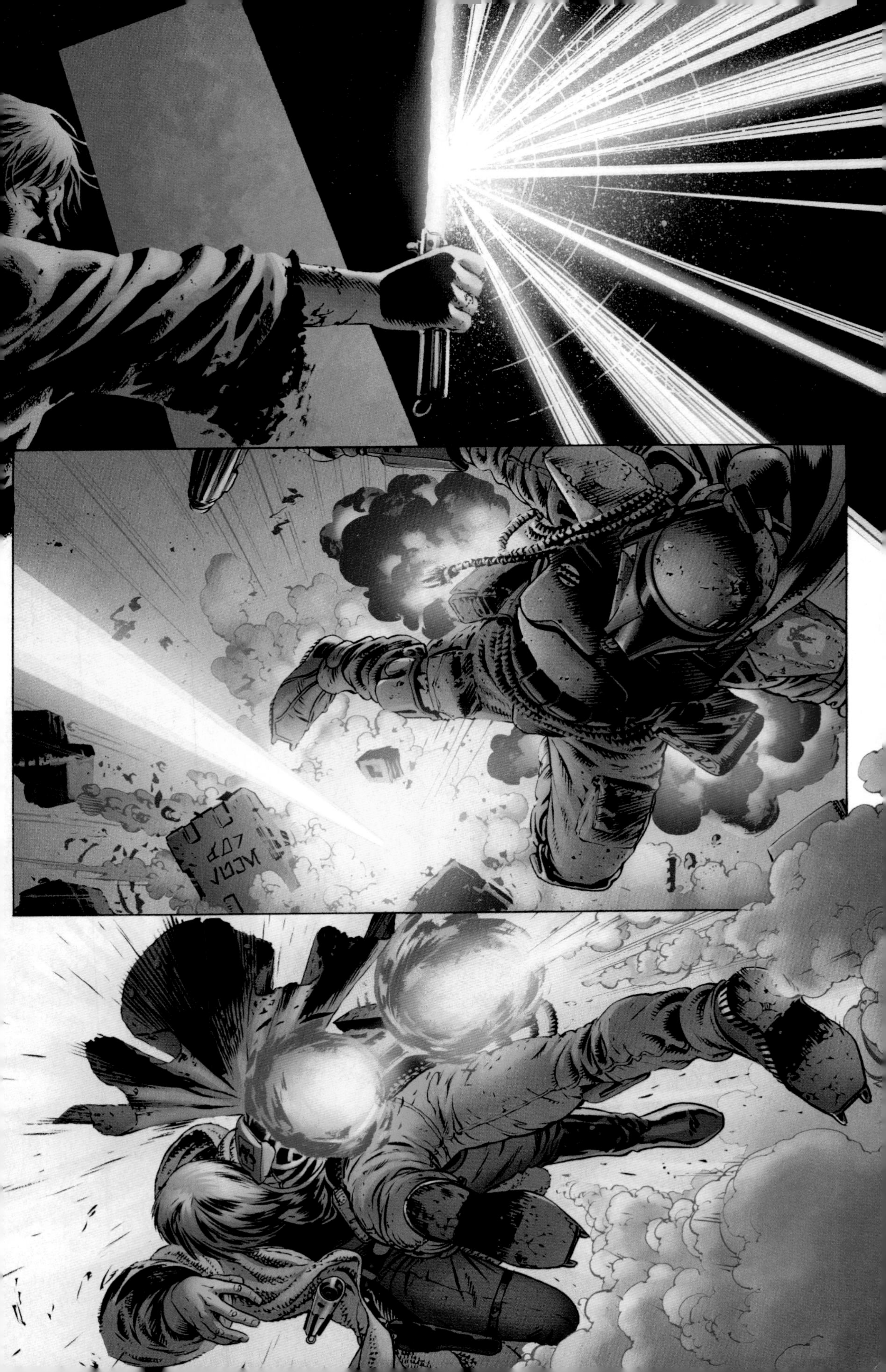

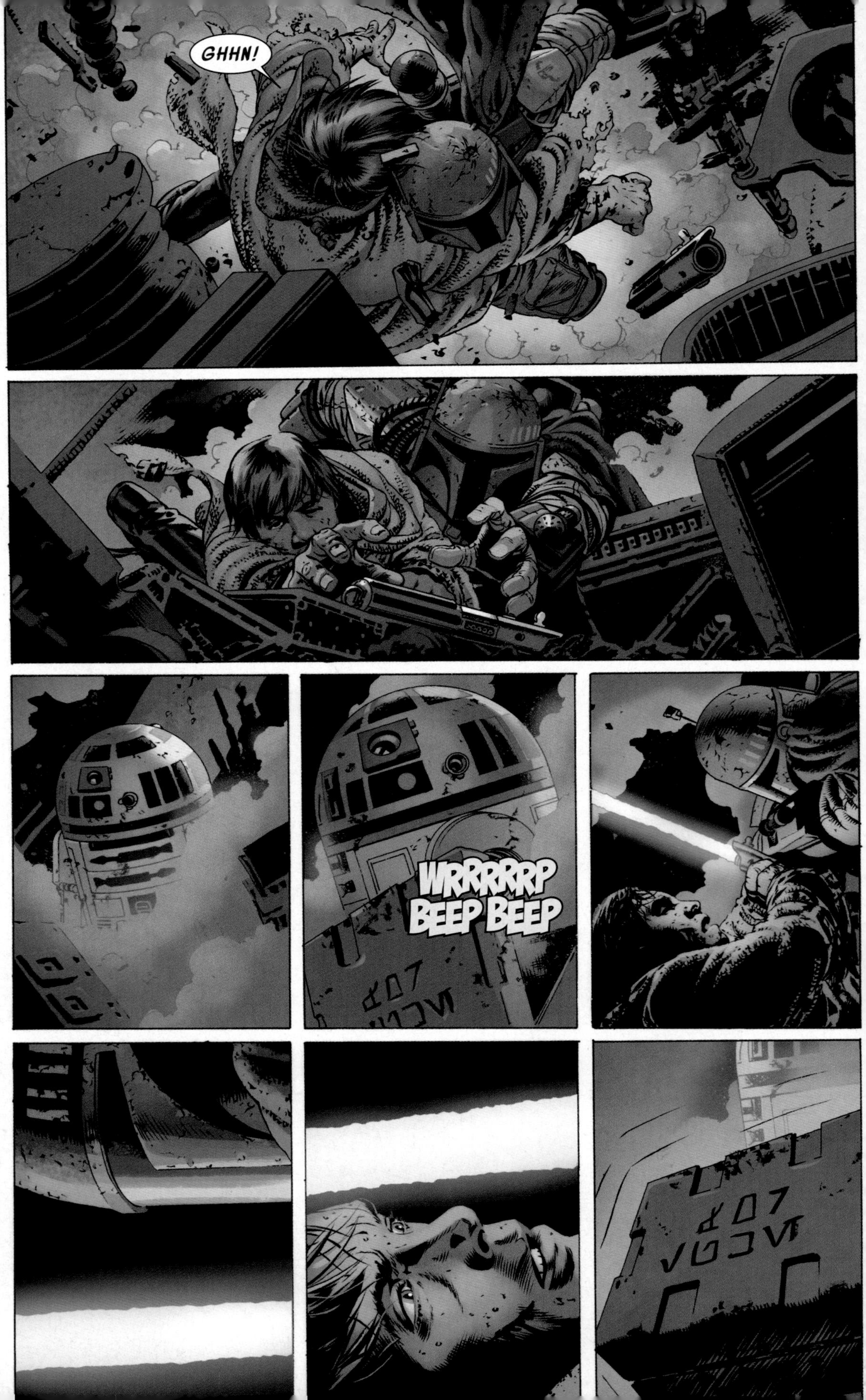
GHHN!
WRRRRRP
BEEP BEEP

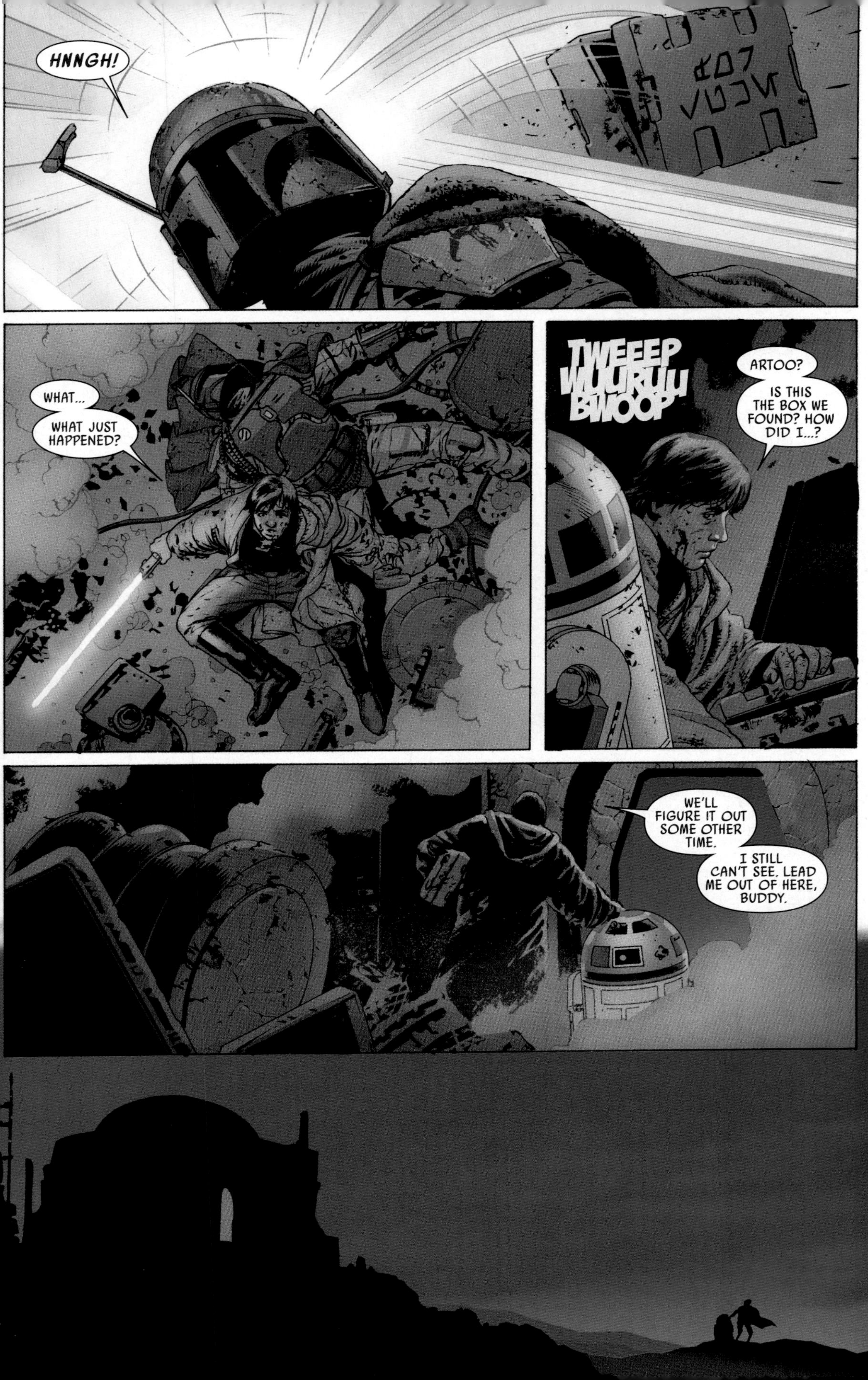
HNNGH!
WHAT...
WHAT JUST HAPPENED?
TWEEEP WUURUU BWOOP
ARTOO?
IS THIS THE BOX WE FOUND? HOW DID I...?
WE'LL FIGURE IT OUT SOME OTHER TIME.
I STILL CAN'T SEE. LEAD ME OUT OF HERE, BUDDY.

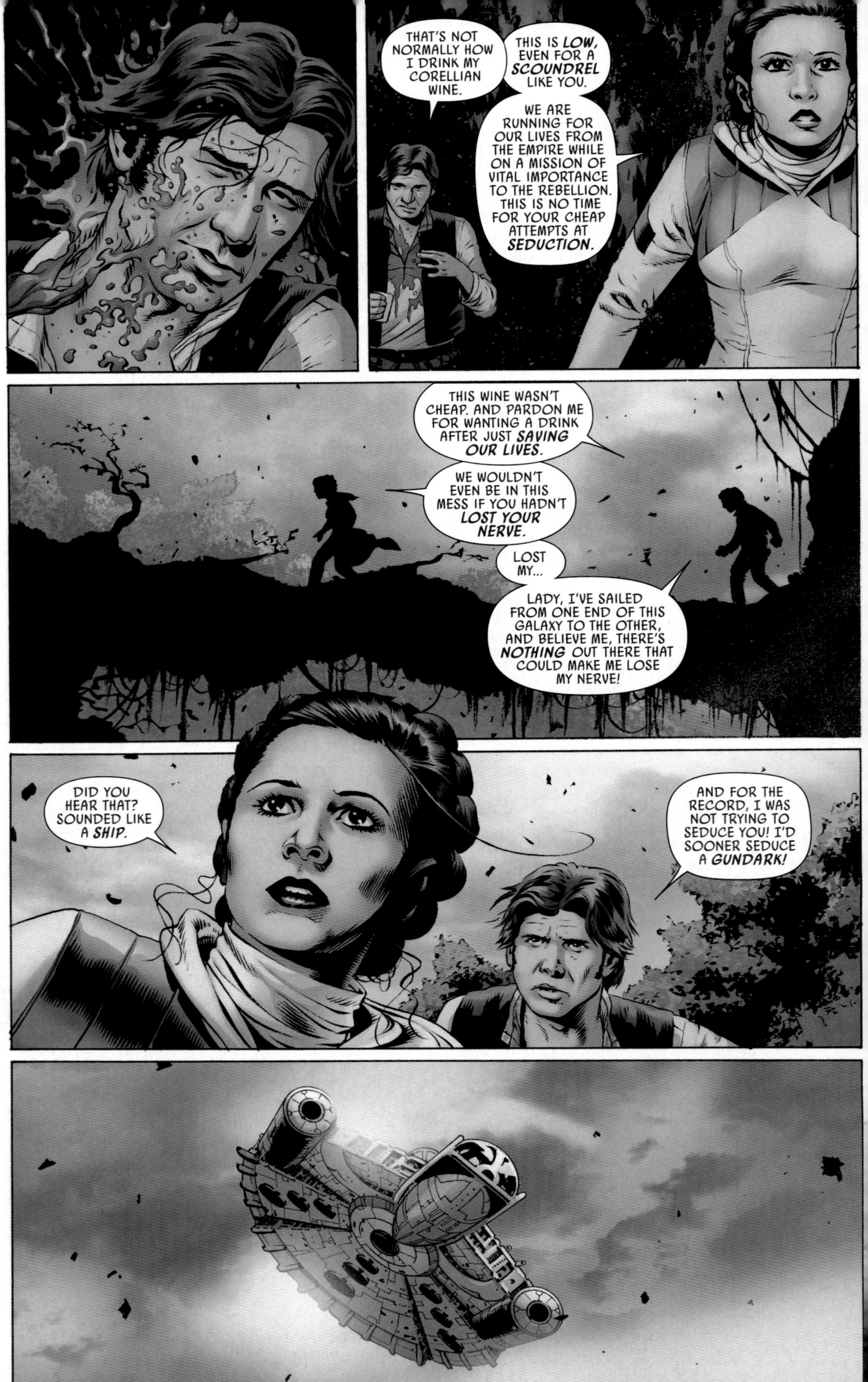
THAT'S NOT NORMALLY HOW I DRINK MY CORELLIAN WINE.
THIS IS LOW, EVEN FOR A SCOUNDREL LIKE YOU.
WE ARE RUNNING FOR OUR LIVES FROM THE EMPIRE WHILE ON A MISSION OF VITAL IMPORTANCE TO THE REBELLION. THIS IS NO TIME FOR YOUR CHEAP ATTEMPTS AT SEDUCTION.
THIS WINE WASN'T CHEAP. AND PARDON ME FOR WANTING A DRINK AFTER JUST SAVING OUR LIVES.
WE WOULDN'T EVEN BE IN THIS MESS IF YOU HADN'T LOST YOUR NERVE.
LOST MY...
LADY, I'VE SAILED FROM ONE END OF THIS GALAXY TO THE OTHER, AND BELIEVE ME, THERE'S NOTHING OUT THERE THAT COULD MAKE ME LOSE MY NERVE!
DID YOU HEAR THAT? SOUNDED LIKE A SHIP.
AND FOR THE RECORD, I WAS NOT TRYING TO SEDUCE YOU! I'D SOONER SEDUCE A GUNDARK!

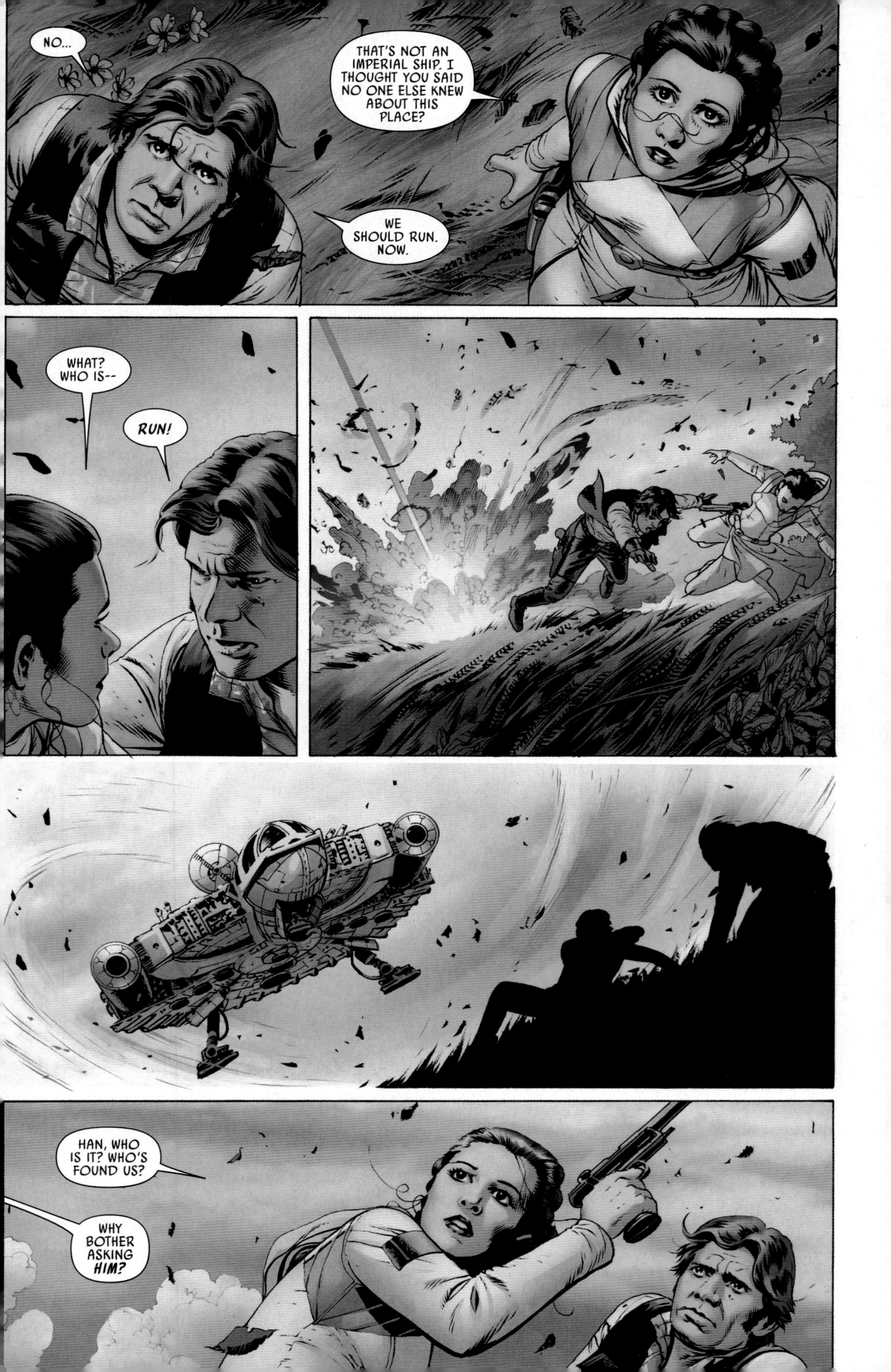
NO...
THAT'S NOT AN IMPERIAL SHIP. I THOUGHT YOU SAID NO ONE ELSE KNEW ABOUT THIS PLACE?
WE SHOULD RUN. NOW.
WHAT? WHO IS--
RUN!
HAN, WHO IS IT? WHO'S FOUND US?
WHY BOTHER ASKING HIM?

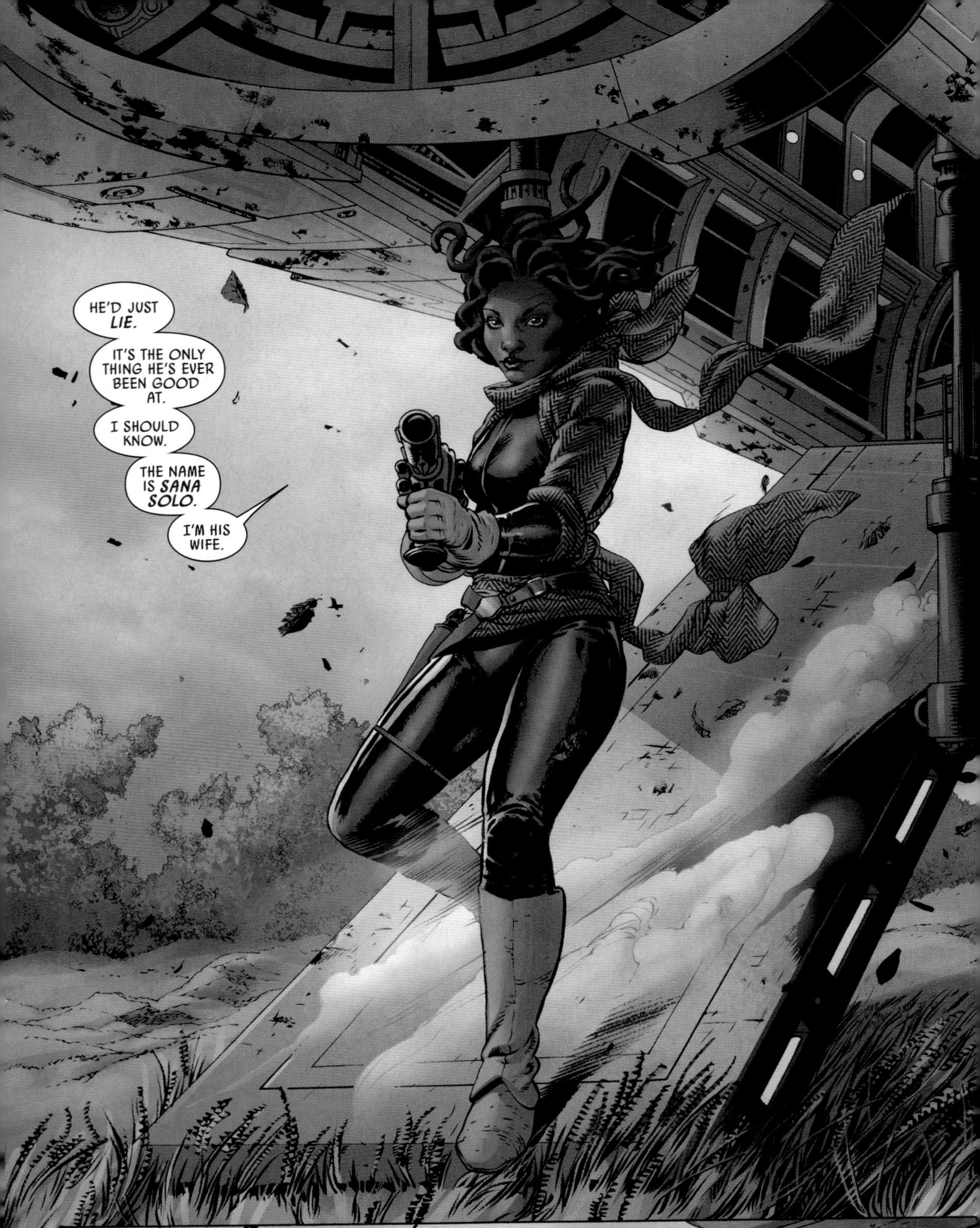
HE'D JUST LIE.
IT'S THE ONLY THING HE'S EVER BEEN GOOD AT.
I SHOULD KNOW.
THE NAME IS SANA SOLO.
I'M HIS WIFE.

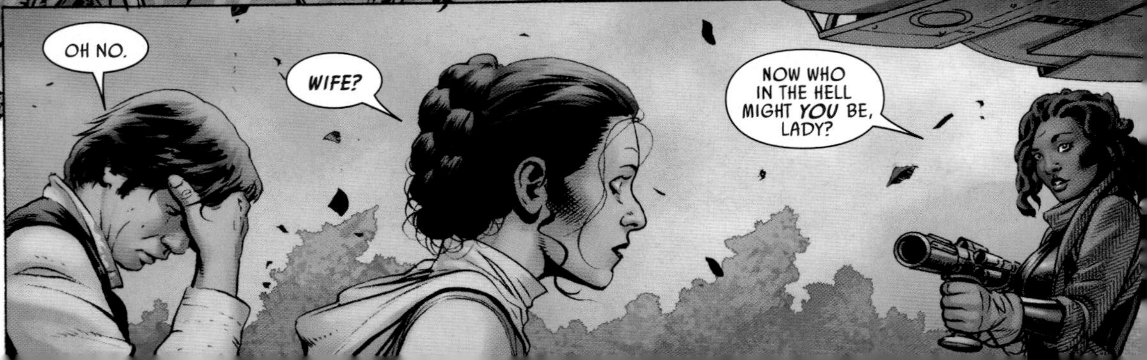
OH NO.
WIFE?
NOW WHO IN THE HELL MIGHT YOU BE, LADY?

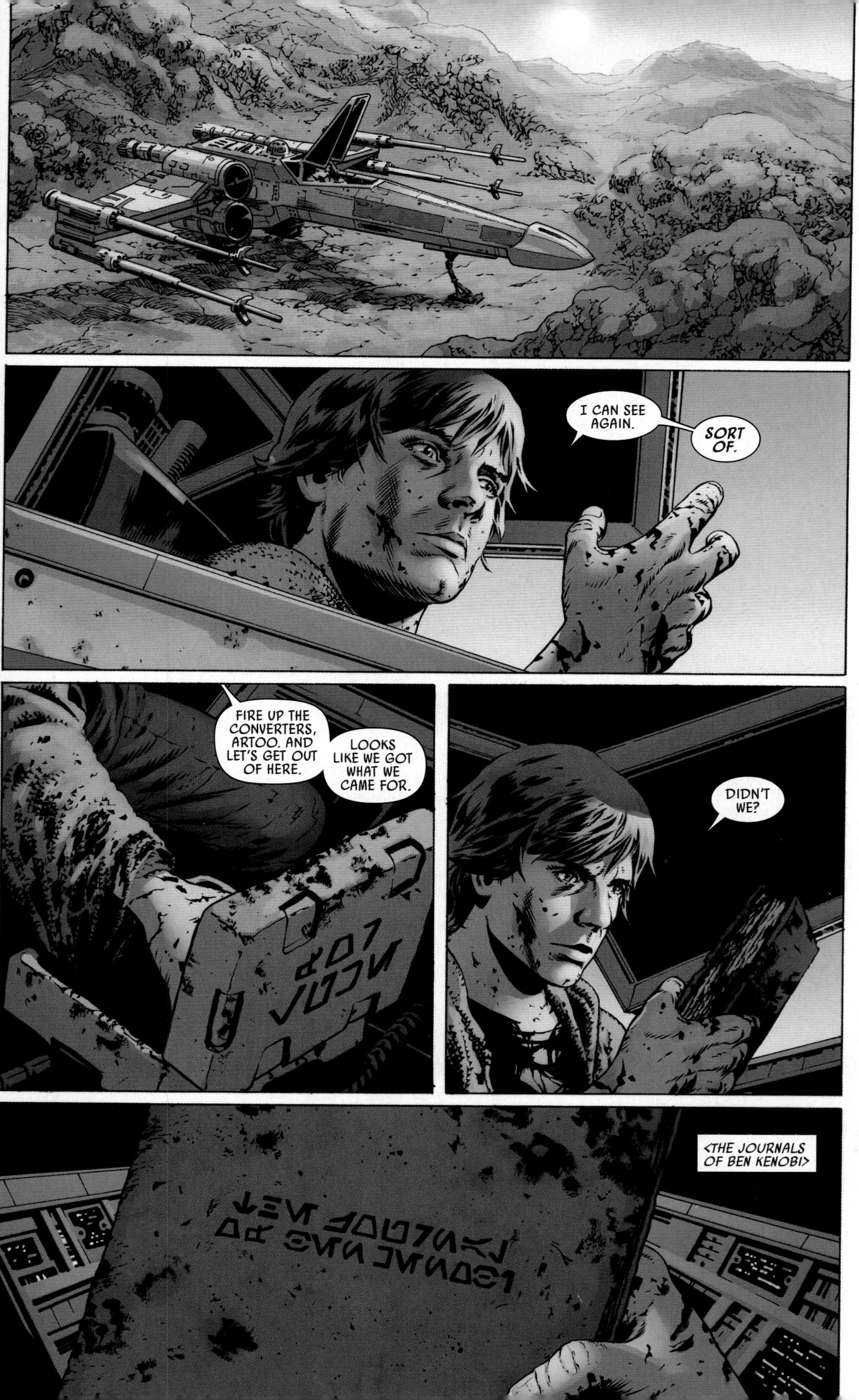
I CAN SEE AGAIN.
SORT OF.
FIRE UP THE CONVERTERS, ARTOO. AND LET'S GET OUT OF HERE.
LOOKS LIKE WE GOT WHAT WE CAME FOR.
DIDN'T WE?
<THE JOURNALS OF BEN KENOBI>

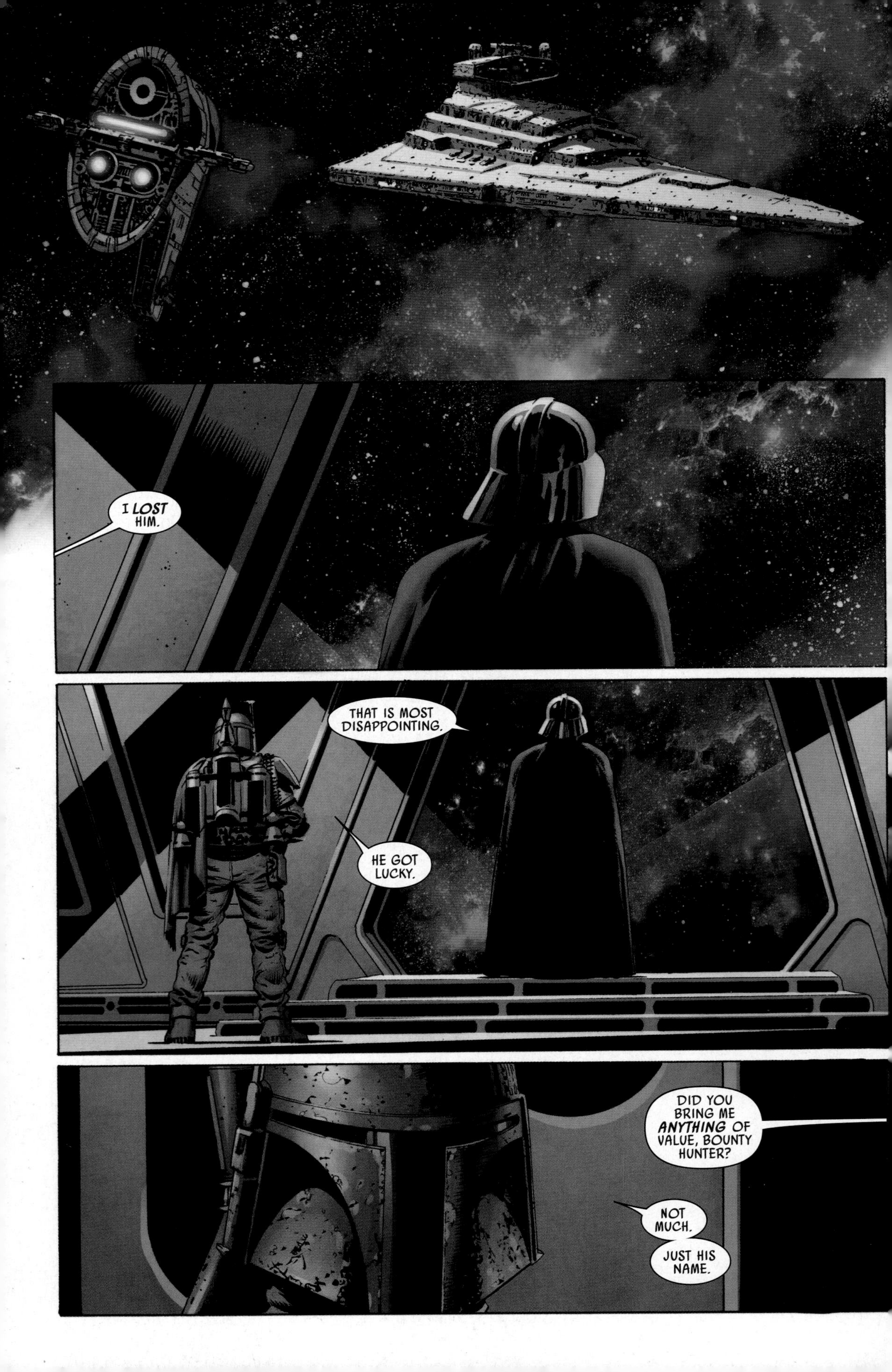
I LOST HIM.
THAT IS MOST DISAPPOINTING.
HE GOT LUCKY.
DID YOU BRING ME ANYTHING OF VALUE, BOUNTY HUNTER?
NOT MUCH.
JUST HIS NAME.

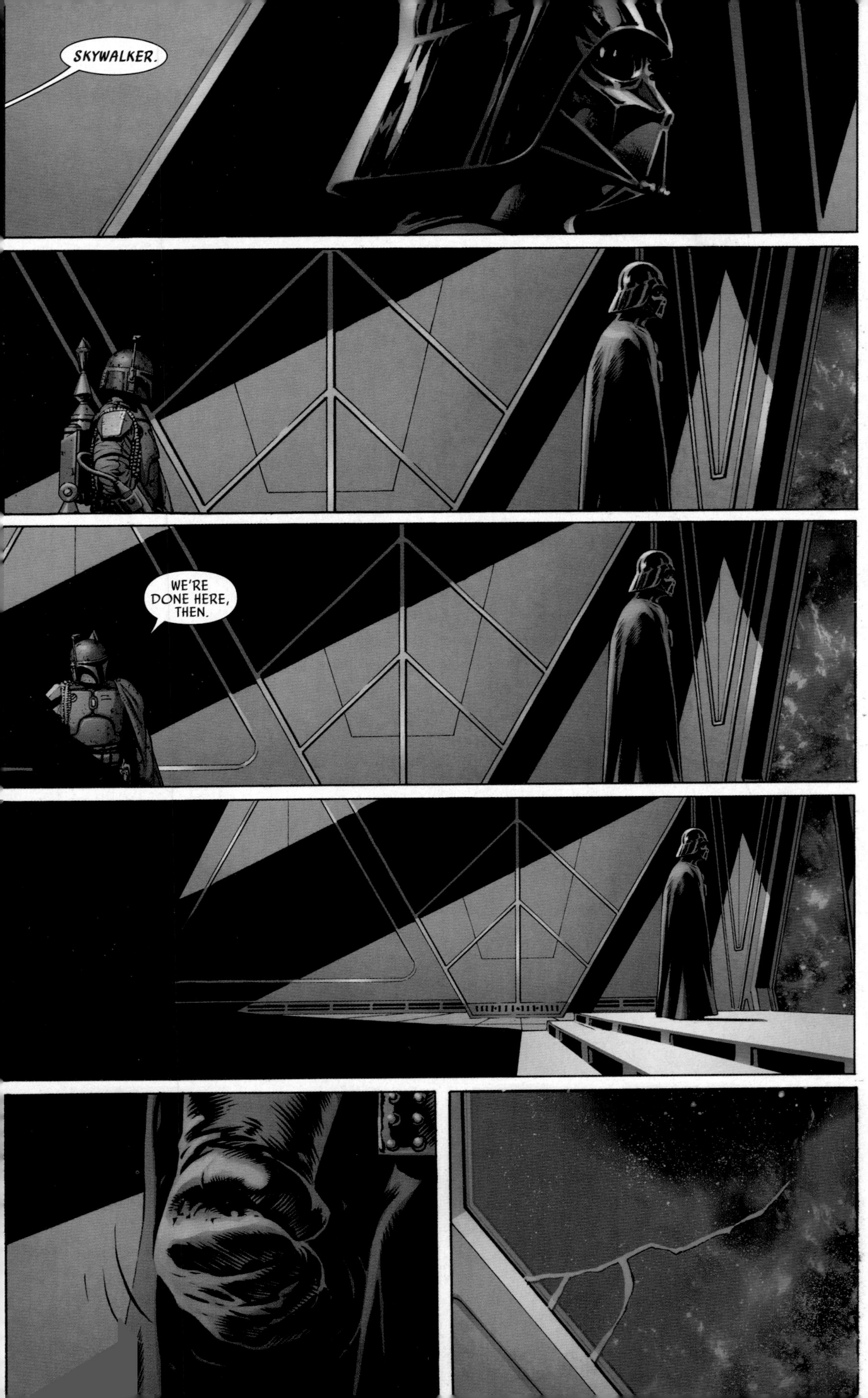
SKYWALKER.
WE'RE DONE HERE, THEN.

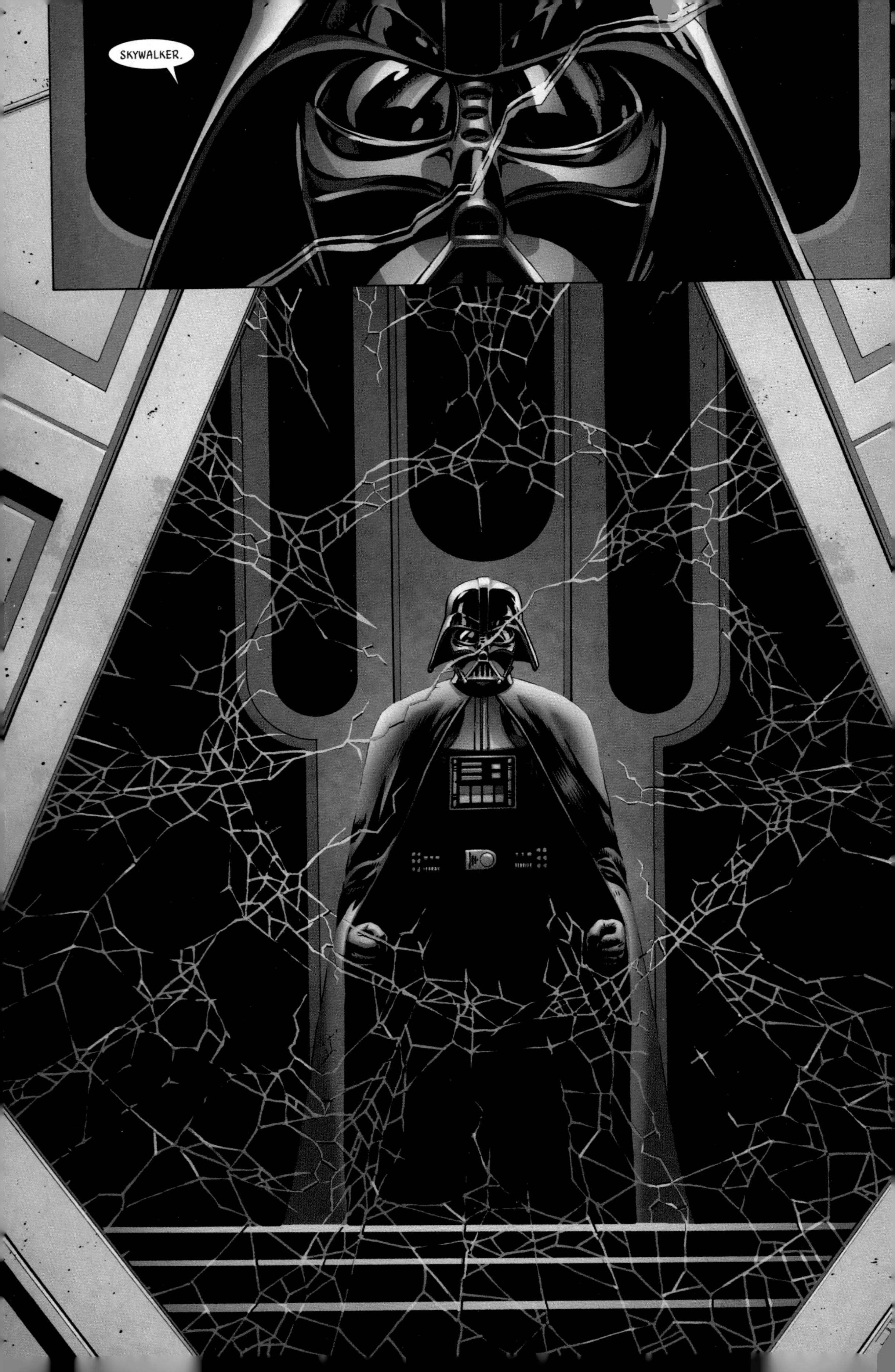
SKYWALKER.